TRACKING MODERNITY

To Ilker,

With best wishes

Marc A...

Tracking Modernity

. . . .

India's Railway and
the Culture of Mobility

Marian Aguiar

University of Minnesota Press
Minneapolis
London

An earlier version of chapter 3 appeared as "Railway Space in Partition Literature," in *27 Down: New Departures in Indian Railway Studies*, edited by Ian Kerr (2007); by permission of Orient Blackswan Private Limited.

Published by the University of Minnesota Press
111 Third Avenue South, Suite 290
Minneapolis, MN 55401-2520
http://www.upress.umn.edu

Library of Congress Cataloging-in-Publication Data

Aguiar, Marian.
Tracking modernity : India's railway and the culture of mobility / Marian Aguiar.
p. cm.
Includes bibliographical references and index.
ISBN 978-0-8166-6560-0 (acid-free paper)
ISBN 978-0-8166-6561-7 (pbk. : acid-free paper)
1. Indic literature (English)–20th century–History and criticism.
2. Railroads–India. 3. Modernism (Aesthetics)–India. 4. Railroads in literature.
5. Postcolonialism–India. 6. Popular culture–India–Social aspects.
7. Mass media–India–Social aspects. 8. Partition, Territorial, in literature. I. Title.
PR9489.6.A37 2010
820.9'3558–dc22
2010030715

Printed in the United States of America on acid-free paper

The University of Minnesota is an equal-opportunity educator and employer.

18 17 16 15 14 13 12 11   10 9 8 7 6 5 4 3 2 1

For Ida Aguiar

The two headed station master
belongs to a sect
that rejects every timetable
not published in the year the track was laid
as apocryphal
but interprets the first timetable
with a freedom that allows him to read
every subsequent timetable between
the lines of its text

ARUN KOLATKAR, *JEJURI*

Contents

Preface

IN NOVEMBER 2008, two disparate images of Mumbai's main railway station appeared on the international cultural scene. A photograph taken by Sebastian D'Souza on November 26 showed a young man strolling with a machine gun through the lobby of Chhatrapati Shivaji Terminus between brightly lit advertisements. The pictures that D'Souza took immediately after, as he followed the gunman to the train platforms, documented for the world the immobile bodies and smears of blood left on the floors beneath the Gothic arches of this colonial monument to mobility once called the Victoria Terminus.[1] The second image, from director Danny Boyle's global hit film *Slumdog Millionaire*,[2] shows that very space as a place of romantic fulfillment (Figure 1). An Indian hero and heroine, separated by the forces of corruption into disparate lives and economic worlds, find common ground between the moving trains. The two sing and dance in this world in motion, joined by other members of the underworld that exists adjacent to the railway lines.

Eric Hobsbawm once called the railway a "synonym for ultra-modernity";[3] given this emblematic legacy, the images taken during the Mumbai attacks seem to suggest that the modern world is forever uncertain, a place where a lively terminal may, on any given day, become a place of death. Yet the scene from Boyle's film recuperates the notion of modernity by showing movement as the key to resolving social and personal problems. Both images, although one is by an Indian (D'Souza) and another by a European (Boyle), grow out of a symbolic history of the Indian train that is over 150 years old. This emblematic legacy, part of a broader culture of mobility, reveals what Rabindranath Tagore, in his Bengali poem "Railway Station," described as modernity's "forever forming, forever unforming."[4]

Figure 1. Final scene from Slumdog Millionaire *on the platform of Mumbai's Chhatrapati Shivaji Terminus. Photograph credit—Ishika Mohan. "SLUMDOG MILLIONAIRE," Copyright 2008 Twentieth Century Fox. All rights reserved. Copyright Slumdog Distribution Limited.*

Symbolic Legacies of the Indian Railway

In India, the train has arguably been the most important material emblem of modernity since the first passenger train ran in 1853.[5] Representations of the Indian railway comprise an enormously important global symbolic history that includes numerous novels, short stories, poems, photographs, and films. Colonial literary writers Rudyard Kipling and Flora Annie Steel, nationalists Rabindranath Tagore and Mohandas Gandhi, postcolonial and diasporic writers R. K. Narayan, Anita Nair, and Jhumpa Lahiri, and filmmakers Satyajit Ray, Manmohan Desai, and Kamal Amrohi represent only some of the writers and visual artists who have imagined the train. What I find so fascinating is not simply the large number of images of the Indian train, but the way that the railway as an imaginative object represents the culture, forces, and processes around it. A look at this phenomenon shows that the railway became a kind of moving theater that staged first a colonial, then a national, and finally a global identity. In this book, I interpret this dynamic process of representation to read the rhetoric of modernity and unpack the tensions within conceptions of the modern.

Tracking Modernity examines the close relationship between images of mobility concerned with a specific technology and the notion of modernity within the Indian context. In exploring this conjunction, I am not suggesting a causal relationship in which the train brought modernity to India in any kind of determining way. I approach modernity, as the introduction explains in more detail, as a rhetoric that has functioned through a cluster of representational and material practices. When this book "tracks modernity," it outlines an emblematic process that illuminates how modernity came to be constituted within the Indian context though a body of images inspired by a particular technology of movement. Modernity, in other words, is read as a dynamic imaginative form. The institutions, paradigms, and subjectivities that make up that form have changed over time, a process I frame in terms of colonial, national, and global modernities. In charting this movement through history, the story I tell here is not simply about the advent of modernity, but also about its dissolution, for modernity's commitment to mobility has consigned it to a reconfiguration that is partially its undoing.

Movement in the Colonial Context

The railway in India was first officially proposed in 1844 in a prospectus written by John Chapman to the East India Company, although the idea had been floating about for several years among British and Indian businessmen as early as the 1830s.[6] Statesman and editor of the London magazine the *Monthly Times*, Rowland Macdonald Stephenson made early private proposals to the East India Company in 1841; later, he journeyed to India appealing to officials of the government of India while waging a media campaign in native and colonial local journals to promote the railway.[7] The railway lines appeared originally in the British popular imagination as part of a national economic space; Chapman commented in 1848 that the merchants of Lancashire, "consider [the railroad from Bombay to the cotton districts] . . . as nothing more than an extension of their own line from Manchester to Liverpool."[8] Just as the railway collapsed space through its speed, the movement of ideas, information, manufactured construction parts, and goods helped make the colony appear more proximate.

Yet Bombay was not Liverpool, and anxieties about the possible vulnerabilities of British economic and political interests gave rise to an increasing preoccupation with securing the geography of the colony. Governor-General Lord Dalhousie, one of the earliest and most important proponents of the railway, revealed these fears as he argued in his influential 1853 Railway Minute that the railway could overcome the distances that would impede communication between colonial centers. Dalhousie's worries about an attack were realized four years later with the 1857 rebellion against colonial rule. The British responded to the uprising with increased attention to railway construction, and during the years that followed, the number of rail lines surged and the geographical body of a colony emerged with its frame assembled for colonial security as well as for economic gain. By organizing a mobile network for passengers, goods, and information, the railway made colonial India a more manageable state.

The railway represented a colonial state committed to increasing mobility as it expanded its own territories and to securing that power through mobility with a distinctive kind of "railway imperialism" that could integrate and annex territory, commandeer resources, and transform the future of a given place.[9] In visual culture, paintings and photographs showed the train as a small but persistent force pushing its way through a hostile and overwhelming landscape (Figure 2). On a material level, the railway would facilitate movement in numerous ways. Its tracks were built by a pool of migrant labor, workers that traveled around India constructing new railway lines.[10] Once built, the train moved along a network, creating a dynamic circulatory geography. As a primary tool of the state, the railway enabled all kinds of information to travel—from military secrets to daily mail. Goods trains moved commodities and altered regional networks of trade. The new mode of transportation also affected the mobility of colonial passengers, allowing them to travel between Calcutta, Bombay, and Madras, and to the Hill Stations like Simla in the summer. On a symbolic level, the train in particular and movement in general became a paradigm for modernity in India. The new technology was seen as a *force* of cultural change by both the British and Indians. This ideological association was a global phenomenon; in the United States, for example, the railway "appeared as self-evident superiority of present to past,"[11] to Euro-American settlers. In India, colonial rhetoric promoted the train as a means of freeing Indians from tradition through increased movement;

Figure 2. 1895 Magic Lantern Slide by American photographer William Henry Jackson, captioned: "Tunnel and bridge on the Northwestern Railway near Quetta (Baluchistan)." Photograph courtesy William Henry Jackson/Harappa.com.

in the process, mobility came to act as a material register for who was modern, a phenomenon that continues to this day.

Despite rhetoric that promoted movement as something new to the Indian subcontinent, there were important networks and practices of mobility in place prior to European colonization. Precolonial India was *already* mobile. People, commodities, and information passed over land on infrastructures like the sixteenth-century Grand Trunk Road that ran across northern India.[12] In 1878, Captain Edward Davidson reflected that "[t]hirty years ago India was practically stationary,"[13] but merchants traveled between arid and river areas and along the coasts before and after the East India Company expanded British political and commercial influence in the eighteenth century.[14] In addition to these land migrations, maritime trade within South Asia as well as with East Asia and Africa was well established. Laborers and merchants journeyed on both land and sea. A 1770 diary depicts a group of men, women, and children, describing them as "a kind of travelling community of their own under a species of

Government particular to themselves, with laws and customs which they follow and observe wherever they go."[15] A regular exchange of laborers was established between southern India and Sri Lanka well before the British colonial period introduced indentured labor and, with the train, a new kind of circulation.[16]

Indians had mobile networks across the globe: maritime workers were systematically hired for voyages on British ships in the Southern Hemisphere; *ayahs* (domestic workers caring for children) were brought to Britain, where they often remained in temporary establishments until they were hired for a return journey;[17] and Indian plantation workers left for Mauritius, Sri Lanka, and the Caribbean, among other places. Inside India, pilgrims regularly made journeys, and travel narratives grew up as a popular genre.[18] Women journeyed to new places after their marriage and returned home for events like the birth of a child. Moreover, fairs and soldiers moved about the country. Hunters and nomadic herders also had a mobile culture.[19] Not only were bodies in motion, but historical revisionists have traced circulatory systems of currency, the dissemination of information by networks of spies and informers, and the interchange of cartographic knowledge.[20] The common idea that colonialism universally *promoted* movement has also been debunked; Claude Markovits, Jacques Pouchepadass, and Sanjay Subrahmanyam assert that, far from actually encouraging total movement, the colonial government in India often sought to impede some traditional patterns of circulation that were seen as a challenge to colonial rule.[21] For example, colonial authorities sought to control and settle transporters such as the Banjara, originally a migrant weaver class that came to organize trade routes (and that ironically later made up an important constituency among railway porters).[22]

Given that there were already well-established modes of movement in India by the mid-nineteenth century, what then was so distinctive about the railway? The railway did, of course, bring a new kind of mobility to Indians. There were many Indian passengers from the very beginning and 80 million Indian passengers by 1880.[23] But this expansion of mobility through technology did not alone give rise to the train's ideological power. More than any previous means of transportation, the railway symbolically correlated modernity and movement. In doing so, it gave shape and substance to the notion of modernity within the Indian context, a modernity mediated by a cluster of associated practices, institutions, paradigms, and subjectivities. In this book, I argue that the emerging rhetoric of modernity in India would be structured by the contradictions evidenced in colonial, nationalist, and global discourse. I call these moments of incongruity "counternarratives of modernity" to signify how they work both with and against the dominant rhetoric of colonial modernity.

One of these paradoxes lay between colonial aspirations for social reform based on a vision of a universal path of development and concepts of difference that lay at the heart of imperial rule. The introduction and chapter 1 of this book examine this issue by considering how colonial writers staged the encounter with India through representations of public railway space. The Indian railway was the largest single foreign capital investment in the nineteenth century for the British Empire; its symbolic importance matched its economic stakes. Political and economic writers Lord Dalhousie and R. M. Stephenson, along with popular travel writers and illustrators, both British and Indian, presented technology as a tool both to control and to educate Indians. Colonial discourse about the train aimed to support the larger effort, typical of a broader colonial rhetoric of modernity, to establish rational and unified public spaces that were culturally secular so as to subsume religion into the order of the state. Even as writers and artists represented the railway as a kind of universal "rational utopia,"[24] however, they worried how Indians might corrupt the public space of the railway. My study of colonial representations reveals how as colonial discourse charted lines dividing European from Indian, or public from private, they presented those spaces as saturated by Indians' religious, domestic, and bodily identities. Two of the most famous literary writers from Anglo-India's late nineteenth- and early twentieth-century period, Rudyard Kipling and Flora Annie Steel, wove cultural difference into their concept of colonial modernity. My analysis of their works shows how, through their representations of technological space, these and other colonial writers opened the door to later versions of modernity that would serve radically different political interests.

Mobility, Stagnation, and Displacement

The rhetorics of colonial, secular nationalist, and postcolonial modernity have celebrated mobility as a means for emancipation and posited it as based in a kind of personal freedom; not all Indians deemed it as such, however, and history proved that mobility was just as often compulsory as it was liberative. Thus, a different narrative of a mobile modernity developed concurrent to the colonial story. Despite the rhetoric that promoted modernity through mobility and the experience of people "dwelling in travel,"[25] as James Clifford puts it, modernity was not always in motion. Some people remained right where they were even after the introduction of the railway heralded their entrance to a modern world. Even with its imbrications with mobility, the rhetoric of colonial modernity depended on stasis; just as movement was both symbolic and actual, so too was fixity expressed in both the logic of categorization and in the materiality of people's lives. This was due, as I argue in the introduction, to the workings of capitalism as well as to the ideologies of colonial rule. For some to move, others must stay put, literally or metaphorically, as in economic stagnation. Such a concept, contemporary critics have argued, structured the very notion of travel as a site of privilege.[26]

Yet by dividing modernity into mobile and static parts, one runs the risk of reproducing the very binary upon which the rhetoric of colonial modernity lay. Indians had lives that were altered forever, sometimes in negative ways, by the new types of mobility, whether they ever set foot in a train carriage or not. Industries were shifted towards the needs of overseas rather than local markets. "Celebrated local handicrafts had been ruined by the cheap Lancashire cloth that flooded north-central India after the completion of the Bombay–Calcutta railroad, and farmers were encouraged to save themselves by using the railroad to export the soft wheat that British millers preferred,"[27] social historian Mike Davis writes. These victims of mobility were also the ones who suffered from famine as the railway carried grain away from where it was needed. The railway's emphasis on an export economy left regions devastated by poverty, famine, and disease. For some late nineteenth- and early twentieth-century Indian nationalists, the train represented a colonizing power, and its network of circulation was seen as a structure binding India to poverty and dependence. These writers challenged the correlation between modernity, movement, and emancipation, and in doing so, they entered an oppositional story of a mobile modernity.

The impoverishment of India through the railway was the subject of heated discussion in the nineteenth and early twentieth centuries among a group known as the "drain theorists." These Indian scholars, including Dadabhai Naoroji and Romesh Dutt, argued that colonial policies had undermined the Indian economy through such practices as promoting agriculture for trade rather than consumption, destroying traditional industries, and mandating financial schemes, such as railway construction, that were unfairly biased toward the British. Although some present-day historians have challenged these assertions that national decline outweighed growth and that privation was primarily derived from colonial policies,[28] there is consensus that some individuals and regions were left outside the promised benefits of the new kinds of commercial activity brought by the railway.

During the same period, the train also became a focal point for a group of spiritual nationalists that included Swami Vivekananda (Narendranath Datta), Aurobindo Ghose, Mohandas Gandhi, and Rabindranath Tagore. The spiritualists were the inheritors of the "drain theory" as well as a social discourse about famine, environmental devastation, labor, and discrimination. Vivekananda, Aurobindo, Gandhi, and Tagore grounded their political, social, and aesthetic commentaries in the space that had been cleared by this earlier group of social critics. They moved away from the proindustrialization politics of their forerunners, however, to radically question technology as a way of being. For these late nineteenth- and early twentieth-century spiritualists, the train's status as an icon of Western culture made it a fraught object in a context in which culture itself had become an instrument of domination. These writers represented empire as a machine that was dangerous because it begat a culturally alien way of being that was mechanistic and thus devoid of moral truth. In chapter 2, I position the essays, poetry, and drama of this group as a response to the colonial discourse described in the introduction and chapter 1. Unlike that discourse, which sought to bring Hinduism within the sphere of the railway, these writers constructed a Hindu identity at odds with the train. As they wrote against the ideology of modernization, they seized the image of the train that had previously been the provenance of the British. I interpret the political and creative writings of these nationalists to reveal an important historical counternarrative of modernity, one rooted in religion but articulated in a discussion about technology.

The rhetoric of colonial modernity had equated movement and freedom, but that was belied by the lived experience of modern mobility, in which not all movement was voluntary. Caren Kaplan differentiates two types of movement engendered by modernity: "travel," which indicates commercial and leisure movement associated with expanding Western capitalism, and "displacement," which references mass migrations. Kaplan's characterization helps make the case for thinking about *types* of movement together as distinct but mutually inflected, "not as synonyms but as signs of different critical registers and varied historicized instances."[29] One excellent example of movement as displacement was in the arena of labor. One often thinks of railway movement beginning with train travel, but the first to move with the train were those who laid the tracks. Laborers participated in mobile economies such as railway construction, some of them prevented by colonial policies from working near their own home and others simply compelled by economic circumstances to live a migrant lifestyle.[30]

The Partition of India in 1947 brought another scene of displacement, as opposed to travel, and generated another counternarrative of modernity. As India came into independence, Partition refugees who fled communal violence experienced a coerced and often violent form of mobility. Movement took on a compulsory character as people fled their homes, fearing for their lives. The train had a critical symbolic importance during this time, and creative works looking back at that period have used images of forced movement (or its opposite, arrested movement) to render the crisis of nationhood during a period of mass migration. Saadat Hasan Manto's striking vignettes written in the immediate aftermath of Partition, Khushwant Singh's classic *Train to Pakistan* (1956), Mukul Kesavan's magical realist *Looking Through Glass* (1995), and Deepa Mehta's contemporary film *Earth* (1998) offer haunting images of the "death train" during Partition, in which trains reached their destinations filled with victims of the violent communal divide that placed Hindus and Sikhs on one side and Muslims on the other.

In chapter 3, I examine this historical moment when inherent tensions within the concept of modernity were cast in relief. The chapter analyzes the many train scenes that have appeared in memoirs, fiction, and filmed works about Partition. These works depict a moment which broke down the ideal of the train as a modern, secular space established by the colonial discourse described in chapter 1. Refugees fleeing the violence of Partition placed their faith in the sanctity of the railway space. The state-sponsored refugee trains on the border of West Pakistan represented the protection of the nation; the Muslims fleeing west and the Hindus escaping east sought refuge in the secular nation. Instead of offering a safe haven, for many the train became the place of death (the train did not play the same prominent role in Bengal's 1947 partition, which created East Pakistan). In my discussion, I look at images of the "death train" that forever changed the meaning of the train in India. Written and visual postcolonial culture representing Partition shows the Indian train as a body rather than a machine, as an instrument of temporal reversal rather than progress, and as testimony to the communal character of a nation celebrating its secular identity. Postcolonial works look back to show the haunting of the railway after India's Partition. This chapter argues that the dialectical nature of modern space—as secular and communal, public and private—emerged in the historical moment of Partition to violent effect and continues to this day, generating another counternarrative of modernity.

By expanding the understanding of modernity to include those *excluded* and those *disempowered* by a culture of mobility, one may begin to step outside the colonial rhetoric of modernity that viewed movement as emancipation. In doing so, one may begin to see mobility in the context of India as something other than the wholesale purchase of a colonial ideology; as Clifford puts it, "Practices of displacement might emerge as *constitutive* of cultural meanings rather than as their simple transfer or extension."[31] Those cultural meanings sometimes aligned with the colonial rhetoric and sometimes ran counter to it. The culture built around mobility challenged the rhetoric of modernity, instead showing the static places inside that modernity and the compulsion of displacement. It belied the promises of equality, progress, and freedom through movement; rather, it revealed how mobility might foster injustices between races, classes, and genders. The culture of mobility showed modernity within the Indian context to be dynamic, disruptive, and productive, and in doing so, formulated alternative versions of modernity through the tensions inside ideas of difference.

National Mobility

As was the case with the colonial state, movement helped constitute the postcolonial nation in India. Chapters 4 and 5 examine this from the perspective of different emphases and genres. In chapter 4, I follow the story of the Indian railway into the postcolonial period. There, I find intimations of a colonial rhetoric of mobility as modernity and an active construction of a national space that recalls how the railway mapped the new colony. I also find the legacies of those counternarratives of modernity put forward by people like Naoroji, Tagore, and Gandhi, who wrote against the empire. Thus, this chapter both traces the well-known story of the railway as the "life-line"[32] of India and examines literature, film, and official discourse to find the contradictions that emerge within that account. One aspect of this story is the relationship between the rural and urban that played an important political and cultural role in India's early postcolonial period. I show how writers and filmmakers like R. K. Narayan, Satyajit Ray, and Phanishwar Renu complicate this relationship between country and city in their creative works. Looking forward to a more contemporary period, I examine the ways that Anita Nair and Shuma Futehally use the setting of the train as a microcosm of Indian society and a way to negotiate different faiths, genders, castes, and classes inside India. They mark the railway journey as a metaphor for personal transformation and a parallel to the broader evolution of the nation. Even as these writers and filmmakers discussed in chapter 4 employ images of mobility to construct an imagined community of the nation, their work also exposes that community's necessarily partial nature—a perspective that I briefly contrast with that of the diasporic artist and contemporary travel narrative. Thus, in their narratives and counternarratives of modernity, these postcolonial artists show how railway mobility both constructs and confronts the nation.

Chapter 5 takes this same discussion into the genre of popular Indian cinema to focus specifically on the gendered nature of this culture of mobility. Hindi action films like *Sholay* (directed by Romesh Sippy; 1975), *Coolie* (directed by Manmohan Desai; 1983) and *The Burning Train* (directed by Ravi Chopra; 1980) construct a rebellious masculinity through images of railway mobility and forge an alternative vision of national subjectivity in a period of state crisis. Melodramas, the main focus of this chapter, reveal a more ambivalent relationship between femininity, mobility, and the postcolonial nation. From the works of the early 1970s like *Pakeezah* (directed by Kamal Amrohi; 1971) and *27 Down* (directed by Avtar Kaul; 1973), to the blockbusters of the 1990s, *Dil Se* (directed by Mani Ratnam; 1998) and *Dilwale Dulhania Le Jayenge* (directed by Aditya Chopra 1995), to the 2007 global releases *The Train* (directed by Hasnain Hyderabadwala and Raksha Mistry; 2007) and *Jab We Met* (directed by Imtiaz Ali; 2007), "Bollywood" is fascinated by romance on trains. This chapter argues that representations of desire and romance on the train highlight how public and private spaces signify in the gendering of India's national modernity. I argue that in these popular films of Indian cinema, the train allows for fantasies, represented in the genre of romance, that transgress social conventions. Far from being simply a mirror of social order, the train offers itself as a way to move across its lines.

This book concludes with the contemporary period and places India in a global relation to suggest the stakes for a discussion of a culture of mobility. The conclusion describes how global modernity enables and arrests movement through cultural visions of the Indian railway. Representations of terrorist bombings reflect one such stasis, and a primary part of this chapter focuses on the train as a symbolic object of terror. The *Samjhauta* (Friendship) Express in Haryana in 2007, the commuter trains of Mumbai in 2006, the *Sabarmati* Express near Godhra in 2002—in the debris of bombed carriages and stations, we find horrific representations of the intersection of private lives and the public sphere. That nexus finds its material forum in the train, the microcosm of society in which relations between communities and classes are worked out in what Suketa Mehta calls a "social laboratory." The conclusion closes by reviewing how the symbolic history of the Indian train allows the critical observer to see how the cultural association between modernity and mobility both obscures and reveals the paradoxes of the modern.

Culture of Mobility

The colonial, nationalist, and postcolonial images of the railway are but one part of a much broader culture of mobility that also included migration and immigration, as well as other technologies of movement associated with modernity, such as telegraphs (which is a technology of movement because it conveys electrical current), steamships, buses, cars, and airplanes. With each of the textual examples, I am mapping a small part of this wider constellation in which modernity has been interpreted through mobile spaces. In other ways as well, this book is a piece of a larger whole. The list of novels, short stories, songs, poetry, photographs, illustrations, paintings, and films with an Indian train in them is vast, and any scholarly work that attempts to account for them all risks becoming merely a catalog.[33] These works are produced in multiple languages; however, this study concentrates on those originally in English, Hindi, Urdu, and Bengali, with the recognition that this shapes the outcome of the project.[34] Moreover, this body of creative work is a small part of the all representations of the Indian railway, which also includes technical reports. It is not my goal to cover all references to the Indian railway, nor is it my objective to produce a comprehensive history. Instead, as a way to tell a story about modernity and mobility in the Indian context and beyond, I look at the work of a group of representative individuals that produced a range of writings and visual materials about the Indian railway. It is my hope that this story might be read fruitfully alongside other works not discussed here, and that other scholars will take up this endeavor.

The authors of the Indian train came from varying historical contingencies and held considerably different political stances. I have grouped their writings and visual materials into conversations that show some of the ways they reproduced, refused, or revised the rhetoric of modernity they inherited through colonialism. Although roughly sequenced in terms of period, these discussions sometimes overlap chronologically; they include the colonial discourse, nationalist debates, creative texts representing Partition, postcolonial renderings, and works representing emerging global relations. What these texts share, despite their dissimilarities in politics, period, and genre, is a way of mapping out a relationship to modernity through the culture of mobility. The chapters that follow show how versions of modernity came to be constituted in India through the culture of mobility and how that same culture exposed the contradictions inside the modern.

Tracking Modernity

What Is Modernity?

The simplest definition of modernity equates it with the new and suggests a determinate rupture with what came before. Although scholars use the notion of modernity to characterize transformations in sixteenth-, seventeenth-, and early eighteenth-century Europe as early modern, others have defined the term around post-eighteenth-century European transformations. Jürgen Habermas and Michel Foucault, for example, have focused on how the term underwent a significant shift in meaning during the period of Enlightenment. Habermas describes how modernity became a mode of relating to contemporary reality; in this mode, the present is continually interrogated by self-conscious subjectivity,[1] creating a forward-driven paradigm that rejects the immediate past and, perhaps more distinctively, propels the present towards a possible future.[2] Foucault advises that modernity represents not only a particular temporality, but also an ethical imperative to change: Modernity anticipates an imminent future as both a task and an obligation.[3]

For many, the idea of modernity has seemed self-evident, yet the term is, in theory, wide open. Modernity is ultimately ambiguous, connoting at once, John Tomlinson suggests, "a category" that emerges from a distinct kind of social formation and its institutions; "a form of cultural imagination" grounded in the epistemology of reason and certain notions of space and time; and "a definite historical period."[4] But although the term "modernity" is indefinite and its meaning contested, the concept has had a powerful historical presence. Modernity appears as an object to be attained (to *acquire* modernity) and a condition to be achieved (to *be* modern). In Britain, the notion of modernity has been given substance since the eighteenth century through a series of ideas, practices, and institutions clustered around it. These include notions of science and technology that became important in the colonial context. This amalgamation also incorporates a new mode of production—capitalism—as well as social processes, such as urbanization, that helped produce a new kind of national identity. New subjectivities have emerged from the ideas, practices, and institutions associated with modernity, bound about the ideals of individualism, secularization, and instrumental rationality. Culturally, they have given rise to new symbols, such as the train symbolism explored in this book, as well as to notions of alienation, meaninglessness, and a sense of impending social dissolution.[5]

Modernity and mobility are closely connected in a relation charged by the power of rhetoric and representation. Modernity has often been allied with mobility through representational forms—textual, spatial, and temporal. A journey, for example, functions as the means and metaphor for personal transformation. A city street filled with people and objects on the go appears as the sign of a society undergoing transformation. "From the democratic spatialization of the public sphere to the interiorized consciousness of the bounded individual subject," Caren Kaplan writes, "Western modernity since the Enlightenment tends to privilege mobility of one kind or another."[6] Despite this, modernity cannot be reduced to mobility. The cluster of numerous concepts, practices, and institutions associated with the modern substantiate modernity even as its meaning remains fluid.

Leaving aside for a moment the problem of defining modernity as such, there is also the issue of defining *a* modernity. Recent critics have challenged the philosophical definition of modernity as derived from particular historical experiences in Europe. They re-situate the idea of modernity to places torn by debates about cultural affiliation, theorizing a modernity of alterity, produced by a "constitutive outside,"[7]—usually an imperial power. In describing this alterity, some scholars show an ambivalent modernity or a dialectical modernity riven by difference. Gyan Prakash, for example, sees a colonial modernity as an "internally divided process,"[8] and Paul Gilroy describes a double consciousness that places modernity *inside* a European tradition of Enlightenment thought as well as *outside* of it, in the sense that the West is forged by relationships with outsiders during the history of the black Atlantic and African diaspora.[9] Timothy Mitchell, like Gilroy, depicts a process by which Western modernity is composed of elements subordinated or excluded, "such elements continually redirect, divert, and mutate the modernity they help constitute."[10] Other critics have argued that European versions of modernity become reshaped along the contours of different and even oppositional local spaces by imaginative and material practices that are both individual and collective, along the lines of Dilip Gaonkar's "creative adaptation,"[11] producing "alternative," or, when they are tallied, "multiple" modernities.

Rather than pursue a comprehensive philosophical definition of modernity across diverse terrain or rehearse this challenge to a Eurocentric definition of modernity, instead I propose approaching modernity as rhetoric and then exploring the history of this rhetoric as it functioned through a cluster of representational and material practices. The historical–political story lies in how that process becomes mobilized, as Frederick Cooper puts it, "how the concept is *used* in the making of claims."[12] By focusing attention on the way that modernity functions through representational and material aspects, one might "trace the effects of its usage and its relation to politics on the ground."[13] The emphasis on how the concept of modernity was deployed—in philosophy, in bureaucratic discourse, in art, or in labor practices—also alters how one defines modernity. The concept of modernity has been filled in by studies that explore the complex responses—repetitions, rebuttals, and rearticulations—made to the versions of modernity authored in the colonial context. By looking at modernity as rhetoric with important historical consequences, it is possible to see both its fluidity as those circumstances change and, perhaps more strikingly, the moments that those meanings congeal into static forms.

Traveling Modernity

Describing the imperial context, Akhil Gupta argues: "To speak of modernity is less to invoke an empirical referent than a self-representation of the West."[14] As the British carried the idea of the railway to India, they brought a rhetoric of modernity—a colonial modernity—the meaning of which was derived from the amalgam of practices and institutional forms that had given it solidity in Victorian England. These included the cluster of concepts, practices, and institutions that had substantiated modernity there, including technology, capitalism, urbanization, individualism, secularization, instrumental rationality, alienation, and mobility.

Although this traveling modernity never had an absolute origin— a place where it existed without contradiction or contestation—it positioned itself as what Timothy Mitchell calls a "world-as-picture," the "autocentric picture of [modernity] as the expression of a universal certainty, whether the certainty of human reason freed from particular traditions, or of technological power freed from the constraints of the natural world."[15] The concept of modernity derived its potential to replicate and expand from this dynamic imaginative quality grounded in claims of freedom from cultural specificity, but the same generative power is a point of instability that allows it to be rearticulated and displaced.[16] The following sections of this introduction interpret that "self-representation of the West"[17] using the rhetoric and practices surrounding the Indian railway. In the chapters that follow, I examine how some of the ideas and processes clustered around modernity would flourish, some would meet resistance, and some would be forever altered by the journey.

Capitalism, Modernity, and the Indian Railway

Economic, technological, and even spatial changes associated with capitalist production gave substance and form to a notion of the modern. Karl Marx's writings in the nineteenth century influenced this understanding, denoting the break of modernity as a transformation in the social relations of production from those of a feudal society to those of a capitalist one. Nineteenth-century colonial and nationalist rhetoric saw the materialization of modernity in the global expansion of financial capital and the extension of commercial markets on a national and international scale. In these formulations, the railway in India appears as a "vector of capitalist modernity."[18]

Capitalism gave rise to forms of mobility, but it was also itself constituted by them in ways that highlighted capitalism's inherent contradictions; Marx recognized that capital draws from processes of circulation and yet cannot be generated solely from inside it. For this reason, Mark Simpson asserts, mobility "[i]s deeply contested under capitalism: a source of contest structural to its operations, and concomitantly . . . a key mode or medium of contest within its histories."[19] These contradictions were made evident in a colonial context in which capitalism depended on the exploitation of labor and natural resources enabled by conquest. This political economy compels other colonial rhetorics of modernity as mobility, such as the equation of movement and emancipation, even as it erodes the logic of these universal claims.

The train was critical to global financial, industrial, and commercial capitalism in the nineteenth century. The Indian railway was itself part of an international economy of finance—it was the largest single investment of the British Empire in the nineteenth century and, indeed, among the largest international investments in that century.[20] The prominent players were British merchants and promoters, although several Indian business-men also actively pursued railway construction. This railway changed the economy of international investment. For British investors, financial gain was secured by the East India Company's 1849 guarantee of free land, facil-ities, and 5 percent profit for twenty-five years, providing an astonishingly secure deal for investors in a climate of uncertain speculation. After 1858, the role of guarantor passed into the hands of the colonial government of India. In the eleven years following, about £150 million of British capital went to India and the railways in particular.[21] The capitalism that devel-oped out of India's railway construction was uneven in the sense that it served more to develop British financial capital than Indian, and this was a primary cause for the protests launched by nationalists against what they deemed a "drain" on India's economy.

Despite bringing some new jute mills, the railway did not industrial-ize India as it had Britain.[22] For the British Empire, and later for India as a nation-state, however, the Indian railway did hold enormous economic importance in developing commercial capitalism. The network func-tioned as a means of transporting raw materials like cotton and coal and for distributing manufactured goods from Britain. The construction of the first two lines between 1850 and 1854 reflected the emphasis on extract-ing raw materials: The East Indian Railway Company (EIR) built a short line north from Calcutta, with the aim of extending it to the coal mines and then to the fertile Ganges Valley; the Great Indian Peninsula Railway Company (GIP) built a line north of Bombay towards the cotton fields of the Deccan.[23] Expanded operation developed new patterns of circula-tion and changed the geography of markets in India. Textile manufactur-ers from Manchester, for example, sought to sell textiles in, as well as to import raw cotton from, India. The new commodity flows transformed the market space, as village artisans were unable to compete with the cheaper manufactured British goods brought in by the railway.[24]

The train itself was a commodity that commanded enormous resources and helped build Britain's industrial capitalist economy. London provided the impetus for India's expanded railway construction, and the move-ment of manufactured parts and labor from Britain and India linked the two places. Iron-girder bridges were produced "to the last rivet" in

British factories and transported by steamship to India, where they were assembled over rivers.[25] It was not until as late as the 1920s that Indian railway companies began to turn to Indian-manufactured parts.[26]

Colonial rhetoric from the 1860s viewed Indian railway construction as a hallmark of capitalism partially because of the way it brought men, women, and children into the sphere of production through wage labor.[27] Bartle Frere, governor of the Bombay Presidency, announced at the opening of the Bhore Ghat in 1862, "For the first time in history the Indian Cooly *sic* finds that he has in his power of labour, a valuable possession."[28] Juland Danvers proposed an extension of the railway in 1877, arguing that one of the prime benefits of the railway to the native was that it allowed workers to engage in wage labor.[29] Although the construction of a "permanent way" did not introduce migrant labor, or even large-scale colonial infrastructural projects, to India (for example, the Ganges canal was built in the 1840s to irrigate areas of Uttar Pradesh), the railway's enormous construction and operation reshaped the structures of labor in India and helped bring workers into a capitalist system of labor. Even before it began to cross the continent of South Asia, the railway became the largest arena of employment within the industrial sphere of India's colonial economy.[30]

Modernity and the State

From its inaugural moment, the public space of the railway, including its tracks, stations, and carriages, functioned as a symbol of British power. The railway might have been funded by foreign investors, but it was built because of the unprecedented state guarantee for those speculative loans. The close connection between the railway and the British colonial state, fostered by the economic conditions of its construction, forever marked the official rhetoric of the railway. The same year that the first tracks were laid, Governor-General Lord Dalhousie penned his influential "Railway Minute" as part of his broader policy of consolidating his rule through geographical connection and entrenching the power of governmental bureaucracy in the colony. The leader of British administration in India systematically argued for an expanded railway network as a means of state security through communication and military transport, and as a way to buttress the political interests of the state with "commercial and social advantages."[31] Dalhousie imagined the railway as a way to map an

Indian state over areas of present and possible rule. In the 1853 "Railway Minute," the governor-general did not directly mention the benefits of the railway to Indians. He only alluded to Indians in a reference to the "hostile attacks" that "may at any time be expected."[32] The railway would shrink these distances and secure these outposts of empire into the bound space of a state.

Following the 1857 rebellion and the 1858 establishment of the British Raj, Queen Victoria announced that new colonial policies would emphasize technology.[33] A newly expanded railway was to play a key ideological function in this process. Framjee R. Vicajee, an Indian scholar lecturing before the National Indian Association in London in 1875, echoed Dalhousie's dominant preoccupations with military security, but he expanded the range for social uplift to include native subjects. The Indian appealed to the anxiety of his European audience over past colonial insurrections, and he argued that the train was critical to the security of empire. "Within the heart of the country, there is scarcely any native principality now subsisting which can hope to become a source of alarm to the Anglo-Indian Empire," the insider reassured his audience, adding, "But attempts of any sinister nature will be effectually stifled by means of the steam-engine before they have time to acquire proportions."[34] For the Anglophile Vicajee, as for Dalhousie, the ability of the train system to move troops at a rapid pace had social effects beyond simply quashing uprisings or winning wars; Vicajee argued that the "iron bands" that bound the country made the state stronger "in extending the silent victories of peace by a strong and efficient policy of administration in matters relating to revenue, justice, or education."[35]

The relationship between the railway and the nation went beyond the civic administration of a colonial state, for the railway played an active part constructing what Benedict Anderson calls a nation as an "imagined community."[36] Colonial rhetoric presented the railway space as a means of amalgamating different religions and castes into a homogeneous nation. The railway's dynamic spatialization, including its tracks, stations, and interior of the carriage, helped produce India. Railway tracks became the skeleton that mapped territory and supported the corpus of the future nation, creating a dynamic social geography (although this body would be partitioned in 1947). This "permanent way" and the movement of trains upon it continually renewed a national identity long past the period of construction. Even today, the train re-inscribes a relation between local and national as a priori; while appearing simply to move between fixed points in a system, the train actually creates these places as points and fosters a relation between them.

For leaders like Vicajee, the trains themselves were to represent the creation of a new collective identity that would amalgamate the many sectors of Indian society. The railway was positioned in representations as a way to assimilate an India seen as multitudinous. This idea of incorporation persisted well into the twentieth century and laid the groundwork for the role of the railway in the rhetoric of nationalists like Jawaharlal Nehru or postcolonial writers like Anita Nair. For early twentieth-century British writers, such representations of the railway offered them symbolic ways to absorb India. In 1934, John William Mitchell published *The Wheels of Ind.*, a railway memoir about his days working for the East India Railway. In it, he describes coming to India as entering a "maelstrom," a "spawning ground of millions," a "huge heterogeneous mass that seethed and moved restlessly and unceasingly."[37] He goes on to elaborate his role in this chaos: "To me was given an opportunity of assisting in the regulating and guiding of this movement by means of one of the greatest gifts of Western materialism to mystical India—the Railway."[38] Calling himself a "cog, if only a small one, in this wonderful organization by which so large a part of India moves and has its being,"[39] Mitchell ornaments his extended metaphor in which India's magical snake becomes Europe's train. The language of order stands out in this passage; words like "regulating," "guiding," and "organization" suggest the imposition of a rational order to contain, as well as better, Indians and India. The railway serves as both the means and the symbol of this order.

In both public discourse and literary representations, British writers imagined this new state forged from different cultures and classes. In *The Journal of Indian Art*, published in London in 1913, Lieutenant-Colonel R. Gardiner described the role of the railway in this process:

> The effect of this vast movement of the people, with the inter-
> course it has brought about between what previously were great
> nationalities practically unknown to one another, is now beginning
> to be felt in the drawing together of the people of India with the
> recognition of common interests, common ideals and ambitions;
> in other words, the birth of a common national and patriotic senti-
> ment which, well directed, should eventually mould India into

a united and loyal people, still the brightest gem in the imperial diadem.[40]

The picture of isolated nationalities was historically inaccurate, but the representation here shows how the British justified their role in India in terms of uniting the subcontinent. The trains themselves were to represent the creation of a new collective identity that would cut across ethnic, religious, linguistic, and cultural differences. As mobile visual displays of this amalgamated self, they were what one critic has called a panorama of Empire: "Trains, with their engines inscribed 'Rocket,' 'Express,' 'Fairy Queen,' or 'Lord Falkland,' manned by European loco men, carrying a different motley crowd—a people —passengers in varied dresses, belonging to different regions, castes, creeds, and colour."[41] The performance was put on for that imagined audience of Indians who were now within the railway sphere.

Mobility, Technology and Social Transformation

Colonial modernity was born out of travel. Movement opened the possibility of contact with new cultures and fashioned a cosmopolitan world vision. Colonial rhetoric justified its role in terms of travel, fetishizing a history of exploration, migration, and mobile technologies. Movement became a way of fulfilling and legitimizing the project of modernity undertaken in Europe, for as James Clifford puts it, "travels and contacts are crucial sites for an unfinished modernity."[42] The rhetoric of colonial modernity animated such ideas as reason, science, and secularism through narratives of progress and expansion, and in doing so, placed centrally, both materially and imaginatively, the paradigm of movement. By the mid-nineteenth century, the rhetoric of modernity had begun to realize this paradigm on a massive scale, both in Britain and in India, through social, economic, and technical changes enmeshed in a culture of mobility. Expressed in material processes, colonial modernity involved different kinds of movement, including flows of knowledge, materials, commodities, practices, and cultural productions. Social and psychical movement, as well as physical passage, comprised this culture. The expansion of markets and the circular flow of goods institutionalized capitalist production. Bureaucratic structures extended tributaries throughout British society and into the colonial sphere. Changes in labor structures forced people to move.

Technological innovations like the railway and telegraph collapsed space through rapid movement and altered relations with the natural world. A culture of mobility became an agent promoting these material changes. That culture also provided a way to describe these revolutions as the *image* of movement offered a way to signify modernity.

The train traveled as an idea from Britain to India, and it brought with it certain notions of the modern, including visions of social transformation and changes in the experience of time and space. The concept of a railway was entwined with particular notions of modernity bound up with the historical circumstances of nineteenth-century Britain. Michael Freeman writes that in Britain, the "railway was deeply embedded in the evolving structures of Victorian society. It both echoed those structures and interacted with them."[43] The railway marked not only these structures, including social, political, and economic aspects of society, but also their development. Early proponents linked the railway to a utopian vision of social transformation connected to the reform movement of the day. Michael Robbins writes of the 1830 opening of the Manchester and Liverpool Railway that people believed the achievement in mechanical science must give rise to political achievement.[44] Wolfgang Schivelbusch summarizes the significance of the train in the cultural climate of the time: "To adherents of progressive thought in the first half of the nineteenth century, the railroad appears as the technical guarantee of democracy, harmony between nations, peace, and progress."[45]

As well as representing a certain version of political reform, the railway in the nineteenth-century British context symbolized spatio-temporal changes. The rhetoric of modernity connoted by a moving train pointed always towards a possible future, a destination toward which one ideally moved quickly. The increase in velocity from the horse-drawn conveyance to the mechanically driven train altered the lived experience of space and time so much that, in the words of one contemporary, "Everything is near, everything is immediate—time, distance, and delay are abolished."[46] Of course, numerous inventions embodied this idea, including electricity, the telegraph, the steamship, and later the automobile; however, perhaps more than any other design, the railway, by "collapsing space and time," came to symbolize the spatial alteration that contemporary theorist Anthony Giddens equates with modernity.[47] These are regulatory orders as well as perceptual ones: The shifting notions of space and time were not merely abstract psychical changes, but changes deeply embedded in social relations.

Even before the first line was built between Bombay and Thana in 1853, the colonial rhetoric of the railway was concerned with using the train as a tool to instill proper public order through social transformation. This rhetoric of reform reflected the political climate of liberalism from 1828, with the administration of Governor-General Lord William Bentinck, to 1857, just after Lord Dalhousie's administration and the uprising against British rule. Representing a movement in Britain, but given new meaning in what became a symbolic forum in imperial India, purveyors of liberalism grounded their ideals in Enlightenment rationality and looked to liberate individuals from traditional religious and feudal powers. A primary aspect of the ideology was the separation of the secular and the religious; this binary held primacy in the ideal construction of the railway even as it was continually troubled by representations of difference, a point I explore in chapter 1. Although a new conservatism took hold after the 1857 rebellion—an ideology that increasingly emphasized what it deemed Indians' essential difference—the notion of imperialism justified by a mandate to bring cultural change remained a powerful force in the colonial context.[48] The train was there to transform Indians as well as India.

During this period, the railway became both a means and a justification for colonial rule. The rhetoric of development as education was central to this form of colonization. David Arnold argues that by the early nineteenth century, "the British saw science, technology, and medicine as exemplary attributes of their 'civilizing mission,' clear evidence of their own superiority over, and imperial responsibility for, a land they identified as superstitious and backward."[49] As rule and technology were made equivalent, India became, in the words of Gyan Prakash, a "context in which colonial governance meant technological transformation."[50] A key process at work in these colonial writings was the function of technology as a symbol of modernity. Dalhousie himself reflected this symbolic role of the railway; looking back at his time in India in 1856, he saw his contribution as introducing the three "great engines of social improvement, which the sagacity and science of recent times had previously given to Western nations—I mean Railways, uniform Postage, and the Electric Telegraph."[51] This process of social transformation took place not only at the level of the state, but also on the micro-level of the construction of railway space. The public space of the train became a site of reform: a "rational utopia"[52] that appeared to embody, in its very spatialization, ideals that would order a seemingly chaotic India.

The colonial discourse that promoted mobility as a means for social evolution was part of this broader set of representations about technology. Science, especially technological development, performed a kind of cultural authority in India.[53] John Chapman, promoter of the Great Indian Peninsular Railway, wrote in 1850 of "the double hope of earning an honourable competency and of aiding in imparting to our fellow subjects in India a participation in the advantages of the greatest invention of modern times."[54] In "The Future Results of British Rule in India," published in the *New York Daily Tribune* in 1853, the year the first passenger railway ran in India, Karl Marx echoed these sentiments, but toward a slightly different end. "England," he wrote, "has to fulfill a double mission in India: one destructive, the other regenerating—the annihilation of old Asiatic society, and the laying of the material foundations of Western society in Asia."[55] Marx anticipated India reaching its complete potential as a fully industrialized society, and he saw the railway as the "forerunner of modern industry."[56] Technology became the concrete sign of a progressive orientation to such an extent that in 1877, a British official wrote: "Any history of the material progress of India may well be divided into a pre-railway and a post-railway period."[57]

Temporal precision promoted by industrial technology became a sign of this modernity. In this regard, the railway emblematized the modern in two ways: First, it spatialized time in the form of a timetable, and second, it ritualized time through scheduled arrivals and departures marked by a signal. The machine even assumed the power of empire through the instrument of temporal precision. In the popular British literary journal *Fraser's Magazine*, a traveler returning from India opined the following:

> We talk of education. What education like that of the glorious,
> much abused, and as yet little understood invention of the railway?
> We preach all science and all virtue, but Blackey will not believe.
> We introduce clocks, and insist on the importance of time, but
> Blackey lingers for his quarter or half-hour of dearly loved daw-
> dling, nevertheless. But the railway comes; and with an awful
> mechanical punctuality—more stern, more silent, more exact-
> ing, more unscrupulous than any punctuality which a man can
> pretend to—the clock strikes, the bell rings, the dead-alive engine
> whistles—moves—departs; the inexorable metal trip succeed in

teaching the lesson which flesh and blood could not impress, and Blackey is never late at a railway station.[58]

The anonymous traveler's meditation is notable not only for its racism, but also for the way it appears to give authority over to the train. In this passage, it is the machine itself, rather than the British, that spreads a scientific world view and furthers the advancement of civilization.

Images of the train such as this one were used to sustain the notion of potential transformation and enforce a cultural hierarchy presented in official writings. Colonial literary and visual texts organized and reinforced the ideal relation between Indians and the train through their depictions of space. They represented the outside, where Indians first encountered the train—the hillside where Indians would view the first trains moving down the tracks; they also showed the inside, where Indians very shortly after entered as passengers—the third-class carriages that would become the designated section for Indian travelers. These colonial representations staged how Indians would encounter Europe through the railway space, first as observers of this mobile memorial to British power and later from the interior space of the carriage. In both places, as the plan went, Indians would be changed by their experience of the technology.

Writers and artists rendered the scene of this transformation, ritualizing in texts the encounter between Indians and this European technological form. In an unattributed engraving published in the *Illustrated London News* in 1863, the idea of progress is narrated by a series of images portraying "Modes of Travelling in India—Tramps—Hindoo Pilgrim—Palky Dawk—Travelling Beggar—Camel Caravan—Charry Dawk—A Bhylie—Riding Elephant—Am Ekha—The East Indian Railway" (Figure 3). The bottom picture of the train shows the final stage of development. In this image, the perspective places the viewer behind a group of Indians watching the locomotive. The Indians gaze intently at the new technology while one man points to it. The passengers are obscured, appearing only in outline, and the viewer's attention is instead drawn to the Indians' wondrous engagement with the train.[59]

Another tableau of first contact appears in narrative form in a travel memoir written by an Indian. Bholanatha Chunder published *The Travels of a Hindoo to Various Parts of Bengal and Upper India* in a series for the Calcutta periodical *Saturday Evening Englishman*. In the collected edition,

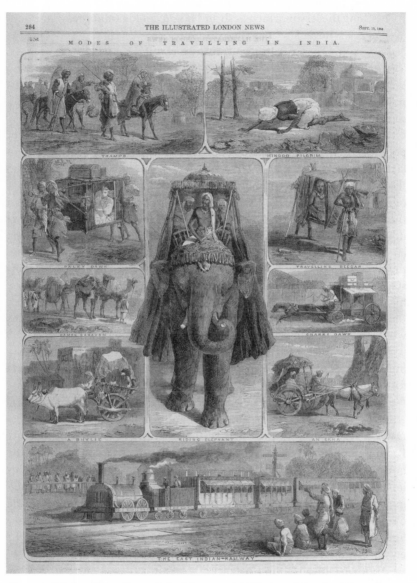

Figure 3. "Modes of Travelling in India," from an 1863 Illustrated London News, *shows a hierarchy of travel culminating at the bottom with an image of the first train;* Illustrated London News *shelfmark 19/9/1863, p. 284. Copyright The British Library Board. All Rights Reserved 03/07/2009.*

published in England in 1869, J. Talboys Wheeler introduced the author as
"a fair type of the enlightened class of English-educated Bengalee gentlemen."[60] In his travel narrative, Chunder presents Indians turning out along
the road to see the "progress of the train, and gaze in ignorant admiration
at the little world borne upon its back."[61] The writer casts the train as the
material embodiment of England's historical role in India. The technology acts as a potential monument: "The introduction of this great novelty
has silenced Burke's reproach 'that if the English were to quit India, they
would leave behind them no memorial of art or science worthy of a great
and enlightened nation.'"[62] Like the image in the *Illustrated London News*,
Chunder's narrative was part of a dynamic colonial imagination interpreting the technology for colonial and Indian viewers alike. The anonymous
illustrator and Chunder presented to British and Indian audiences what
the railway should mean to Indians—namely, an object that secures the
colonial authority in cultural terms. The popular discourse, like the official
rhetoric, advanced the train as a way to enact social change.

Modernity and Religion

In 1853, the London-based *Railway Times* laid out these ambitions as it
announced the first Indian railway: "In a few weeks, therefore, the iron
road that is probably destined to change the habits, manners, customs,
and religion of Hindoo, Parsee, and Mussulman will commence its work
in the Indian Peninsula."[63] The same year, Karl Marx looked even further ahead to see the railways changing the Indian economy, and thus
Indian social relations: "Modern industry, resulting from the railway system, will dissolve the hereditary divisions of labour, upon which rest the
Indian castes, those decisive impediments to Indian progress and Indian
power."[64] Although he viewed the social reform of the Indian caste system emerging from a new organization of labor, Marx reproduced the
rhetoric that placed Hinduism, understood as caste, in opposition to the
railway.

As seen in these quotations, colonial writers representing the railway as
a means of reform concentrated on the charged arena of religion. A broad
set of writings circulated in both India and Britain describing the railway
as a public space that would engender social transformation by overcoming certain aspects of Hinduism (less so Islam), especially caste structures
and the perceived role of Brahmin priests.

The British relationship to caste was twofold. Notions of caste were increasingly used over the nineteenth century to classify Indians under British rule as part of a broader effort to categorize Indians in terms of social, economic, and occupational categories, often reduced to essential attributes.[65] At the same time, the idea of overcoming caste was posited as an objective in much of the nineteenth-century colonial writings. One sees in the construction of caste as inherently oppressive intimations of what was happening in the political scene of Britain itself, which during this period was marked by efforts for political, social, and economic reform.

This liberal ideology found a symbol in representations of Brahmin priests. Colonial scholar-officials often, though not exclusively, saw Hindus entrapped by a Brahmin-centered value system that was, from this perspective, rigidly hierarchical.[66] Following the 1857 rebellion, this kind of classification was given added force and anti-caste writings more directly challenged the legitimacy of Brahmin priests. In 1864, East India Company official Sir John Kaye depicted a new knowledge, embodied by the "fire-carriage on the iron road," performing a kind of epistemic rupture that "disquiets" the mind of all the Hindus who apprehend the new technology.[67] Kaye's attack on the social inequity inherent in a religion allegedly controlled by a "scheming" Brahmin priesthood clearly indicated an attempt to undermine the power of a rival group of leaders. Indeed, although Enlightenment principles legitimized the separation of the secular and religious, the division drew its historical force in India from the project of removing power from the precolonial states associated with religions. Kaye drew on the writings of liberal leaders like James Mill, who depicted Brahmins, who were civic as well as religious leaders, as detrimental to India's progress.[68] More to the point here, Kaye cast Hinduism as an impediment to the development of this technology.

In the beginning, the mere sight of the train would overthrow or transform Hinduism, but later, the interior of the railway space was presented as the classroom for social change. Writing the introduction to Chunder's travel narrative, Wheeler rhapsodized that the easy distance of the rail has overcome "the strongest possible prejudice against traveling [that] existed in the minds of the Bengalees."[69] Government Director of Indian Railway Companies Juland Danvers outlined the benefits of the railway, which would remove prejudices and improve habits by placing natives in proximity to Englishmen: "As they go to and fro, they will see and learn much that they never thought of before. There will also be more intercourse and friction. The power of caste will likewise be shaken."[70] Popular travel writers also endorsed the railway as a way to overcome the perceived inequities of caste, if not caste itself. Edward Davidson wrote in 1868, "A sacred Brahmin now sits in a third-class carriage in contact with a Dome (the lowest caste of Calcutta, employed in killing dogs and burying dead), and preferring a saving in money to his caste exclusiveness, drops his prejudices."[71] In these writings that elevate cultural assimilation, the railway as both a mobile space and a public space became a site for working out a colonial relationship to Hinduism.

Race, Class, and Gender

In 1854, an image appeared in the *Illustrated London News* showing a railway platform with Indians traveling alongside Europeans in an idealized concept of a mixed traveling public (Figure 4). The station space, bound by a fence and a telegraph pole, is cordoned off from the background vegetation

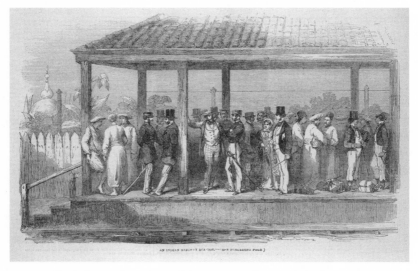

Figure 4. "An Indian Railway Station," from an 1854 Illustrated London News, *presents an idealized scene of Indians and Europeans sharing a platform.* Illustrated London News *shelfmark 2/9/1854, p. 208. Copyright The British Library Board. All Rights Reserved 03/07/2009.*

and temple, showing that this new public space is both a part of and apart from the India around it. A few years later, one traveler described a typical train: "the two second-class [carriages] scantily occupied by a mixed population of Europeans, half-castes, and natives; and six or seven third-class, in which the great multitude, on whom the fortune of the Calcutta Railway depends . . . were herded together in a manner more profitable to the Company than pleasant to the passenger."[72] When the train was first built, European railway officials welcomed Indian passengers fairly quickly, recognizing the profit that lay in such an enormous population of potential travelers: 80 million in 1880, 200 million in 1904, and more than 500 million by 1921.[73] As a new public space, the train brought to India new ways of organizing its interlocking societies of Europeans and Indians, yet in doing so, the rhetoric and material practices of the railway often reestablished old standards in new ways. The idea that the railway would open social boundaries was matched by a contradictory response that stratified categories of race, class, and gender.

The workings of capitalism, as well as other ideological aspects of colonial rule, gave rise to these formulations. The function of capital in the colonial context depended on the production of difference. Describing the relationship between mobility and arenas of stagnation, Mark Simpson argues, "To the extent that mobility is not so much a common condition as a social and material resource crucial to the production and reproduction (the 'uneven development') of national, racial, engendered, classed subjectivities, it becomes the locus of contest."[74] This contest was made evident not only in protests against such schemes of categorization and their accompanying hierarchical practices, but also in the contradictions of the colonial discourse itself.

Although the 1854 illustration of the platform presented an image of a secular, interracial shared travel space, the racism that characterized the workings of the British Empire had begun to be encoded into laws regulating the platform and carriage space, as well as employment practices that prevented Indians (other than Anglo-Indians) from holding senior positions. Early mandates prevented Indians from coming onto the platform until a few minutes before the train arrived. Class divisions that made up the structure of the railway carriages enacted racial segregation; even Indians who could afford first- or second-class tickets were forced out of these areas by these practices when Europeans were present. Although longstanding, the conditions became a flashpoint for protest by early twentieth-century nationalist movements. One writer in 1910 decried the way that Europeans and Indians clashed almost daily in the first- or second-class carriages and Indians were forced to move to third class.[75] A body of nationalist writing critically described the crowded carriages in which more than 90 percent of Indians rode and the lack of access to drinking water and sanitation facilities.[76]

The relationship between class and the railway had a fraught history in Britain, where the dynamic spatialization of the railway had helped secure class structures even as the idea of the train played a role in a broader cultural discourse about class liberation.[77] In India, the structures of class became one of the defining orders in colonial and, later, postcolonial contexts; as in Britain, class was simultaneously undermined and reinforced by the railway. People from different economic backgrounds gained mobility through the railway, many of them traveling on pilgrimages. Ian Kerr argues that the railway made pilgrimage a more accessible popular practice: "[M]ass transportation has intensified the interflow between widely held values, experience, remembered experience, and imagined possibilities."[78] For example, agricultural workers were able to fit pilgrimage into their everyday lives, sometimes even on a single-day trip there and back. Despite this freedom, the train forced Indians into class identities imported from Britain through the type of tickets they carried, because railway space was divided by class; these divisions might otherwise have been made on the basis of region, language, religion, occupation, or caste. In the practices of railway regulation as well, class served to stand in for other signs of difference; Manu Goswami argues that the practices that distinguished between race and class "placed Indian bodies into the homogenized category of third- and fourth-class passengers. . . . [and] tended toward flattening of the internal divisions within 'communities.'"[79]

The tension between the railway as an arena for emancipation and as a place of class stratification becomes especially evident in railway officials' correspondence about redesigning the space of the railway to accommodate upper- and middle-class Indian women, many of whom were in *purdah*, the custom of women remaining secluded from public view that was, at that time, practiced by some Hindus and Muslims. One railway official, opposing a separate carriage that would protect the privacy of these women, put it thus in 1869: "In these days of progress and social improvement, I think it would be unwise to introduce any system that would tend to encourage and perpetuate class prejudices, especially when Railways have already done so much to cause their disappearance."[80] Popular opinion went another way, however. Official records include letters from prominent Indian men who argued to the railway administration that "this want of distinction often proves fatal to those who have not sufficient money to pay for a reserved carriage, and at the same time cannot submit, in consideration of their rank and privilege, to the degradation of traveling simultaneously with the common male passengers of a different creed and color."[81] As advocates of the railway sought to expand Indian traffic on the railway in the nineteenth century, the issues of colonial racial segregation collided with class conventions in the forum of the public space. European women rode in the first-class carriages, but racial hierarchies that figured in colonial administration would often not permit Indian women to join them there. Moreover, European men would also be in those carriages. Upper-class Indian women could (or would) not travel in the third-class carriages that carried 90 percent of Indians because that would undermine their status. They were left only with a mixed-gender second-class carriage as a traveling possibility, and they were sometimes forced out of that class when Europeans were present.

After tossing around the idea of having a seatless carriage laid with rugs where women could sit as if in a *zenana* (the enclosed room where a woman in *purdah* meets only her husband and close male relatives), the railway officials settled on a second-class carriage with the women's compartment separated by a corridor to an open compartment for male relatives, and a third-class carriage with two adjacent compartments for women and men. The secluded first-class carriages, where Indian women would not travel if there were European passengers on board, required no changes. Laura Bear argues that these changes effectively forced women to identify with class more strongly than they had previously.[82] For the woman in *purdah*, the secluded carriages reinforced divisions of gender while separating them from their lower-class counterparts, who traveled in what were sometimes multigender carriages.

This extensive correspondence about women travelers, which I discuss more in chapter 5, highlights how the representational as well as material practices of the railway secured gender as well as racial and class binaries. These conversations that took place in the late 1860s regulated space through a discourse about female purity. In characterizing the problem, this correspondence collected in the colonial Public Works Department records became a way of defining Indian culture for European officials by depicting the relationship between women and the public space. Both colonial and elite Indian voices, all male, appear in this correspondence; one Baboo Joykinshen Mookerjee wrote in a letter to the magistrate that "it is death to [women] to walk up to the train from out the station."[83] Thus, one may see in the discourse around railway space a complicit patriarchal discourse devoted to maintaining a private female space inside the public space of the train. Notions of both womanhood and Indian identity were constructed in this correspondence, constituted not within the home but within the spaces of mobility. The categories of race, class, and gender relied upon boundaries and the railway provided a way to fix the binaries that maintained these categories.

The porous nature of colonial administrative categories of identity were made apparent in the creation of the new community designated Anglo-Indian, which was fundamentally tied to the railway. The definition of "Anglo-Indian" is a tricky one, for the lines of demarcation do not fall strictly on racial lines but also include elements of the colonial category of domicile; bureaucratic attempts in the 1920s to differentiate "European," "Anglo-Indian," "Eurasian," and "Indian" took into account such factors as family relations (for example, contact with relatives abroad) and documentable heritage.[84] Moreover, the popular usage of the term has shifted over time. Thus, some refer to a European born in India, such as Rudyard Kipling, as Anglo-Indian, while others use the term exclusively for those with mixed-race heritage. As a result, Anglo-Indians as a group have always fallen between identities—historically considered not quite European by those in Britain and not quite Indian by many nationalists.[85]

One of the most distinct aspects of Anglo-Indian identity has been its close relation to the railway. In 1923, nearly half of the Anglo-Indian community were employed by or associated with the railways. This was originally the product of racist colonial administrative procedures, in which Indians were kept in the lowest levels of railway employment while Eurasians and Europeans born or living a long time in India were given relatively better jobs, such as drivers. The identification between Anglo-Indians and the railway was fashioned in the social arena, as well as through employment practices. Institutions such as the Railway Institute club or schools became places where Anglo-Indians cultivated a separate identity from other Indians. As a kind of cultural borderline, these institutions had an ideological charge; Bear argues that they "attempted to produce distinctions between physical and moral qualities of British civil society and

Indian forms of sociality."[86] This task extended into the domestic sphere, as homes located in railway colonies built to house European and Eurasians reflected through space the hierarchies within this distinct community and regulated its difference from both European and Indian constituencies. These practices of economic, institutional, and spatial practices were the basis for forming a "railway caste."[87]

John Masters's 1954 novel *Bhowani Junction* focuses on the conflicted nature of Anglo-Indian identity during the independence movement. Masters, from a military family in India, is himself considered Anglo-Indian, although in his narrative he identifies more closely with the British officer than with the mixed-race characters. His novel portrays a love quadrangle between an Anglo-Indian woman named Victoria Jones; her old lover, the Anglo-Indian Patrick Taylor; her prospective groom, an Indian nationalist named Ranjit Kasel; and a British colonel named Rodney Savage. Although Victoria finds true love with Rodney and receives a marriage proposal from Ranjit, she ultimately reconciles herself to a future with Patrick, a resolution that shows Masters's faith in the determining structures that keep Anglo-Indian identity separate from European and Indian.

Masters's novel shows the close alliance of Anglo-Indian identity to the railway. All the characters work on or live around the tracks and know intimately the schedule. Victoria feels a visceral connection, for the train symbolizes her sense of self, including her sexuality. Through Victoria, Masters presents a "railway caste's" relation to India. As her father blows the whistle of the 98 Up, Victoria muses, "That was not music for the soul; it was one of our people, his hand on the whistle cord, sending the shrill voice of the engine out over the roofs of the city, over the plains, reminding them of steel and people and wheels grinding on the rail."[88] This train constitutes a community and claims India on its behalf. For Masters, as India moves into independence, the borderline community forged from conflicting bureaucratic categories of race and residence ultimately will carry on the colonial technological project in the subcontinent.

With depictions of the universalizing force of technology, the colonial authors of the railway sought to overcome difference between Indians— difference that might otherwise unbind the colonial state. The discourse of the railway attempted to subsume aspects of Indian culture within the broader order by means of a public space, and in the process render it, from the colonial perspective, both more egalitarian and more rational. At the same time, the colonial rhetoric of development and education played an important role in delineating this space of alterity, in which difference justified colonial rule; technology in the form of the train performed a key ideological and symbolic function in this discourse as well. The images of Indians awed by European technology, which pointed toward a singular path for development, reinforced the difference between Europeans and Indians. At the same time, the category of Anglo-Indian, produced out of the material conditions of colonialism, belied these racial divisions. Chapter 1 analyzes visual and literary representations of the colonial railway, further exploring this contradiction between a rhetoric that touted an ideal of universalism and a simultaneous discourse of difference—a difference that continually troubled the dominant narratives of colonial modernity.

The Permanent Way:
Colonial Discourse of the Railway

Panoramas of Empire

In 1888, Rudyard Kipling and A. H. Wheeler Co., an Allahabad firm that monopolized the bookstalls of Indian railway stations, created a book series called the "Railway Library." The goal of the series, authored by Kipling, according to promotional materials, was "to be illustrative of the four main features of Anglo-Indian Life, viz: THE MILITARY, DOMESTIC, NATIVE, AND SOCIAL."[1] Travelers consumed the small gray volumes, bought for one rupee at station bookstalls, their progress marked by turned pages and the invisible rails beneath them. The books offered a mobile means for seclusion and observation, much like the train carriage itself. As the first-class carriage presented a discrete vista of the world that it revealed through the windows, so too did the narratives show a panorama of India. Sitting in a first-class car, passengers read about the world they inhabited, and the stories organized that world for them. As they read, they became part of a colonial discourse that delineated the public space of the colony through the railway and through narrative. As the goal of Kipling's library suggests, native identity was to be cultivated as well as controlled in this space. Of course, the image of seclusion was a fantasy; just as the space of the carriage was permeable to the India that it seemed to leave outside, so too was that carefully constructed notion of colonial public space subject to the features that it attempted to exclude. The stories became a way to mediate that gap, bringing into the textual realm the aspects of Indian identity that seemed to lie outside the idealized order of technology. Yet, ironically, in attempting to contain India's variance, these texts ultimately served as a record, a way to maintain the difference of India. This notion of difference, an unstable delineation between colonizer and colonized that created binary notions of race, ethnicity, culture, religion, and even temporality, was a defining characteristic of colonialism.

It was no coincidence that the railway was simultaneously the means for distributing the books, the scene for reading them, and often their subject. For colonial writers in India, the train as a vector of progress mobilized the imagination in a way no other public space could, because it presented and ordered a unique relationship to the world outside through the paradigm of movement. The colonial origins of the railway, which was first constructed in 1853, have forever marked this relationship between the train and its surroundings for both Indians and foreigners. This chapter emphasizes the latter, while the rest of this book considers how Indians have represented an ambivalent relationship to a national icon originally built by the British.

In a trope developed during the colonial period but continuing to this day in works like American director Wes Anderson's 2007 film *Darjeeling Limited*, the setting of the train has inspired the foreigner's imagination by placing India behind the traveler as a panoramic—and often static—background. In an early unattributed image from the *Illustrated London News*, for example, a European traveler lounges on his carriage couch. India has given him informality, and his coat is unbuttoned and his feet are on the cushion. He looks neither out the windows at the Indian landscape nor inside his carriage; instead, his blank gaze turns inward as he smokes.[2] In depictions like this one, an idealized European traveler is removed from both India and Indians, allowed to contemplate both as images in the window rather than as realities to be negotiated on the ground.

In the early twentieth-century vignette "A Railway Soliloquy," authored by a "Mrs. Shoosmith" (actually M. C. Reid), the narrator rhapsodizes about the introspective possibilities of Indian railway travel:

> A railway traveller in England develops an active hatred of his
> fellows: in India he sinks (or perhaps rises) into a dreamy self-
> absorption which almost denies their existence. There is a peculiar
> other worldliness about travelling alone in India: the two or three
> days enforced "retreat" from the ordinary pursuits of life, the
> calm with which the long journey is undertaken, the monotony
> of the scenery which must often be shuttered out together with
> the sunlight, the station noises which strike weirdly upon an ear

hypnotised by the rattle of the train, all combine to bestow an inner serenity which might be envied by the Jesuit Fathers.[3]

In Shoosmith's account, India is emptied; instead of the world of political movements and international exchange that the country was in the 1920s, it is an empty shrine for the spiritual rebirth of the English traveler. Intriguingly, the suspended railway traveler is relieved of his role in progress: "One can do nothing to help onwards the march of events," the narrator concludes, "There is a blessed tranquility in feeling that one has handed over for a while."[4] The passenger gives way to the movement of the train that carries him along; so too does the individual hand over the imperative to progress to the machine of empire. Despite pervasive images of the railway as a place temporarily separating weary Europeans from an overwhelming subcontinent, colonial writers and artists often actively used representations of the train to negotiate a relationship with India and Indians.

This chapter considers how colonial writers and artists staged the encounter with what they perceived as India's difference through depictions of the public railway space. That space was not a static field; it had a socially constructed meaning reflecting broader ideologies and crystallized in material practices. I argued in the Introduction that the political and economic writers Lord Dalhousie and R. M. Stephenson, along with British and Indian popular travel writers and illustrators, presented technology as a tool to both control and educate Indians. Colonial discourses about the train aimed to support the larger effort, typical of the rhetoric of colonial modernity, to establish rational and unified public spaces that were culturally secular, in which religion was subsumed into the broader order of the state. As these official and popular writers and artists imagined how the train would transform Indians, they also increasingly worried that Indians might change the nature of public space. In this chapter, I study these railway narratives and images to reveal how colonial culture used the train to construct binaries that elaborated features of Indian difference—the religious, the bodily, and the domestic in particular—aspects that seemed to lie outside the secular public sphere of the railway; they represented these binaries as a way of constructing a notion of modernity within India. I also show how these cultural works incorporated such representations of difference back into the image of the railway, challenging the very binaries that they constructed and producing a counternarrative of modernity.

Technology as a metonym for modernity became the staging ground for this friction between the primacy of colonial homogeneity and the articulation of Indian difference. Statesmen, artists, travel writers, and novelists alike transposed the linear narrative of progress into a story in which the train provided crucial aspects of form and mobility while carrying historical, cultural, and even spatial differences in its seemingly neutral moving box. The radical possibilities of that vision of modernity emerged only when the story of the train was later hijacked by people with vastly different interests, a phenomenon described in subsequent chapters of this book. Colonial narratives of the train never fully challenged the right of British rule. However, they did offer visions of the modern space as private rather than public, as religious rather than secular, and as Indian rather than European. To some degree, all the nineteenth-century colonial discourse presented a tension between two ideals of similarity and difference—for example, in writings that sought to reform Indians even as they deemed them essentially fixed into biologically determined racial categories.[5] Literary writers offered a particularly compelling vision of how an evolving colonial order attempted to reconcile the conflicting nature of a symbolic space that was at once public and private, universal and particular. In representing railway space as a site for the resolution of these conflicts, these creative writers generated a new vision of an inhabited modernity opened to the domestic, bodily, and religious aspects that it ostensibly set aside. Two prominent colonial writers of the nineteenth and early twentieth centuries, Rudyard Kipling and Flora Annie Steel, especially placed the image of the train centrally in their literary writings, imagining a lived-in modernity though this railway space, a vision that challenged the founding binaries of a colonial modernity.

Social Construction of Space

The social construction of Indian railway space, born in the other context of nineteenth-century industrializing Britain, made possible this imaginative dynamic in which the train articulated colonial rule. Several spaces are simultaneously claimed by the railway: the interior of the cars, the body of the trains, and the surrounding landscape experienced fleetingly by the observer yet occupied permanently by the tracks. The railway operates within these multiple spaces as an object that is both mobile and fixed, for it is both the vehicle and the road. These spaces of inside and outside are marked as separate; one need only think of the relationship between observing traveler and observed native to reflect on the hierarchical but fraught relations between interior and exterior highlighted by the window. So too, the train is constructed as a privileged enclosure offering a place of observation that is also one of retreat. In India's colonial context, it was promoted as an engine of modernity, a moving box in which cultural, racial, and historical differences could be amalgamated under a civic, secular, and public order — a "rational utopia."[6]

The spatialization of the railway carriage is one of regulation: in its strict bifurcation of inside from outside and in the way it has traditionally been heavily structured within its interior. A train carriage, in its ideal, offers the traveler the regulation of what Michel de Certeau calls a "rational utopia,"[7] in contrast to an outside perceived as chaotic. For colonial representations of the railway, only the first-class carriage — an exclusively European space — holds that ideal, and these works divide the inside of the first-class carriage from the outside, including other parts of the train that are deemed native (the second-class carriages also held Eurasians and thus are not part of this ideal). Colonial descriptions of railway stations consistently depict disorder in this exterior space: the crowd of Indians traveling "with their pots, pans, and other chattels hanging about them,"[8] and the "station noises which strike weirdly upon an ear."[9] These representations contrast the outside with a first-class carriage that appears like an intimate, but mobile, European domestic space. "An Indian railway carriage is a very luxurious one," one women's magazine wrote of the first-class carriages promoting honeymoons in India. "It contains a table, berths, and dressing-room, with shutters to exclude the glare of the sun, or quaint cocoanut fibre blinds, through which, when wetted with spray from a hose, delicious gusts of scented tropical air permeate refreshingly."[10] In visual culture, a divide is marked by the presentation of the carriage interior in several ways. Often a sink appears in the margin of the image, offering a sign of cultural order in the form of cleanliness.[11] The carriages suggest a middle-class Victorian living room transposed to India. However, the most important image marking cultural difference is the panoramic window: the framing barrier of glass that separates inside from out.

The idea of separation is, of course, one of fantasy because a carriage is always part of the world around it: A train is never truly impermeable. This is even more so when the carriage is forever conjoined to that outside world in the form of the second- and third-class carriages. Yet the fantasy speaks to the function of permanent order within a culture of mobility. Michel de Certeau has eloquently theorized the ideological coding of interior railway space as one of dialectic:

> The unchanging traveller is pigeonholed, numbered, and regulated in the grid of the railway car, which is a perfect actualization of the rational utopia. [...] Only a rationalized cell travels. A bubble of panoptic and classifying power, a module of imprisonment that makes possible the production of an order, a closed and autonomous insularity — that is what can traverse space and make itself independent of local roots.[12]

De Certeau describes the contradiction embedded in mobility — namely that the vehicle that expresses freedom through movement also rigidifies what might otherwise be fluid, fixing it through surveillance that separates inside from outside, and, in this context, colonial from native.

The Problem of Difference in Public Space

The 1857 rebellion against British rule gave rise to a more conservative government that emphasized what it saw as the irreducible difference of Indians. On the cultural front, Victorian scholarship sought to categorize — and therefore contain — conceptions of this difference. However, the liberal discourse of civilization remained a part of these newer theories of difference. British writers negotiated these two seemingly contradictory ideologies throughout the later nineteenth century, avowing sameness as they institutionalized difference; as Thomas R. Metcalf explains, "The task was never to be easy, nor was the result to be a coherent ideology of rule."[13]

Even as colonial writers and artists looked to use the public space of the railway to transform Indians, they were apprehensive about letting Indians into the public space. The railway space was a "contact zone," a social space "where disparate cultures meet, clash, grapple with each other, often in highly asymmetrical relations of domination and subordination."[14] In colonial discourse, the tension in the technological contact zone showed itself in the twin sentiments of racism and fear. The India suspended outside the window of the European traveler reading in her private carriage pushed in through the "slender blade" of the window frame.[15] As certain classes of

Indians entered the shared public spaces of platforms and the train itself (albeit in different classes)—and they did so as early as 1854[16]—colonial travel writers worried about the ways that the nature of that space would be changed. In response, these writers used the train to register an insurmountable cultural barrier.

English travel writers enumerated multiple ways that they saw Indians misusing the public space of the railway. In their eyes, Indians mobbed the stations, talked excessively, brought their pots and pans, and turned the secular world of the train into a place for religious rituals. One common depiction was the representation of Indian passengers as so excessively verbal that the contemplative Englishman could barely hear himself think. In his essay "The Indian Railway," published in 1863 and later part of a series of fictionalized letters collected in *The Competition Wallah*, George Otto Trevelyan describes Indians inappropriately trying to bargain about the ticket price before being forced to pay the posted rate and shoved onto the platform, "where he and his companions discuss the whole proceeding at great length and with extraordinary warmth."[17] Trevelyan also characterizes "an interminable row of third-class, packed to overflowing with natives in high exhilaration, stripped to the waist, clattering, smoking hubble-bubbles, chewing betel-nut."[18] Michael Furnell, in his 1874 memoir *From Madras to Delhi and Back via Bombay*, describes a group of pilgrims aboard his train near Allahabad as a "helpless" group, always "chattering."[19] He quotes one guard describing the group: It "is worse than 'osses,"[20] the man complains, a sentiment the author both mocks by rendering the guard's dialect and reproduces himself with his representation of an animal-like group.

The image of physical excess was also prevalent. Such racist representations, though they began during the nineteenth century, lasted well into the twentieth century. In John W. Mitchell's 1934 travel memoir, the railway official describes the Indian passengers "dashing hither and thither in that aimless way which seems to obsess them, at all times, on a railway-station platform when the train is in."[21] He describes the scene as "pandemonium" and "bedlam," producing an image repeated as a dominant trope in numerous representations of Indian railways. Mitchell inveighs against the Indians who abuse the rail system, from fare-dodgers to begging fake "sadhu" holy men, from men who con illiterate pilgrims with the offer to help them return home to passengers who sleep with their feet hanging out the windows.

Legal changes lay at the root of some of the early antagonism. In the effort to recognize an aristocratic Indian class along the lines of the British, Indians at first shared the platforms waiting for the trains, a situation idealized in the 1854 *Illustrated London News* image (see Figure 4 in the Introduction). Shortly after, officials from the Public Works Department decried the use of the railway platforms by natives and suggested that the accessible public space led to idle gossip or possibly subversive gatherings.[22] In her study on the production of state space in India, Manu Goswami describes the "microgeography of railway travel" constituted in colonial India by a racial hierarchy. She catalogs regulations by the Public Works Department that restricted the access of Indians to the spaces of the railway. Indians were either prohibited entry onto platforms or allowed only immediately before boarding. They were required to use separate sanitary facilities at the stations and sometimes the third-class carriages they rode in did not have bathrooms either. The series of carriages in the train were defined minutely into first-class European, second-class European, Eurasian, third-class Indian, and "coolie" class, reflecting the "obsessive concern to calibrate the movements of differentiated bodies, and reproduce the reified binarism of colonizer and colonized."[23]

The colonial fears that prompted racist writings and legal practices were concerned with proximity between the races and the subversive possibilities enabled by this new kind of mobility. On a subtler level, they represented anxieties about possible changes to the public space of the railway. That space and its rational order were important to colonial ambitions for social change—and for a colonial mandate for rule. But what if, instead of the public space changing Indians, Indians changed the public space? As early as 1863, Trevelyan reversed the notion that the railway would make Indians more industrious. He characterized the eminent symbol of progress as "a species of locomotion which pre-eminently suits [Indians'] lazy habits."[24] From the perspective of some European travelers, as Indians were invited to share the technological gift of the railways and to better themselves by doing so, Indians appeared to alter the nature of the railway.

Two pervasive images in particular support this position: the image of the train as a domesticated space and the scene of the railway as a place of religious ritual. Furnell describes in his memoir a scene in which a woman yells out to her family after she squeezes through the door only to realize she has left her party behind, a "performance repeated with slight variations at least a dozen times."[25] The view of the Indian railway space as an inappropriate extension of family space became a trope in colonial narratives. John W. Mitchell's portrayal of the Hindu household carrying its pots and pans shows the continued existence of this image sixty years later.[26] In Mitchell's mind, the Indian passengers break the rules of railway space by washing their clothing in the surrounding pools of rain rather than in the provided taps. Mitchell connects the domestication of the public space of the railway to the entrance of religious practice in the "rational utopia" of the train. Noting that "the Hindu faith is insistent upon many purifications," he attributes the passengers' care for washing to religious motivations. The indignant tone of Mitchell's passage suggests that the representative British passenger is bothered by more than the accompanying delay. The Indians are remaking the secular space of the train with their rituals of purification.

Literary representations like those of Mitchell and Furnell present both an idealized order and the aspects of difference that frayed that tightly woven image. The preoccupation with these deviations from the railway ideal implies a tension over regulation and order in the practices of the colonial railways. The vignettes of Indians misusing the public space might have provided comic relief for an audience back home, but they also implied uneasiness in the minds of the authors. Even as they inscribed the public space as a place of order, writers and artists were acutely aware of the porous nature of railway space, in which what was deemed private continually seeped into the public.

Reflecting fears that these alterations to the "rational utopia" of the railway might have a permanent effect on the Europeans who brought the train, colonial writers and artists occasionally showed the railway as a place of disorder undoing the civility of the British. Travel writer Trevelyan hints that the railway in India carries a new kind of "undone" European, including the *sahib* who arrives at the train with "a dirty alpaco coat, no collar, no waistcoat,"[27] as well as other European passengers in the first-class carriages who commit unseemly acts. These passengers include a newly married couple engrossed in "that charmingly selfish concentration of affection which is sometimes a little out of place in general society,"[28] and a "languid, bilious mother" and her "three little ones sprawling on the cushions in different stages of undress."[29] In the 1874 memoir described above, Furnell himself gets "carried way by the Babel of voices and struggling pilgrims."[30] He almost misses his train—an anathema

because, as a character muses in E. M. Forster's novel *A Passage to India,*
"[Englishmen] never do miss trains."[31] Furnell's comment suggests a fear
that competing notions of public space would prompt the degeneration of
European civilization.

In Forster's 1924 novel, the branch line train reflects this disintegration,
suggesting this change to the significance of the railway as part of a more
general loss of meaning for the British. The train scenes are pivotal in
A Passage to India, both as devices for forwarding the plot and as symbolic
passages elaborating Forster's themes of colonialism and modernity. After
the British professor Fielding misses the train, the main Indian character,
Aziz, is left alone to host two European women, Mrs. Moore and Adela,
on an expedition to see the Marabar Caves. In keeping with colonial representations of the Indian railway, Forster shows Indians domesticating the
railway space, with "dependents swarming over the seats of the carriage like
monkeys" as the train pulls in; as dawn arrives, "the smell of tobacco and
the sound of spitting arose from third-class; heads were unshrouded, teeth
cleaned on the twigs of a tree."[32] Shortly after, in another scene, however, he
focuses on the relationship between Adela and the train, echoing the earlier colonial texts in which the traveler turns inward in the isolation of the
Indian railway carriage. As Adela muses on her plans, "the train accompanied her sentences, 'pomper, pomper,' the train half asleep, going nowhere
in particular and with no passenger of importance in any of its carriages, the
branch-line train, lost on a low embankment between dull fields. Its message—for it had one—avoided her well-equipped mind."[33] The nonverbal
signifier "pomper" anticipates the crucial "boum" that Mrs. Moore hears
in the caves, and like that sound, the significance of "pomper, pomper" lies
beyond comprehensibility. The sound is both mundane and impossible
to penetrate, an idea elaborated throughout this text as reflecting the inef-
fective situation of the British in India—and, more broadly, the condition
of modernity. Forster's branch line train is a place where it is impossible
for the mind to take hold; such a depiction contrasts sharply with other
literary representations of the Indian railway in which the train is exactly
where the mind takes hold and where colonialism gathers significance.
Forster here focuses on the periphery of the colonial world, for this branch
line train is contrasted with another train: "Far away behind her, with a
shriek that meant business, rushed the Mail, connecting up important
towns such as Calcutta and Lahore, where interesting events occur and
personalities are developed."[34] The author, seemingly simply, contrasts a

backwater and a metropolitan arena; by locating his narrative in the static space of colonial modernity, however, he in fact calls into question the relevance of those important people and places signified by the hypermobility of the Mail train. The scope of his critique emerges with a haunting image of the return journey, in which "the train itself seemed dead though it moved—a coffin from the scientific north which troubled the scenery four times a day."[35] Forster references the technological mandate of colonialism emblemized by the train and transforms the symbol of modernity into a final resting place for a moribund colonial world.

Writers in the late nineteenth and early twentieth centuries made the space of the railway a contact zone where the cultures would both clash and grapple with each other. Writings that described Indians as incapable of using public spaces demonstrated the tenacious racism that coexisted with programs of social reform; these works also revealed the unstable nature of difference inside a technology posited as a homogenizing force. The same writers who deemed Indians incapable of using the railway also imagined the space of the railway as a medium to transform them. At the same time, some of them intimated that the space itself was being rewritten. The next section looks at the complex ways in which colonial writers and artists managed this contradiction by claiming the terms of difference.

The Discourse of Wonder

The notion of difference—racial, cultural, and even epistemological—had always been central to the narratives of colonialism. Even as scholarship and literature elevated the variance of other cultures, this writing often used difference as a way of justifying colonial rule through negative representations of the Other. In colonial India, diversity destabilized a technological rhetoric based on the ideal of a universal rational utopia. However, rather than simply suggesting that Indians should not use the railway—an unprofitable option—most colonial writers and artists sought to contain rather than deny difference. The representation of alterity, especially the distinction between Indians and Europeans but also the variation between Indians, became an important consideration when constructing railway space.

The discourse of social betterment did not seek to overcome all aspects of religious identity; in fact, certain kinds of commitments were encouraged overtly. Promotional materials touted the railway as the ideal vehicle for pilgrimages,[36] an objective that conveniently served an economic as well as a social agenda. An exhibition in the 1911 Festival of Empire showed a model of the station at Howrah, a terminus for Hindu pilgrims. The catalog for this exhibition describes a display section devoted to "illustrating progress under British rule since about 1858." It goes on to note:

> Nothing has been more remarkable, of course, than the facilities
> for travel, especially on the railways, which have been remarkably
> attractive to Indians, enabling them, for example, to go with ease
> to remote places of pilgrimage, at very little risk to themselves,
> whereas in the past few who journeyed to distant shores ever
> expected to return.[37]

The railway, it seems, enabled Hindus to be better Hindus. Bholanatha Chunder's advocate, J. Talboys Wheeler, saw Indians, especially upper-class Indians, as overcoming superstition even as they increasingly visited shrines, so long as they did so through the "safe and speedy mode" of railway travel.[38] His introduction to Chunder's travel memoir and these promotional materials suggest that the British saw Hinduism, when contained within the order of railway travel, as compatible to their ideals of civil order.

By promoting the railway in the service of religious identity, these writers sought to contain India's difference — for they consistently saw that difference as centered in religious identity — within the order of the train. Long before colonial writers embraced the use of the train in the service of religion, however, they made room for difference in their representations of the new technology. They assigned a central role to wonder, a condition equated with the prerational religious world of the Indians, within notions of technology. The 1863 *Illustrated London News* image of the first train in India promoted the rational ideal associated with the train by showing a hierarchy of travel (see Figure 3 in the Introduction).[39] In this representation, Indians do not work out the superiority of the European technology through the processes of logic; instead, they are entranced by the supernatural power of the machine. In the bottom part of this series of images, a group of Indians point with wonder at the new technology. Indians are initiated into the world of reason through the ineffable power of the sublime.

Colonial writers connected this condition of wonder to Hinduism. Chunder visually equates the railway and the Ganges, naturalizing technological space and validating the technology in terms of the sacred Hindu space. He merges the colonial discourse of education with that of religious fulfillment. "Surely, our ancient Bhagiruth, who brought the Ganges from heaven," Chunder writes, "is not more entitled to the grateful remembrance of posterity, than is the author of the Railway."[40] Chunder also likens the work of railway planning to the creation of a Hindu god, and both types of creation to his own writing through the use of the word "author." Offering the perspective of the "native" audience apprehending the train, the educated Indian writing in English represents the railway as fulfilling Hindu mythology:

> The first sight of a steamer no less amazed than alarmed the Burmese, who had a tradition that the capital of their empire would be safe, until a vessel should advance up the Irrawady without oars and sails! Similarly does the Hindoo look upon the Railway as a marvel and miracle—a novel incarnation for the regeneration of Bharat-versh.[41]

Once again, Chunder uses the discourse of wonder to ritualize the history of colonization, describing the train as a "marvel and miracle." He imagines himself at this place of first contact and suggests that the Indians understand the new technology in terms of Hindu mythology; the "Hindoo[s]" who look at this train see a reincarnated version of Bharat, a sacred word synonymous with India. In this way, Chunder uses the train to inscribe the new order of the colonial state in terms of a mythological, original India. He goes on to describe rail travel itself as the fulfillment of Hindu mythology:

> In [the train], a Hindoo is apt to feel the prophecies of the sage verified in the Rail—riding upon which has arrived the Kulkee Avatar of his Shasters, for the regeneration of the world.[42]

In this passage, the author draws another parallel between European modernity and Hinduism: The idea of reincarnation gives way to the modern rupture. The passage offers a way for Indians to understand modernity on their own terms. Although Chunder positions himself as an inside informant, the representation of the train in terms of Hindu mythology was not limited to Indian writers. Kipling's short story

"The Bridge-Builders," discussed later in this chapter, features a good example of the same kind of imagery. What is important to understand here is not that Indians needed to understand the European technology in religious terms, but that they were represented as needing that lens by both British and Indian colonial writers. The images that show credulous Indians apprehending the train and the travelogue that interprets that new technology through Hindu mythology demonstrate how colonial writers and artists managed India's seemingly absolute difference by framing that difference inside their representations of the railway.

To summarize, colonial writers needed to maintain India's difference, even as they promoted the train as a means for surmounting it. One way that they did this was by ritualizing the scene of Indians' first contact with the railway. They showed this initiation to the new technology not as a rational process but as one based in transcendence. This is ironic because the machine was the symbol of rationality. Colonial writers and artists connected this experience of wonder to Hinduism and translated the technology into the mythology of Hinduism. They selectively reproduced Indian writing that reinforced ideas of European technology as having a mystical force. One reason that colonial writers and artists wanted to pre-serve alterity, even as they promoted technologies as universal, was the centrality of difference to the imagination. Recall from the beginning of this chapter that the colonial imagination did not depend on the isolation of the "rational cell" but on the relation between that cell and an outside "different" India. The next section shows how literature became a way to negotiate these competing narratives of a universal, isolated, rational utopia and a particular, corporeal, and often sublime difference within the colonial context.

Inhabited Modernity: Rudyard Kipling and Flora Annie Steel

Rudyard Kipling and Flora Annie Steel were two of the most famous European authors from India's late nineteenth- and early twentieth-century colonial period. Their portrayals of the railway may be seen as an exten-sion of early images that used a discourse of wonder to present a "native" response to the train by retelling the story of technology as an experience of the sublime. Like these artists and writers, Kipling and Steel sought to portray difference in their imagery of the railway; in the process, they incorporated that difference into the concept of colonial modernity.

The result was an image of an Indian colonial modernity as a doubled space, one that was both an extension of Britain and a place for the articulation of alterity. Although Indian nationalists also simultaneously rewrote the colonial project of modernization in their own terms, a project that I consider in chapter 2, Kipling and Steel approached the same process as advocates for colonial rule. In their fictional works, the railway functions as what Michel Foucault called a "heterotopia," a "counter-site" in which "all the other real sites that can be found within the culture are simultaneously represented, contested, and inverted."[43]

Edward Said's work on Kipling helps historicize the literary writer's doubled space of colonial modernity. Said locates the Kipling of 1901 within what he called "competing truths." On the one hand, Kipling was writing "from the perspective of a massive colonial system whose economy, functioning, and history had acquired the status of a virtual fact of nature." As a journalist for the *Civil and Military Gazette*, Kipling closely followed civil engineering projects in India for a British colonial audience. In his letters abroad, political commentary, and fictional writing, he promoted these public works, contributing to the technological rhetoric that legitimized colonialism in terms of development. On the other hand, Said argues, Kipling wrote at a specific historical moment when the relationship between the British and the Indians was changing and decolonization movements were gaining strength.[44]

In his short story "The Bridge-Builders," several of Kipling's characters assume the positions of late nineteenth-century Indian nationalists like Dadabhai Naoroji, the president of the Indian National Congress in 1886. Kipling reproduces, then ultimately dispenses with, Naoroji's and others' arguments against the railway. Ironically, Kipling portrays through the imagery of Hindu mythology the historical materialist critique known as the "drain theory"—a secular theory promoted among certain late nineteenth-century nationalists arguing that colonial commercial, agricultural, and infrastructural practices, including the construction of the railway, had hindered rather than helped Indians economically. Thus, Kipling pushes the emerging voice of nationalism into a familiar construction of difference. In the novel *Kim*, Kipling uses the train as a framework to order a multitudinous India within the larger structures of modernity. Yet in both works, the notion of difference ultimately troubles the ideals of order.

"The Bridge-Builders" portrays the contradictions of a colonial technological narrative. Kipling first published the story in 1893 in the *Illustrated*

London News, six years after he had written two articles on bridge works for the Lahore-based *Civil and Military Gazette;* it was republished in the 1897 collection *The Day's Work.* The story has been read as evidence of Kipling's belief in the power of modern technology as a legitimizing force of empire; for example, Gyan Prakash argues that: "Kipling's short story depicts the triumph of reason over India's unruly nature and mythic culture."[45] However, "The Bridge-Builders" is more complex and ambivalent than this assessment suggests.

Throughout the story, Kipling uses a dialogical narrative to explore the nature of technology, articulating a prodevelopment stance as well as an antimodernization, even anticolonial, rhetoric that counters the protagonist's visions of progress. In the story, an English railway engineer, Findlayson, meets several Hindu gods who debate the merits of the new technology. Findlayson has been consumed by the construction of a railway bridge over the river Gunga [Ganga/Ganges], which is nearing completion. The engineer's initial perspective offers the bridge as a display of scientific empire: "Behind everything rose the black frame of the Kashi Bridge—plate by plate, girder by girder, span by span."[46] Contrary to the rhetoric of development that presents the colonial feats of engineering as self-evidently superior, however, the mastery of British technology must be established in the story through a debate on the part of Indians in terms of their own culture—or Kipling's version of it. Like the travel writers who presented the train through the discourse of Hinduism, but offering a critical rather than an awestruck view of it, Kipling assumes the voice of India to critique development. The author contains an "Indian" cultural view inside a European's perspective by identifying the Hindu mystical vision with an opium dream. When a monsoon causes the waters to rise, Findlayson's concerned Indian helper, Peroo, offers him some opium to relieve his anxiety. The Englishman sets out on a hallucinogenic quest to save a fleet of boats and washes ashore onto an island where an abandoned Hindu shrine rests. Kipling plays with the idea voiced earlier by Peroo that those who die in the Ganges go to the gods; the engineer is thrust into "Mother Gunga's" world, as he finds himself in a land inhabited by gods in animal form.

As the gods congregate on the overgrown island, they debate the merits of the railway. Initially skeptical, they decry the trapping of Mother Gunga between the support walls, her humiliation before guard towers, her pollution by the corpses of disease-riddled workers, and the mockery of her holiness by the British workers. Assuming the voice of India (equated with

Hindu gods), the narrative criticizes the by-products of development, including environmental destruction and exploited labor. It also censures those in Britain who reap the economic benefits of perilous railway construction. The god Ganesh says: "I, looking over their shoulders by lamplights, see the names in the books are those of men in far places—for all the towns are drawn together by the fire-carriage, and the money comes and goes swiftly, and the account books grow as fat as—myself."[47] Kipling describes a broader context "drawn together by the fire-carriage" in which Britain and India are locked in an uneven economic relationship.

After laying out political, social, and economic arguments against railway construction through a group of gods, Kipling extends the dialogical narrative to include "native" proponents of a transferred technology. Ganesh reminds the other gods that the traffic in pilgrims attending shrines has increased since the advent of the "fire-carriage." The monkey god Hanuman then suggests: "They will only change a little the names of their Gods. . . . Beloved, they will do no more than change the names, and that we have seen a thousand times."[48] The gods here propose seeing the railway world as a continuum of their timeless world, and the changes taking place as part of a series of alterations that have "a thousand times" recast the old in the guise of the new. By presenting a forum for gods who claim the railway for their own purposes, Kipling complicates the notion of a European technology in ways that anticipate his representation in *Kim*.

Kipling gives the final word to Krishna, whom he makes the most human and sympathetic god. Krishna warns: "Great Kings, the beginning of the end is born already. The fire-carriages shout the names of new Gods that are *not* the old under new names."[49] Krishna's idea that the fire-carriages will bring new gods, not gods with new names, represents the idea that the transformation brought by the railway will inaugurate a rupture within Indian society between the old and the new. The god views this break as an initiation into time because he deems the previous world as anachronistic, and in doing so, Krishna articulates a concept of transformation central to the rhetoric of modernity. Thus, Kipling puts the debate over the advent of modernity into the mouths of Indian gods, ventriloquizing technological debates within the colonial sphere. He reassigns decision making to a collective subject, a group of gods representing India, which claims the technology on its own terms.

The subversive possibilities of this dialogical narrative have been a point of some debate. Zohreh Sullivan places "The Bridge-Builders" within a body of Kipling's work produced in the 1880s and 1890s that was haunted by the potential loss of India as a British colony.[50] She notes that during the 1880s, Kipling consistently allocated authority to narrators drawn from the margins of imperial power, narrators who created a kind of dialog with the imperial power. Yet according to Sullivan, the author's dialogism is necessarily limited because it is constituted from a position of authority.[51] Kipling's voice as author presents one aspect of this authority; he also spoke within a broader system of authority. As I mentioned, Kipling's gods reproduce the actual protests already lodged by 1893 by writers like Naoroji. As chapter 2 argues more fully, these "drain theorists," who argued that Britain had underdeveloped India with the railway, were working within a historical, materialist, scholarly tradition. In "The Bridge-Builders," Kipling authorizes the voice of this anticolonial critique, only to constrain that voice within an Orientalist discourse of empire that equates India with religion and ultimately renders India an insubstantial place.

A quick look at the criticism of this story shows a general agreement on its significance as a kind of suture between a conception of India and a narrative of technological progress. Benita Parry notes the doubled worlds of this story in her insightful reading, in which she focuses on the constructed nature of Kipling's traditional India. She points to "The Bridge-Builders" as a milestone in the author's vision of a transcendental India: "Through this allegory Kipling achieves his most consummate evocation of India's unique identity as it was imaginatively conceived in myth and legend."[52] Parry sees the bridge as representing both the path of ideas that traveled from the British to Indians and a metaphor for the transition between the finite and infinite. Peroo personifies the bridge as a character who "has accepted the science of the West but not its ethics, nor its aggressive confidence in the omnipotence of reason."[53] Parry suggests that Kipling uses the railway bridge to represent the opposing realities of the rational and the metaphysical, which are in turn given the cultural valence of British and Indian. Ravi Ahuja makes a similar point about Kipling in slightly different terms, suggesting that Kipling is "mainly concerned with the propagation of *technological* and not of *social* 'reason' and 'progress.'"[54] In other words, Peroo is placed inside the framework of Western science but allowed to opt out of its epistemology on the basis of cultural difference.

These interpretations focus on the constructed nature of Kipling's traditional India rather than on the ambivalent nature of British technological narratives, yet Kipling's representation suggests contradictions on both sides of this binary. Although a teleological narrative of progress concludes the story, the representation as a whole offers more complexity in its presentation and reversal of two worlds. It is not just the Indian mythological world that is dematerialized in the story, but also the bridge, which becomes a vision. In his hallucination, Findlayson remembers, "Somewhere in the night of time he had built a bridge—a bridge that spanned illimitable levels of shining seas."[55] Kipling reverses the real and the imaginative, as the spaces of technological development become the dream and the sacred vision of the gods becomes reality. Here, the author highlights the visionary aspects of the narratives of progress, which rely upon sublime processes of transformation—it is imperial modernity that is really the mystical dream spanning levels of seas. In "The Bridge-Builders," Kipling undermines these binary oppositions—sacred and secular, dream and reality, tradition and modernity—deconstructing the linear path that forms the overt ideological vector of his story. He elaborates this doubled space eight years later in his novel *Kim*.

In *Kim*, published in 1901, the public space of the train functions as a representational entry point, a place where Indians literally and symbolically encounter the colonial order. Kipling uses narrative space to map the British and Indian worlds and the relations between them. The two worlds intersect in the space of the train, creating the hybrid space that the characters call the "*te-rain*."[56] The novel's geography briefly follows the tracks of the railroad before it moves into the discontinuous spatial reality that Kipling ultimately associated with the "real India." During the course of the novel, Kim repeatedly uses the train to move from one important location to the next, and the scenes on the train itself are key to the story's unfolding events. Examples of this include when Kim and the lama acquire patrons, when the officers capture Mahbub Ali's pursuers, and when Kim helps disguise agent E.23.[57] As Kipling uses representations of railway space to delineate, and thereby contain, the bodily, the domestic, and above all the religious, he produces a different image of public space, one that merges representations of governmental, secular space with a religious, bodily identity.

In *Kim*, Kipling establishes the railway—the train, the tracks, and the surrounding area—as a governmental space of order, a representation that recalls Lord Dalhousie's vision of the railway as a way to institute, promote, and secure the state. British soldiers and railway workers are always proximate to the train and oversee its operations; the spy Mahbub Ali uses this knowledge that British officials are always near the train to save himself from his two would-be assassins by telling the assistant district traffic superintendent that the men are stealing grain from the railway stores.[58] For Kipling, the British presence on the train suggests security: Kim reassures secret agent E.23, who has recently been beaten, "thou art safe in the *te-rain*, at least."[59] Indeed, E.23 does find safety with a British soldier who boards the train. The security associated with the train is not limited to the physical presence of the soldiers, however; Kim cannot believe that E.23 was beaten within earshot of the train, suggesting that most people understood the railway system as a symbol of a broader colonial order.

The space of the railway offers a way for Kipling to elaborate the relationship between the people of India and the state. As protagonist Kim and his hesitating friend, the Tibetan lama, look for a place aboard a train to Umballa, a Sikh character calls out: "Do not be afraid. I remember the time when I was afraid of the *te-rain*. Enter! This thing is the work of the Government."[60] The assurance rests on the assumed shared belief in the ensured safety of the colonial government project, and the railway as the embodiment of that promise. Through the voice of a Sikh, Kipling calls forth a common subjectivity among the Indian passengers through the evocation of a shared dominion of the British Raj.

Echoing the first writings that promoted the train as a way to overcome difference, Kipling depicts a railway space as overcoming the prohibitions of caste. As the Tibetan lama is helped onto the third-class carriage and offered a seat, he protests that "[i]t is against the Rule to sit on a bench," to which a moneylender replies, "there is not one rule of right living which these *te-rains* do not cause us to break. We sit, for example, side by side with all castes and peoples."[61]

Although Kipling does present the carriage as a place of colonial order, there are other ways that he challenges the ideal of technology as a rational utopia and instead creates a culturally and ideologically hybrid space. Kipling depicts the train as a local space, the *"te-rain."*[62] Kipling's railway space amalgamates India's diverse regions, religions, occupations, classes, and ethnicities. The carriage contains a Hindu Jat, a courtesan from Amritsar, a Punjabi soldier, and a Sikh artisan, as well as the Anglo-Indian Kim and the Tibetan lama, outsiders who make their home in India. Moreover, although the author introduces the interior space as one in which all "rule(s) of right living" must be broken, his subsequent description of the evening and morning in the carriage reveals a space transformed by cultural particularity. The passengers occupying the carriage perform the rituals of their everyday lives and bodies, making their morning meals, preparing and smoking their pipes, chewing *paan* (a preparation of betel leaf and spices chewed as a stimulant or digestive), praying, "spitting and coughing and enjoying themselves."[63] They remake the rational utopia by domesticating and inhabiting the space. In the *te-rain*, the lama begins to preach to an enraptured audience. Kipling's representation of sound, furthermore, suggests the hybridity of this space; as the meter of the Buddhist incantation to the click of a "rosary" overlaps with the clatter of the train, and the seemingly secular space of the railway also becomes a sacred space. Kipling does, however, present limits to this transformation. In the end, the guru is ultimately unable to be incorporated into the train, or even into the *te-rain*, and must set off on foot. The machine ensemble as "the work of the government" circumscribes the construction of this hybrid space and marks the boundaries of mutable space.

Kipling extends the symbolic use of the train to his characterization of Kim. The body of the main character becomes the site where the rational utopia converges with the difference of India. In the final pages of the novel, Kim asks: "I am Kim. And what is Kim?"[64] He thus continues the existential search that has marked the novel. Once again, a train appears in a key scene. As Kim struggles against tears prompted by his own question, "with an almost audible click he felt the wheels of his being lock up anew on the world without. Things that rode meaningless on the eyeball an instant before slid into proper proportion."[65] Kipling turns Kim's being into a train carriage on the tracks of an external world. The emblem of the self-as-train supersedes the emotions — the "meaningless" ride of the tears over the eyes — that hitherto guided many of Kim's actions. Kim's existential search for self embodied by his question, "who is Kim?" then "slid into proper proportion," finding meaning within the structures of the railway. Directly after, the epiphany has Kim in a phenomenological connection to the earth: "He felt it between his toes, patted it with his palms, and joint by joint, sighing luxuriously laid him down full length along the shadow of the wood-pinned cart."[66] As Kim on the track becomes one with the clay beneath him, he becomes part of a "permanent way" (a term for the railway) that grasps the whole of India on its own terms. The key to understanding this scene as more than a victorious narrative of progress, in which Kim assimilates India by imitating a train, lies in recognizing the hybridity of Kim's character. Kim was brought up by an Indian nurse and passes for Indian, but he later finds that he has an Irish soldier father. Bart Moore-Gilbert has described the character Kim as between two cultures, and he offers the following pertinent insight on the colonial context: "Hybridity, it seems, is the key to continuing British control of India; yet hybridity, of course, undermines any claim to authority on the grounds of an essentialist notion of the innate nature of British identity, let alone its intrinsic superiority."[67] As Kipling reconfigures the space of the railway as a hybrid space, he challenges the coherence of the colonial technological narrative.

In Flora Annie Steel's 1897 short story "In the Permanent Way," the railway also appears as an ambivalent object that sutures together the ideology of a colonial state with a traditional India viewed from the perspective of a colonial writer. Steel was a widely read colonial writer and novelist whose experience with rural Indian life and interest in women's issues gave her a markedly different perspective than that of Kipling. As it did for Kipling, however, the railway forms a dominant trope in several of her stories, including "In the Permanent Way." In this story, Steel uses the imagery of the train to present both conquest by means of technological development and Indian resistance. The British are charting space, entering it into an imperial, empirical order by "driving a straight line through the whole solar system and planting it out with little red flags."[68] India's resistance is represented by the figure of the "Hindu saint,"[69] a man who is meditating on a sand hill and refuses to move from the path of the surveyors. The guru is "in the permanent way," a pun using the moniker for the railway that Steel uses to reveal how the colonial state views the indigenous culture that held the land over which they are laying the tracks. When they are unable to move him, the surveyors turn the guru into a survey mark, symbolically requisitioning him to map space.

The story develops the relationship between the meditating man and the lead surveyor, Craddock. When the railway tracks are laid, Craddock solves the problem of the Indian in the way by picking the man up and setting him down a few feet over; he continues this practice when he becomes a driver on the same line. From the point of view of the Englishman, which is the only perspective that readers are given, the two have an invisible, intimate relation; even driving the train in the dark, Craddock instinctively knows exactly where the guru sits on the track. This relation to the "still figure" to whom the mobile man is "strangely bound"[70] ultimately causes the Englishman's death. On a night when Craddock has had too much to drink, his friend takes over the driving. The invisible bond causes Craddock to awake suddenly from his stupor and run out from the train onto the tracks to save the Indian from the oncoming train. The conclusion to this story, in which both men are hit by the train and killed, suggests a certain fatality in relations between Indians and Europeans when it comes to the grand imperial project—a relation as deadly to the English as to the Indians.

As Steel uses the train to present a relationship between the English surveyor and the Indian "marker," she offers a way to read a relationship between the colonial technological order and the differentiated India that was inherent to its narrative. At the end of the story, the identity of the two men has become confused: "When a whole train goes over two men who are locked in each other's arms it is hard—hard to tell—well, which is *Shivers-Martha Davy*, and which is *Whishyou Lucksmi*," a reference to Craddock's confused description of the guru and himself.[71] The hybrid corpse of the Englishman and Indian recalls the final passages from *Kim*, in which the character, who is himself an amalgamation of India and Europe, imagines his body as the railway line. Steel embeds this dialectical cultural relation into her vision of the railway with an image of a memorial: two squares of smooth stucco set in the tracks, an oval black stone laid in vertically and a round purple one set in perpendicular to that. The two stones mark the death site of the Indian guru and British railway officer, who died as they lived, locked in the intimate relation of opposites. The "altars"[72] are "in the permanent way,"[73] and as the narrator's rail-trolley must disassemble and go around them, Indian resistance is structured into the very narrative of colonial modernity as a technological development.

Legacies of the Colonial Railway

In Steel's story, the seeming immobility of India, represented by the stationary guru, ultimately poses the biggest challenge to the dominant colonial narrative of modernity. Mobility is, after all, the primary function for a train; it was also the rationale for a colonial power that justified itself by the transferability of its ideals. For Europeans who read Kipling or Steel while traveling on the railway, the imagined space of the railway presented a kind of theater in which they could work out their relations to India and Indians. In fact, the space itself, as it was rendered in the public sphere as well as in literary and visual texts, became a dynamic expression of these relations. This space offered itself as the concretization of a rational utopia, the order of which reflected the order of colonial rule. It was the means as well as the model for social reform. Kipling's and Steel's works set on the railway provide a literary counterpart to a broader cultural discourse in which the public space became a place where the elaboration and containment of an India seen as different occurs. These writers left as their legacy in India the narrative of technology, especially the train, as a rational utopia, a story critical to the construction of an independent nation under the leadership of Jawaharlal Nehru. With that said, in using the images of the train to inscribe difference, they began to elaborate the contradictions of this technological space in India. Furthermore, even as this discourse charted lines dividing European from Indian and public from private, it presented the railway space as saturated by identity, whether it was religious, domestic, or bodily. Colonial writers and artists recorded cultural difference into their concept of colonial modernity. Through their representations of technological space, they produced an early counternarrative of modernity, opening the door of the moving box to later versions of modernity that would serve radically different political interests.

CHAPTER 2

The Machine of Empire:
Technology and Decolonization

I N 1854, an account appearing in the English-language Calcutta journal *Bengal Hurkaru and India Gazette* narrated the travels of a scholar who went by train to Hooghly, "but declined to undertake the return journey, because, said he, too much travelling on the car of fire is calculated to shorten life, for seeing that it annihilates time and space and curtails the length of every other journey, shall it not also shorten the journey of human life?"[1] Although such criticisms on the part of Indians were dismissed by most British as the worries of "antiquated Hindoos,"[2] they presented a sociological and even ontological critique of the values of a technology-centered modernity. The Victorian imagination had heralded the railway's "annihilation of time and space" as paradigmatic for a modern consciousness modeled on the efficient machine. As early as 1879, however, a concerned colonial official had warned that British rule in India was "so hard and mechanical in its character" that "to the great mass of the people, the English official is simply an enigma . . . a piece of machinery possessing powers to kill and tax and imprison."[3] The official's comment differed sharply from the dominant colonial discourse, which had idealized the science that produced the railway. That discourse had designated the train as both the emblem of a universal rational utopia that would be Britain's lasting gift to India and the site for articulating and containing what most colonial writers viewed as India's irreducibly different culture. The voices that emerged from that space of difference, however, challenged the dominant narrative of the train, and, by extension, the culture of colonialism.

Writers put forward two types of challenges to the colonial discourse of the railway: One group questioned the justice of the railway's implementation in India; the second group condemned a modern consciousness based on the paradigm of the machine. These different types of challenge to the machine mark a dividing line, containing within an intelligible group on each side a diverse array of writers who otherwise might diverge on the political spectrum. The first group, roughly termed here the "social critics,"[4] worked within a post-Enlightenment theoretical framework. This group was made of both proindustrial Indian nationalists and progressive British journalists, philanthropists, and concerned colonial officials. These individuals narrated the history of the Indian railway through a discourse of political, social, and economic critique, including a critique of underdevelopment known as the "drain theory," and a public discussion of famine, environment, labor, and racial discrimination. This group produced, as the critic Manu Goswami phrases it, "an insurgent grammar of political economy"[5] that countered the discourse of technology justifying a colonial presence in terms of the railway.

In contrast, the second group challenged on moral grounds the theoretical framework of the Enlightenment, specifically its devotion to science. They turned to Indian tradition—a specific version of Hinduism in particular—for a radical reform movement. For spiritual political leaders Swami Vivekananda (Narendranath Datta), Aurobindo Ghose, and Mohandas Gandhi, and for literary writer Rabindranath Tagore, the machine acted not as a symbol of emancipation, as had been cultivated by the British, but as a powerful emblem of the British way of ruling. Among them, there were some important political differences: Tagore, for example, opposed the authoritarian nature of nationalism and publicly argued with Gandhi on the methods of nationalist movements. Yet as a group, these "spiritualists" focused on the railway as representing a modality, a way of being, that was both culturally alien and morally corrupt. Britain, they charged, had the soul of a machine. Using two different epistemological frameworks, the social critics and spiritualists confronted the dominant colonial narrative that elevated the train as a means for India's emancipation and challenged colonialism itself in the process.

Social Critics

As early as the 1860s, through the more radical nationalist politics of the 1920s, social critics recorded the economic problems that colonialism presented. According to their writings, colonial policies had forced a change to commercial agriculture from subsistence farming, destroyed traditional industries to make way for imports, and promoted unfair business practices.[6] These critics also charged the railway with having a role in the worsening of conditions for Indians, including increased peasant debt. They enumerated the railway's failure to bring emancipation through mobility: how the railway had promoted economic inequality, led to famine and environmental devastation, and contributed to labor exploitation and racial discrimination. The record of these failures was nearly absent from the victorious narrative of technology-driven economic development. The social critics were a diverse group with social and political differences: they included both Indian and British figures who wrote from their dissimilar cultural, political, and economic positions in a colonial context in which race largely defined people's positions. Even among writers on the same side of the colonial divide, there were divergences: The Indian writers took part in movements that ranged from colonial reform to nationalism; the British writers were an assorted group comprised of radical journalists and conservative, but frustrated, colonial officials. The people within this group of social critics had different audiences, both national and international. Finally, they registered their protests in different genres as they gave speeches and penned treatises, wrote journal articles, and published letters to the editor. Yet even noting those differences, one may see them all together as a group of social critics who, through their discussions of economy, civil rule, and society, reoriented colonial narratives of progress to account for justice.

In their critical representations of the railway, the social critics bypassed the dominant colonial measures of technology as a symbol of advancement and freedom. Using the image of the railway as a symbol of enslavement, extortion, bereavement, and humiliation, the social critics altered the ever-malleable symbol of the train to do several things. First, they questioned how well the train had upheld the promises that were made in its name. Second, they called into question the rhetoric of progress as universal; there was a price to be paid for this advancement, as they knew all too well from the experience of Indian workers building the railway. Third, they shifted the terms by which this technology would be judged. The official letters and published papers of colonial writers during the mid- to late nineteenth century, from Lord Dalhousie's strategic "Minute" in 1853 to Juland Danvers's 1877 defense of railway administration, emphasized the profitability or pace of construction of the railways. The social critics, on the other hand, looked at their effect on the Indian people. They turned the language of economy—for there is no word more pervasive than "cost" in their writings—into a humanist discourse that decried the price paid in the currency of Indian lives. Finally, they seized the image of the railway, which was a simulacrum for colonial presence, and used it to challenge the colonial enterprise.

One defining focus of the social critics' protest was the economic inequality expressed in the terms of railway construction; a subset of this larger group, Indian nationalists committed to political economic analysis, led this charge. In speeches, letters, and essays, Dadabhai Naoroji, president of the Indian National Congress in 1886, exposed the biased arrangement that favored the British investor over the Indian investor, consumer, and taxpayer. It was not that he undervalued the contributions of the British with regard to railways, Naoroji asserted; it was that the Indian nation could never profit from this industry under the terms of British railway investment. According to the financial terms for the early railway, if the railway initially made less than 5 percent profit, the difference would be made up by Indian state revenues that were, in turn, gathered from Indians through sources like taxes. If the railway made more than 5 percent profit, the state received only half of the surplus. This, retired civil servant and economic historian Romesh Dutt argued, was in contrast to other railways worldwide that were built on borrowed capital, but where the income (aside from interest and capital repayment) remained in the domestic economy.[7] After 1869, which marked a turning point away from the guarantee system to state sponsored construction, the Indian government paid expenses (such as the entire income of the European staff), provided free lands, and was a "captive, publicly subsidized market for English steelmakers and locomotive builders."[8] Under this system, Indians incurred the losses but none of the gains presented by the railways. Naoroji offered the following critical appraisal:

> Thus, the whole burden of the debt is placed on the shoulders of the people of India, while the benefit is largely enjoyed and carried away by the people of England, and yet Englishmen raise up their hands in wonder, why India should not be happy, pleased, and thankful![9]

In this passage, Naoroji evokes the familiar image of the Indian coolie, envisioning India carrying the burdens as Britain strides forward on the road of progress. But it was another image, that of the "pitiless drain," that provided a name for these nationalists who cataloged how India's wealth was seeping away through the construction of the railway.

Proponents of the "drain theory" saw the political economic problems of India as based on more than the initial terms of British railway investment; the railway had transformed India's state economy in ways that disproportionately benefited its colonizer. From the perspective of even the proindustrialization Naoroji, India was being "underdeveloped" by the railway, to use a contemporary term that focuses on the ongoing deleterious effects of the relation between a metropolis and a satellite country.[10] G. V. Joshi, a scholar of political economy, argued in 1888 that though he was not against the railways per se, the economic results of railways had impeded industrial growth, and he denounced their "tendency to prevent, in a country like India, a healthy material advance on *normal lines*"[11] (italics in the original). Normal, in this case, would be the concurrent development of domestic industry.[12] Joshi pointed out that the changes that had accompanied railway development reoriented production to a different market; industries were shifted towards the needs of an overseas rather than a local market. Given the subsidies of the railway, he argued,

> India is thus asked to make room for the foreign trader by paying him or his country-men a bounty to facilitate his competition with the native producer, and to give him land free of cost, and to arrange that the interest payments shall be punctually made in gold from year to year at any sacrifice, and finally to see with patience the native manufacturer and trader pushed out of his sphere of domestic industrial activity.[13]

For example, inexpensive manufactured British cloth drove handicraft production out of business after the Bombay–Calcutta line was completed. In addition, desperate farmers began to produce a particular type of wheat for British millers in the meantime.[14] These nationalists focused on political economy to describe a domino effect in which the changes brought by the railway were the first of a series of deleterious transformations. As Goswami puts it in her analysis of Indian railway space, "Nationalists such as Dadabhai Naoroji, Mahadev Ranade, and Romesh Dutt reversed the logic of colonial discourse that presented railways as a universal magical agency for development by recasting them as particular vehicles of intensified imperial exploitation."[15]

It is worth pausing at this point to note that some contemporary scholarship challenges the validity of "drain theory." Tirthankar Roy's research suggests that India displayed an overall positive economic growth during the colonial period.[16] Responding to the idea that commercialization killed India's traditional industry, Roy offers a more differentiated picture by noting that commercialization was limited to certain areas; moreover, there is no way to assess how large these sectors were compared to traditional sectors. Thus, slow growth, where it did occur, was regional rather than throughout the subcontinent. Roy argues that inequality did not grow during the colonial period so much as change hands between groups of ruling classes; furthermore, he asserts that although there was an increase in indebtedness, it was not entirely due to large-scale dispossession of land. With regard to railways, Roy asserts that they brought down transportation costs, increased foreign demand for certain crops, and encouraged changes in cropping patterns.[17] My point here is not to validate or refute the drain theorists' claims but to identify a rhetoric of modernity that existed in the late nineteenth century and explore how it functioned as a broader cultural understanding that competed with pervasive (on both the British and Indian sides) affirmations of technology. The drain theorists reframed a colonial narrative of technology as they reinforced a sense of a national whole.

These writers focused on political economy turned to both the English-language press and the popular vernacular press to describe to a general audience the costs of the railway. Romesh Dutt detailed the history of railway construction and use in India up to 1903, summarizing that "over-all economic effects of the railways 'had not been beneficial.'"[18] Indian politician G. K. Gokhale wrote at the turn of the century: "The Indian people feel that this construction is undertaken principally in the interests of English commercial and moneyed classes, and that it assists in the further exploitation of our resources."[19] The vernacular press presented the railways as impoverishing the country and undermining Indian prosperity.[20] Hindu nationalist Bal Gangadhar Tilak referenced the custom of adorning one's wife with jewelry as a sign of both regard and prestige when he described the economic gift to Britain of the Indian railway as "decorating another's wife."[21]

As these Indian nationalists created a critical body of writing around the history of the railway, they altered the symbolic import of the technology from the paradigms advanced by colonial rhetoric by reinventing the language and imagery of the train. In the colonial discourse, as chapter 1 showed, the railway was imagined as a box moving along a vector of progress, amalgamating difference into a "rational utopia." The nationalists humanized the economic relationship that brought the train to India by using the literary technique of personification and images of labor. Those representations of labor were all but invisible in colonial writings on the railway.[22] "As India is treated at present," Naoroji wrote in 1887, "all the new departments, opened in the name of civilization, advancement, [and] progress," are a "burden on exhausting India."[23] Modernity was not gliding on the wheels of change: it was being dragged along by India. In the popular press, the tracks triumphantly "driving a straight line through the whole solar system,"[24] as colonial writer Flora Annie Steel had described them, became, in the imagery of social reformer G. S. Iyer, a means to bury the country. In a 1901 article in the early Calcutta newspaper *Statesman*, Iyer wrote: "Every additional mile of railway constructed in this country drove a fresh nail into the coffin of one industry or another."[25]

The writers who produced the political economic critique of the drain theory were nationalists, but in their historical methods and post-Enlightenment theoretical framework, they may be seen as part of a broader constituency that cut across racial and national lines. That broader group of social critics included progressive British writers and reform-oriented Indians, as well as these Indian nationalists, as it spoke in a polytonal voice against one of the most important global sociopolitical issues of the late nineteenth century: famine. The railway tracks had been promoted as a lifeline to save regions from hunger,[26] but instead, according to these writings, they had done just the opposite, as construction commandeered already-scarce capital resources. Moreover, the emphasis on an export economy based in a large-scale commercial crop and the increased production of cotton, both aimed at an international market, left regions devastated by famine. Food shortage was not entirely the issue: During the 1876 famine, for example, India was exporting rice and wheat to Britain. Moreover, free market fundamentalists like Viceroy and Governor-General Lord Lytton worked alongside corrupt Indian middlemen to use the railway to transport grain away from areas where even the railway workers were starving to export stations where the grain was stockpiled.[27]

Progressive writers in Britain moved away from notions of profit to itemize the material cost of the railways by tallying the bodies of Indians. In an effort to raise consciousness about the failure of the British to live up to their colonial rhetoric, famous engineer and philanthropist Sir Arthur Cotton wrote in his 1877 exposé *The Madras Famine:*

> Now we have before our eyes the sad and humiliating scene of magnificent Works [railroads] that have cost poor India 160 millions, which are so utterly worthless in the respect of the first want of India, that millions are dying by the side of them.[28]

Florence Nightingale penned a letter to the *Illustrated News* the same year on this topic.[29] Given that the railway was Britain's largest single area of foreign investment, Cotton and Nightingale were making an important intervention in the public concerns of their day. They were offering a view of these railways that had not been encountered by a British readership. Cotton and Nightingale were successful in fostering the debate in Britain's domestic public sphere, prompting concerned queries like that in 1861 by "An Indian Stock and Railway Shareholder," who wrote a letter to the editor of *The Times* of London appealing for support for famine relief.[30] Such apprehension by investors must have placed pressure on the railway officials in India, but it seemed to have little effect on Lord Lytton. William Digby, author of a scathing 1878 exposé on the Indian famine, wrote: "The railways, by the conveyance of grain to the affected districts, preserve the lives of millions, but they do this at the cost of making the people everywhere pay so high a price that a daily sufficiency of food becomes impossible to ever-increasing millions."[31] Dissident British journalists on the ground in India's famine districts, which included the Madras Presidency, the Bombay Deccan, and the North West Provinces, described how administrators of the famine relief works of Sholapur, Maharashtra, sent away anyone who, even for reasons of starvation, could or would not work as a "coolie" on a public works project.[32]

British social campaigners linked famine to the environmental cost of colonial public works. Progressive journalist Vaughan Nash detailed these in his 1900 book *The Great Famine and Its Causes*, charging that, "The Forest Department has a pretty long queue of sins waiting at its door for the day of reckoning, as so have the Indian railway companies."[33] In the late 1860s, Madras Railways deforested the future famine districts of Salem, Cuddapah (Kadapa), and North Arcot (Ambedkar)[34] because the tracks required 1 million wood ties a year and the trains burned wood fuel. Sir Arthur Cotton saw the railway as a misguided project, a less viable alternative to canals, which would provide a more sustainable means for transportation.[35] The British reformers wrote for an audience that included Indians and Europeans in the subcontinents and interested parties abroad. By offering images of starvation and environmental devastation alongside these massive public works projects, they were challenging in these public spheres the very measure of success for the colonial enterprise.

By the turn of the century, Indian political commentators, economic historians, and journalists were reporting the human price of the railways to an educated Indian audience. An author writing in 1910 under the name "Indo-American" in the Calcutta *National Review* detailed the problem:

> Even during the stress of severest famines, the Railways keep
> depleting the country of grains of all kinds, carrying them to the
> sea-ports, from thence to be shipped abroad. Thus the railways
> have not only sadly failed in mitigating the sad state of the famine
> sufferers; but also have contributed directly toward the aggravation
> of the calamity by draining the country of resources which were
> sorely needed at home.[36]

From the perspective of the anonymous writer, it is not simply that the railways could not overcome the problems of famine: The railways were themselves directly contributing to famine.

Together, the "drain theorists," who wrote about political economy, and the progressive writers from Britain and India, who linked that economy to famine, presented a powerful social critique of the colonial discourse of the railway. They offered a radically different view of what the railway *meant* in India than those like R. M. Stephenson, who had argued for the economic benefits of the train, or even those like the Indian correspondents to Stephenson, who endorsed the "mighty changes [that the railway] would tend to produce on the political, social, moral, and religious condition of the millions who inhabit this vast territory of British rule."[37] Through their political and economic writings, these writers shifted the focus onto a humanistic discourse.

To complete this task, the social critics also had to look at what the railway meant to individual Indians. That included both the "coolies" who laid the tracks and the Indians of various classes who took the train in increasing numbers. The railway appeared to divide India into two parts: a without, where Indian workers toiled to make that dream happen for others, and a within, where the train promised the mobility to transcend conditions like famine. Yet the divide between these two places was not as distinct as it initially seemed, because the status of Indians as second class vis-à-vis Europeans was evident in both locations.

Social critics of the railway uncovered the racism that permeated both the conditions of labor and the experience of riding the rails. They wrote against a colonial discourse that rendered invisible the men and women who built the lines of Britain's largest overseas public works project (Figure 5). The safety of Indian workers was a low priority for the British, who kept records only of British victims. Such an omission may be found in a paper read at the Society of the Arts in 1877, in which Juland Danvers, director of the Indian Railway Companies, memorialized the wayside graves of only the Europeans buried along the lines. He recalled the "great undertakings" carried out by human exertion, but focused exclusively on the European engineer. "He not only had to overcome the natural physical

Figure 5. 1895 Magic Lantern Slide by American photographer William Henry Jackson, captioned: "Indian Workers Building Railway." Photograph courtesy William Henry Jackson/Harappa.com.

difficulties of the country," Danvers stressed, "but he had to submit to a hostile climate and to the pestiferous vapour of the jungle. The labour at his command was inferior and at first difficult to manage."[38] It is no wonder the labor was difficult to manage: Indian workers' wages were invariably low, frequently in arrears, or often paid short.[39] Railway workers, both men and women, recruited from across populations that included urban middle classes, migrant peasants, tribal peoples, as well as industrial and rural laborers, were removed from their social networks.[40] They did dangerous labor: Workers were injured or killed by drowning, by being crushed under collapsed embankments and tunnels, by falling off bridges, or by being maimed or killed by machinery.[41] Moreover, these workers were subject to devastating diseases such as cholera, malaria, smallpox, typhoid, and pneumonia that swept through the ranks. Records were not kept for Indian deaths, but historian Ian Kerr suggests that one construction site, which had 75 percent of its workers down with fever during the worst period of the year, was typical; a common way of remembering the uncounted dead has been to mark each death by a sleeper tie, the wooden ribs of the track, of which there are some 1,700 a mile.[42]

In terms of promotion, the British discourse of education stopped short when it came to educating Indians with the technological knowledge necessary to run the railway. Discrimination was pervasive: "The European or the Anglo-Indian engine drivers treated their 'native' firemen like their valets. . . . This master craftsman–apprentice relationship among the engine crew was by the 1920s acquiring racial ferocity."[43] In remote sites, Indian workers faced racially motivated violence, often fueled by a culture of alcohol.[44] When later administrative measures aimed at appeasing protests attempted the "Indianization" of the upper levels of the railway, it created antagonism between Europeans and Anglo-Indians on one side and Indians on the other.

For Indians, even the interior of the train was no escape from the harsh material realities of colonialism. Letters to the vernacular press deplored the treatment of the Indian passengers who filled the third-class carriages. Writing in the influential, Calcutta-based English-language periodical *Modern Review* in 1910, Abinash Chandra Chatterjee condemned the treatment of third-class passengers, who were crowded into carriages without access to drinking water.[45] In his exposé, he also detailed the systematic theft by railway employees of goods shipped by railway.[46] Throughout the nineteenth and early twentieth centuries, Indian newspapers reported the repeated humiliation of Indians on railway platforms.[47] The racism of the colonial system did not allow Indians to ride peacefully in anything but the third-class section when Europeans were present. A contemporary writer testified that Europeans and Indians clashed in the first- or second-class carriage on a daily basis; Indians who paid for the more exclusive carriages (only to offend their fellow European passengers) almost always had to travel in third class.[48]

The treatment of traveling women, who were subject to a spectrum of violence ranging from humiliation to rape, formed a rallying cry in the pages of the nationalist newspaper *The Bengalee*. In her book on the Indian railway, Laura Bear details how editor and activist Surendranath Banerjee provided monthly accounts in this newspaper of "outrages" against Indian women travelers on the railways:

> The stories were framed by descriptions of how the loss of a ticket, an accidental overrunning of a destination, the lack of money to pay an excess fare, and the separation of a husband and wife into male and female compartments produced devastating violations. The perpetrators were always Europeans or Eurasians, and they were marked by the signs of colonial authority—wearing the cap of their office or dressed in the uniform of the Railway Volunteer force.[49]

The case of one woman in particular became a focal point in the demand to equalize the railways. The Calcutta daily newspaper *Amrita Bazar Patrika* described how a young girl named Rajabala Dasi lost her ticket and, after being forced off the train, was raped by four European railway officials. As Bear goes on to argue, these accounts that detailed this incident and similar episodes of harassment aimed to foment anticolonial sentiment by focusing on the violation of virtuous women.[50] The entrance of women into the public space had been one of the most contested areas in Indian discussions about the social effects of the railway. Stories like that of Dasi tapped into those concerns, making the railway an arena for the articulation of anticolonial sentiment.

Viewed as a broad group, the social critics focused on the financial, environmental, labor, and public conditions of the Indian railway to challenge the colonial enterprise. In the process, they altered the very meaning of the train from a symbol of progress to a symbol of exploitation, including slavery. In Indian newspapers, both vernacular and English-language, journalists denounced the railways, charging that the "extension of iron roads means iron chains."[51] In the pages of the *Modern Review*, a critic writing under the name "Indo-American" in 1910 contended:

> It is by means of the railway, trolley, telegraph, and such other agencies that 200,000 foreigners can hold 300,000,000 natives in subjection and the Englishman, gifted with foresight, foresaw this contingency and thus furnished the impetus for railway building in Hindostan.[52]

Historian Lajpat Jagga characterizes the sentiments of this period: "To the British [the railways] were a symbol of the Raj but to the Indian mind they had come to signify its opposite—the colonial reality, its exploitation, humiliation, and the imperial arrogance of the *ferenghi*."[53] But although the image of the railway was central to an emerging nationalism, it was also important to British liberals who were critical of what Britain was doing in India. As a whole, this group of social critics supplanted the colonial meanings attached to the Indian train—including progress, emancipation, and civilization—using the language of economic exploitation, enslavement, and morality. They provided a new vocabulary for talking about technological development that included the word "drain" to describe India's loss of sustainable industries under colonialism and the word "price" to inventory the sacrifice of life made under conditions of famine. They sought to show the human side of a railway built largely by hand. Finally, they showed that mobility was not the same as emancipation. Although among them they had different audiences and political goals, together the social critics forged an important radical discourse of the nineteenth century that defied the dominant rhetoric of colonialism by arguing for the injustice of its use. Another group, the spiritualists, would go even further to confront the very nature of the machine.

The Spiritualists

Late nineteenth- and early twentieth-century nationalist movements in India encompassed several different strains. A diverse group of Indians were writing their own visions of the nation, drawing from different types of intellectual and religious sources and often combining these traditions. The "drain theorists" described previously based their writings in a secular tradition of political economy. Figures such as Syed Ahmad Khan (who preached in, among other places, railway stations across India) formed a divergent strain of Muslim nationalism. Regional nationalism included a movement growing from nineteenth-century intellectual and political concerns in Bengal, such as challenges to the British partition of that province in 1905, a decision reversed six years later. As Sugata Bose put it, "Indian anticolonialism was nourished by many regional patriotisms, competing versions of nationalism, and extraterritorial affinities of religiously informed universalisms."[54]

Vivekananda, Aurobindo, Gandhi, and Tagore are often seen as part of this latter group of nationalists, who drew inspiration from a Hindu revivalism that stretched from the 1880s to the first few decades of the twentieth century. They championed a vision of a spiritual India that would oppose the degeneration of Indian society by technology-driven modernization and consequent Westernization. There were certainly differences among them—for example, Gandhi and Tagore drew from different cultural inspirations and argued for different methods of nationalist struggle.[55] Despite these important distinctions, this group collectively provided a critique of modernity. The railway as an emblem of the West figured prominently in their writings, for it represented the very aspect of a European society that they condemned—the ideology of the machine.[56] Unlike the colonial discourse that sought to bring Hinduism within the sphere of the railway, these writers constructed a Hindu identity at odds with the train; as they did so, they once again transformed the meaning of the train.

Swami Vivekananda, born in 1863, began his work earlier than the others, and his writing influenced Aurobindo, Gandhi, and Tagore. Drawing on a vision of an essential soul of India, Vivekananda looked to Indian spirituality based in Hinduism to unify India's different languages, sects, regions, and even religions. Despite his emphasis on mysticism, Vivekananda was very much invested in the social issues that had been advanced by liberal reformers of the time. Moreover, he saw the modern form of the nation as the means by which India could regain its spiritual past. Yet Vivekananda challenged the version of nationalism based on industrial-driven social reform, such as that espoused by Naoroji, and looked to foster a new kind of nationalism with a basis in spiritual regeneration.

This regeneration was to draw its paradigms from the natural world as it denounced a mechanical way of being. In an 1898 letter entitled "Our Present Social Problems," later collected and translated from

Bengali as part of a series of volumes setting forth his spiritual teachings, Vivekananda argued that the Indian enraptured by the culture of the machine would be subsumed by it and lose the agency of self-government:

> The huge steamer, the mighty railway engine—they are non-intelligent; they move, turn, and run, but they are without intelligence. And yonder tiny worm which moved away from the railway line to save its life, why is it intelligent? There is no manifestation of will in the machine, the machine never wishes to transgress law; the worm wants to oppose law—rises against law whether it succeeds or not; therefore it is intelligent.[57]

More broadly, in this essay Vivekananda makes a claim for political autonomy on the basis of the natural state of self-determination—and self-preservation. Moving away from the language of economy that characterized much of the social critics' writings, Vivekananda instead summons the opposition of machine and nature. The railway embodies the force—the "huge steamer"—and the logic—"the railway line"—of colonial rule. It also represents the unquestioning subject that never wishes to oppose the law. Vivekananda alters the symbol of the train; it is no longer the colonial symbol of emancipation through mechanization but rather the embodiment of unintelligent passivity.

In another section of "Our Present Social Problems," Vivekananda sets up the railway as an automaton: "If living by rule alone ensures excellence, if it be virtue to follow strictly the rules and customs handed down through generations, say then, who is more virtuous than a tree, who is a greater devotee, a holier saint, than a railway train?"[58] Vivekananda's ironic image of the train as a saint for culture that values only blind adherence uses the icons of spirituality to undermine the paradigm of the train as well as to criticize colonial rule. The critique is political and moral, but it also calls into question a scientific epistemology, an Enlightenment framework, in which the machine offers the way to truth.

Another key Indian figure associated with a spiritual-based nationalism, Aurobindo Ghose, spoke of the machine in general, rather than specifically discussing the railway. Aurobindo was in many ways Vivekananda's heir, and he refined the notion of autonomy by elaborating the concept of *swaraj*, or self-rule, which was being revived by radical writers by the late nineteenth century. For Aurobindo, the term carried from its Sanskrit etymology the idea of soul rule, and consequently the impetus to liberate the consciousness from a Western mentality.[59] Some present-day activists have disinherited Aurobindo because of his role as an inspiration for the conservative Hindutva movement that selectively employs his rhetoric on Hinduism and India, but as Peter Heehs points out, these statements were made in a particular historical and cultural context within the struggle for decolonization, and therefore Aurobindo cannot be held account-able for the beliefs of Hindutva.[60] Moreover, Aurobindo was an intellec-tual hybrid, inspired by European Romanticism as well as by the sacred texts of Hinduism (that were ironically brought to him through the cir-cuitous route of European Orientalist writings on the East). Aurobindo's writings locate a Romantic critique of European "mechanism" within the anticolonial struggle and emphasize the relevance of that critique to social and civic rule. Although he had earlier been a leader in the radical nation-alist movement, following his 1908 incarceration he scarcely mentioned the cause of nationalism, although in *The Life Divine*, first published in Aurobindo's monthly review *Arya* between 1914 and 1920 and later col-lected in a series of volumes, he equates the state with a machine.[61]

Aurobindo managed the cultural aggression of colonialism by "seeking to make sense out of the West in Indian terms"[62] and by condemning the mechanization that had wreaked devastation in World War I. In his 1940 essay "War and Self-Determination," the famous figure of ascetic renun-ciation wrote a political exposé warning of the dangers of a resolution to global strife modeled on a technological paradigm. He described the League of Nations as a coin-operated machine: "Get the clock work going, put your penny-worth of excellent professions or passably good intentions in the slot and all will go well, this seems the principle."[63] Like Vivekananda, Aurobindo challenged the values that privileged the machine:

> The one way out harped on by the modern mind, which has been as much blinded as enlightened by the victories of physical science, is the approved western device of salvation by machinery; get the right kind of machine to work and, everything can be done, this seems to be the modern creed.[64]

With the phrase "salvation by machinery," Aurobindo bases his anti-machine rhetoric on authority centered around morality. The notion of a divine Absolute provides a moral authority that supersedes that of government—such is a powerful challenge to the state.

Aurobindo, with his notion of individual freedom based on spirituality and his language concerning machinery, anticipated Gandhi, who used the railway as a metaphor for the cultural and material binds of colonialism. Gandhi's antitechnological discourse appeared very early in his writings. In a 1900 letter to Henry Polak, a South African lawyer who was a close friend, he wrote, "It is not the British people who are ruling India, but it is modern civilization, through its railways, telegraphs, telephones, and almost every invention which has been claimed to be a triumph of civilisation."[65] In his famous 1909 mandate for self-rule, *Hind Swaraj*, published in Gujarati and then translated into English by the author, Gandhi argues that "but for the railways, the English could not have such a hold on India as they have."[66] Karl Marx heralded the development of railways "when that once fabulous country will thus be actually annexed to the Western world"[67]; Gandhi recognized that if India was indeed a space fastened to the West, it was so as an economically dependent territory rather than an equal one. Gandhi bemoaned the transformation of the economic and social structures that he viewed as fundamental to Indian identity. The railway was central to these transformations, both materially (in the sense that it altered the geography of production and circulation) and symbolically (in that it emphasized an increased production and consumption over the attainment of truth).

Gandhi invoked the language of justice and a spiritually based morality in his condemnation of mechanization. In *Hind Swaraj*, he wrote, "Machinery has begun to desolate Europe . . . . Machinery is the chief symbol of modern civilization; it represents a great sin."[68] Gandhi extends his theory in a 1909 letter to Lord Ampthill, a former governor of Madras: "Railways, machinery, and corresponding increase of indulgent habits are the true badges of slavery of the Indian people as they are of Europeans."[69] In a 1926 article entitled "The Morals of Machinery," published in the journal *Young India*, Gandhi resists the idea of the universal right of machinery: "The use of machinery is lawful which subsumes the interest of all, meaning, only when the greater good of people is put first and the machine is strictly in the service of that does the machine have legitimacy."[70]

Gandhi focused on the emblematic status of railways, describing them as a "symbol" of sin, and "badges" of slavery. Investing machines with an agency of their own, Gandhi wrote in 1931, "Machinery is a grand yet awful invention. It is possible to visualise a stage at which the machines invented by man may finally engulf civilisation. If man controls the machines, then they would not; but should man lose his control over the machines and allow them to control him, then they will certainly engulf civilisation and everything."[71] The railways were a material symbol recalling the imperialism that had absorbed India and forecasting a world marked by the loss of human agency.

Like the nationalist proponents of the "drain theory," Gandhi sometimes described the machine as a neutral tool that has been used to exploitative ends, especially in his later writings, as he worked out the anticolonial strategy of *swadeshi*, or economic self-sufficiency. Facing some criticism, he clarified his stance to a Japanese correspondent in a 1936 letter: "I am not against machinery as such, but I am totally opposed to it when it masters us."[72] Moreover, Gandhi made extensive use of the railway network as part of his campaign for nationalism. Even so, Gandhi differed from critics such as Naoroji on the issue of technology. Gandhi continued to position himself strategically, not only against the conditions of the railway but against technology itself: Even in the previous statement, for example, Gandhi describes "it," or machinery, as master, rather than the colonial power.

Contemporary scholars have pointed to the symbolic nature of Gandhi's condemnation of industrialism. Robert Young, in line with the work of Ashis Nandy, characterizes Gandhi's contribution as follows: "Gandhi's brilliance was to use theosophical thought to focus not on colonialism itself but to provide a critique of modern western civilization—of modernity as such."[73] Partha Chatterjee argues that Gandhi's pronouncements must be read as a "total critique of the fundamental aspects of civil society:"[74] the values of bourgeois society based in a market sensibility, private property, the mediation of Parliament in the expression of political subjectivity, the excessive desire for innovation and change in science, and the supremacy of reason in matters of ethics and aesthetics.[75] For Chatterjee, Gandhi positions himself through his critique of civil society outside the thematic framework of post-Enlightenment thought. Gandhi's outside status furthermore places him into an ambivalent position in relation to nationalist thought, "in the way in which [Gandhi's position] challenged the basic premises on which [nationalist thought] was built and yet sought at the same time to insert itself into the process of a nationalist politics."[76]

One of the primary ways that he inserted himself was by challenging, through his writing on the machine, the epistemology of a scientific mode of knowledge. Gandhi saw that scientific knowledge could not fully explain human experience.[77] In setting himself against the machine as such, Gandhi moved away from the position of advocates of the drain theory, who saw the machine as misused rather than misconceived.

Rabindranath Tagore took up some of the same ideas on the machine in the literary realm that Vivekananda, Aurobindo, and Gandhi expounded upon in their essays and letters. Rabindranath, ironically, was the grandson of the Indian businessmen Dwarkanath Tagore, who had attempted to create a railway empire in the first years of railway construction. Yet the younger Tagore, whose literary work in Bengali has been described as "rural lyricism,"[78] was profoundly ambivalent about British technology. Tagore well understood the close relationship between colonialism and the railway, as well as the place of the railway in the rhetoric that justified the British presence in India. Like Gandhi, his criticism was leveled not simply at the conditions of the railway, but at the culture of the machine itself.[79] Tagore sharply disagreed with Gandhi over the nation as a form of political emancipation, but he affirmed Gandhi's stance on the train in a 1921 essay that otherwise distanced itself from the sacred figure, stating, "Where Mahatma Gandhi has declared war against the tyranny of the machine which is oppressing the whole world, we are all enrolled under his banner."[80] Tagore's response to mechanization focused on the transformation of time and space heralded as perhaps the most valuable contribution of the railway. According to historian Michael Adas, "Tagore concluded that the accelerated pace of living made possible by Western machines contributed to disorientation and constant frustration, to individual and societies out of sync with the rhythms of nature, each other, and their own bodies."[81] The Indian writer represented these sentiments in two of his plays, *The Waterfall* (*Muktadharaa*) and *Red Oleanders* (*Rakta Karabi*).

In 1922, Tagore published his Bengali play *Muktadharaa* (Free Current) with his own translation, which he entitled *The Waterfall*. In this play, Tagore censures civilization as dependent on the logic of the machine. He depicts a kingdom called Uttarakut that venerates "the Machine." The technological wonder has stopped up the flow of a waterfall, and stolen the waters from a minority community in the kingdom called Shiu-tarai. Tagore represents "the Machine" as an amalgam of technologies: although it is a dam, the feat of twenty-five years of engineering also resembles a train. For example, the technological devotees sing saluting the Machine, "Loud with its rumbling of wheels, / Quick with its thunder flame."[82] In the same song, Tagore evokes the blasting, smelting, and digging of railway construction with a machine, "Fastening its fangs / into the breast of the world. / Hurling against obstructions / its fiery defiance / That melts iron, crushes rocks, / And drives the inert from its rest."[83]

Clearly, in his representation Tagore wished to call to mind the railway built by the British, but his critique extended more generally to censure a European society that had come to idolize technology. Chief engineer Bibhuti, a main character in the play, is the epitome of the technophile, whose mind contemplates the "majesty of the Machine."[84] Bibhuti diminishes the sacrifice of these workers who, like those who made the railway, have been smothered by sand and earth or drowned in floods, and states that his object has been accomplished by the completion of his project.[85] In what is perhaps an allusion to the social critics' position, the Machine has brought famine to the province of Shiu-tarai. Bibhuti shows his indifference to this destruction using a language that echoes the British discourse of technology: "My object was to make Man triumphant over the sands and water and stones, which conspired against him. I had not the time to trouble my mind about what would happen to some wretched maize fields of some wretched cultivator in some place or other."[86] Bibhuti's fierce indifference recalls the social critics' characterization of a British colonial administration that ignores the creation of famine in the interest of advancing India through technology. The machine is placed in contrast to the structures of religion; "like a spasm of agony in the heart of the sky,"[87] the machine's spire competes with the nearby temple. The play ends on a hopeful note with the destruction of the machine's embankment, as the river, which is once again free, and the temple reign supreme, a resolution that demonstrates Tagore's idealization of spiritual tradition.

In Tagore's 1924 play *Rakta Karabi*, translated by the author into English and published a year later as *Red Oleanders*, Tagore returned to similar themes, setting a natural spirituality in opposition to the rule of a bureaucratic kingdom that assigns people numbers and forces people underground to harvest "blocks of stone, iron, gold."[88] The character of Nandini, an enchanting woman described as "the light that breaks through a cracked wall," gives voice to Tagore's critical sentiment; she states, "It puzzles me to see a whole city thrusting its head underground, groping with both hands in the dark."[89] The concept of a network forms a primary motif in the play, for the king remains separated from everything by a barrier that is alternately called a screen and a network. With this division, Tagore emphasizes a dominant preoccupation in his work with the binary between interior and exterior, the *ghare* (home) and *baire* (outside) that make up the title to his famous novel *The Home and the World*. Tagore comments on the king's flawed leadership by placing him as the ruler on the inside, but the screen that holds him links Tagore's critique of this monarchy to the ideology of the railway. When a scholarly and traditional character seeks refuge, another character steeped in science sneers, "You see how our Antiquarian has quietly slipped off, thinking he'll fly and save himself. After going a few steps, he'll soon discover that there's a wire network stretched from post to post, from country to country."[90] Tagore explicitly links the dominant symbol of the net to modern technology in the form of the telegraph that ran along the railway lines. Inside the kingdom, the king is "shrouded in his mist of netting," but outside in the mining empire, "the net is spreading farther and farther," for it is, in Tagore's view, the individual consciousness that enables the dehumanizing empire of the machine.

Inside and Outside Modernity

As they wrote against the ideology of modernization, Vivekananda, Aurobindo, Gandhi, and Tagore seized the image of the train that had previously been the provenance of the British. They produced an important counternarrative of modernity: a critical vision of the modern that was rooted in religion but grounded in a secular, historical, materialist critique of technologically driven development. These writers' critiques of technology emerged from within a struggle to gain self-rule in the form of the nation, itself a modern construct. As such, the writings of Vivekananda, Aurobindo, Gandhi, and Tagore should not be seen as antimodern or isolationist.

This is true for another reason as well: Their work was born of transnational relationships and influences. All these spiritual writers had personal connections to, or audiences in, Europe and the United States. Vivekananda, born Narendranath Datta, came from a family of Calcutta lawyers and received a European-style legal education. He gained international renown as a speaker at the 1893 Chicago Parliament of Religions.

His mysticism was validated by Western writers such as Max Müller, who looked east to essentialized versions of Vedic philosophy as part of their own visions of modernism. Aurobindo was brought up from age seven by a family in Manchester, England, before he went to St. Paul's secondary school and later to Cambridge University. Like Vivekananda, Gandhi was educated as a lawyer. His views, as scholar Robert Young puts it, "were irredeemably syncretic and often, despite his affirmations otherwise, dialectical in their operation."[91] Gandhi's sacred transhistorical rhetoric drew upon a wide range of influences, from nineteenth-century European writings to vernacular interpretations of Hinduism. David Arnold has argued that his writing was influenced by Edward Carpenter, who is cited in *Hind Swaraj;* John Ruskin, whom Gandhi translated; and Leo Tolstoy, with whom Gandhi corresponded.[92] Moreover, Gandhi staged his rhetoric for a European rather than just an Indian audience—a number of Gandhi's writings are to be found in letters to Europe. As Young has argued, Gandhi was an early master of the society of the spectacle, strategically choosing his clothes and media appearances to use the technology of the camera to make the greatest impression on the Western world.[93]

In addition to their personal biographies of movement and influence, all the spiritualists produced work of transnational significance. Although these writers opposed the railway as a symbol of Westernization, their anti-technological discourse was part of a broader, global critique of mechanization that included Western writers. Like many prominent European modernists, Aurobindo and Tagore created their works in the shadow of World War I, and their writings may be seen as part of a global modernist response to war.[94] European writers of the period certainly understood this: Tagore's play *The Waterfall* was promoted to a European audience by the French writer Marc Elmer, who celebrated Tagore's work as part of a post–world war renunciation of mechanization and materiality.[95]

Like the social critics, the spiritualists wrote from within the conditions of modernity; unlike the social critics, the spiritualists imagined an outside of Western modernity by turning to the past, a theological-textual past in particular. Like Walter Benjamin's angel of history, they looked backward while being propelled inexorably into the future.[96] The storm of their present was comprised of a particular expression of modernity: a colonial modernity, the conditions of which were embodied by the spatial and temporal paradigms of the railway. Manu Goswami has argued that the desire implicit in Gandhi's traditionalism was embedded in his ambivalent experience of this colonial modernity:

> The contradictory texture of colonial state space—the proliferating economic and cultural distinctions together with various effects of homogenization—engendered longings for a transcendent organic space-time. Among the most passionately felt responses to colonial unevenness was Gandhi's articulation of eternal, organic, self-enclosed forms of community.[97]

The work of these spiritualists may thus be seen as both inside and outside of modernity—technically occupying modern modes of space and time while simultaneously endorsing a return to more natural ways of being—disrupting notions of the modern like the "rational utopia" to produce what might be called a counternarrative of modernity.

Tagore's Bengali poem "Railway Station" provides a literary illustration of this inside/outside position and the aesthetics of this counternarrative of modernity. The poem expresses profound uneasiness with shifting modes of being represented by the space of the railway station. The narrator describes a mobile world of contingency and anonymity:

> Day – Night – clanking and rumbling,
> Trainloads of people thundering forth.
> Changing direction at every moment,
> Eastwards, westwards, rapid as storms.[98]

The narrator's fascination with the flow is soon superseded by his apprehension about this new subjectivity as he watches those at the station in motion and stasis, "succeeding, failing, boarding, or remaining."[99] The passengers participate in "[a] whimsical game, a self-forgetting"[100] produced by their departure. The railway world is one of appearance rather than substance, and the rapid movement emerges as a form of artifice: "The hurry disguises their jobs and sorrows/Masks the pressure of gains and losses."[101] For the narrator, their lives are a picture that becomes a shredded canvas with its strips discarded, and their movement at the station becomes a metaphor for the virtual nature of the world.

"Railway Station" has been read as giving "an image and definition of spiritual failure"[102] by showing a world in which the brushstrokes of representation only obscure inner truth. The poem's narrator sees himself as different, as a stationary entity observing "alone in the midst of the to-ing and fro-ing."[103] The line that complicates the narrator's self-positioning, however, sets up a parallel between the contingent movement of trains and language, "forever forming, forever unforming, / Continuous coming, continuous going."[104] Here, through the narrator, Tagore implicitly critiques his own poem and its inability to capture the truth. For just as the narrator is positioned inside the transitory world of railway space, so too is the author "forever forming, forever unforming" inside of modernity. The inside/outside position of Tagore's narrator in relation to the railway space acts as a spatial analogy to the ideological position of all the spiritualists described in this chapter. Just as the narrator finds himself framed by language, the spiritualists wrote from inside the machine of colonialism, and, as Western-educated writers, from within its paradigms as well. The narrator, like Tagore, Vivekananda, Aurobindo, and Gandhi, imagines a self outside the impermanent contingency represented by the railway world.

A New Cultural Provenance

The political discourse of the social critics had specified that it was the way the railway had been used by the British, rather than the railway itself, that gave rise to such conditions as famine. The spiritualists, in contrast, set themselves against the epistemology of the railway, its way of being and knowing, for colonial discourse had posited the railway as a means for social transformation through a new form of knowledge—a secular knowledge—materialized by technology. Yet despite their differences in ideologies, political programs, and even race, the social reformers and the spiritualists shared more than a focus on the machine. Both groups shared the concern for justice and moral integrity. Their language reflected that common ground: although the social critics described previously based their case against the railway primarily on secular grounds, they often used the language of morality. Furthermore, despite the fact that spiritualists departed from the Enlightenment-influenced epistemology of the social critics, Vivekananda, Aurobindo, Gandhi, and Tagore grounded their political, social, and aesthetic commentaries in the space that had been cleared by this earlier group of critics. Put another way, although the spiritualists wrote from within the moral authority of tradition, they were motivated by the same economic and political circumstances as the social critics, and learned of these circumstances by studying the social critics' work. Mohandas Gandhi wept when he read Romesh Dutt's *Economic History of India*, which linked the railway to the impoverishment of India.[105] The discussion of famine became an important motivator in the nationalists' political program to decolonize India; Gandhi cited the frequency of famines and the railway's role in this in *Hind Swaraj*, his 1909 call for self-rule.[106] The social critics were able to articulate in their "insurgent grammar of political economy"[107] the very conditions that gave rise to distinctions evident in the third-class railway carriage. The contradictory nature of the experience of the railway prompted Gandhi to devote the third chapter of his autobiography to railway outrages and to reject the paradigm of the train as his model for Indian identity in favor of the village. Finally, like the social critics but using a different set of tools, the spiritualists challenged the dominant discourse of the railway and all that it represented.

These Indian writers and their British sympathizers responded to the colonial rhetoric of development. That rhetoric offered the railway as both a means and a symbol of transformation. The railway became a focal point as a symbol for those who criticized or outright opposed British rule in India. For some, it represented the unequal distribution of wealth and a "drain" on Indian resources. Its public spaces were a place where the discrimination of colonial India revealed itself in plain sight. Many of these writers maintained faith in the rhetoric of technological advancement as they sought a civil society under independent rule. Other writers, however, examined the meanings of the train as an emblem of a new way of being and warned of the dangers of a society based on a technological ideal. These writers instead turned to ethical ideals based on spiritual teachings as a counterpoint to the machine. Whether they used the ideas and modes of writing derived from European political economy or the language of spirituality and morality, the nationalists and dissident British writers challenged the symbolic import of the train, turning it against its cultural provenance. By the moment of India's Partition and independence, the train was for many Indians a symbol of a newly independent nation. It was also the site of some of the most intense religious violence in modern history, as the myriad symbol of the railway gained yet another new meaning denoting the failure of secular ideals.

CHAPTER 3

Partition and the Death Train

Ladies and gentlemen, my apologies. News of this train's arrival was delayed. That is why we have not been able to entertain you lavishly — the way we wanted to.

Saadat Hasan Manto, "Hospitality Delayed"

THE 1947 VIGNETTE "Hospitality Delayed" ("Kasri-Nafisi"),[1] by Urdu writer Saadat Hasan Manto, takes a paradigmatic moment in the railway journey—the official welcome of travelers to a new place—and turns it into a nightmare of civic ceremony. An assassin makes a pleasant speech to a crowd that has witnessed a massacre, implicating the survivors in the brutality that they have witnessed against the other, unnamed community, and suggesting that even this display has fallen far short of what they all had wished. The vignette imitates and distorts two narratives of travel and civility in South Asia: the duty of the proper host to entertain a guest and the official discourse of the railway as a state bureaucratic space. The horror of the communal violence that characterized India's Partition gains the terribleness of irony. What is being rewritten here includes not only the normalcy of life, but also the notion of a safe, secular modernity that was central to the promise of national independence. As Manto's vignette suggests, this ideal—and its negation—came to be represented by the railway, a process that brought to light the unstable character of modernity.

Partition, Violence, and National Subjectivity

As Sir Cyril Radcliffe drew a line in 1947 dividing the former British colony in South Asia into India and East and West Pakistan, the political decisions surrounding his action gave rise to some of the most intense displacements, interethnic violence, and systematic sexual assaults of the twentieth century. Estimates place the number of deaths between 100,000 and 500,000 (the huge range reflecting discrepancies between unofficial and official sources, as well as biases within those official sources). Recent histories like the scholarly works by Urvashi Butalia, Ritu Menon, and Kamla Bhasin have recovered the experiences of some of the more than 75,000 women who were the victims of rape, mutilation, and abduction.[2] The political decisions and the imminent violence forced between 10 and 12 million people (16 million by unofficial count[3]) to leave their homes. While well-to-do refugees traveled by airplane or car, and some of those heading to Bombay from Karachi took a ship, the vast majority walked or rode in bullock carts (a two-wheeled wooden vehicle pulled by oxen) in enormous caravans that stretched for miles. A number also traveled in buses and on the railway (Figure 6). The trains carried more than a million and a quarter Hindus and Sikhs to India from Pakistan from August to November of 1947.[4] Sometimes 5,000 people crushed into a train meant for hundreds, with a third of the passengers relegated to the roof.[5] Reflecting a similarly massive migration in the other direction, one train in November 1947 carried 6,550 Muslim refugees and government employees toward Pakistan.[6]

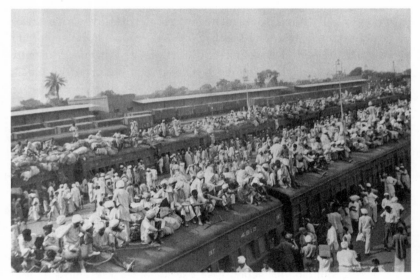

Figure 6. Refugees crowd trains in Amritsar in October 1947 during Partition. Photograph courtesy AFP/INP/Getty Images.

Political leaders saw the railway as a vehicle to make concrete political plans for Partition and arranged for special trains as part of the relocation efforts. During the first months after Partition, more than 700,000 evacuees were carried by these refugee trains;[7] the two states put these operations under the charge of the Indian and Pakistani Military Evacuation Organization Government. Railway officials viewed the train as a safe vehicle for relocation, for the rhetoric of modernity that was the legacy of the colonial period promised that the state space of the railway would supersede what appeared as localized violence. Many refugees believed strongly in the vision of the railway system as inviolable, a faith that can be linked back to the notion of the train as a civil arena. The state-sponsored refugee trains on the border of West Pakistan represented the protection of the nation; symbolically, the Muslims fleeing west and the Hindus fleeing east sought refuge in the nation as they boarded refugee trains. They saw the railway as a national, secular space that could transcend the religious difference that now manifested itself in violence.

The trains were not safe, however, for they did not have proper state protection, and the soldiers who did travel on-board often had their own communal allegiances. An article in an October 1947 issue of the *British Railway Gazette* noted that 3,000 passengers had been killed on a Muslim refugee train in Amritsar.[8] To the world, the American photographer Margaret Bourke-White offered a snapshot of this violence, with photographs of bodies lying along the tracks and images of refugees that personalized the mass migration for readers of *Life* magazine (Figure 7).[9] For many Indians and Pakistanis, the image of the train was held even more intimately in the collective memories of displaced families that might have grandmothers and uncles who were witnesses to the violence, or even missing children and aunts.[10] The massacres, beatings, and rapes in and around the trains eroded the ideal of the secular nation, breaking down the civil dreams of modernity.

Political decisions by Hindu, Muslim, and British leaders prompted the announcement of Partition. Although the Muslim League had existed since the first decade of the twentieth century, it gained more currency among Muslims after riots took place throughout the country in 1946; the organization then focused its demands on the creation of a separate state that would fulfill the dream of a Muslim brotherhood.[11] The Indian National Congress, the most powerful party in Indian politics, agreed to the division against

Figure 7. Margaret Bourke-White's photo of Muslim refugees boarding the train in New Delhi on August 7, 1947, to travel to Pakistan. Photograph courtesy Keystone Features/ Stringer/Hulton Archive/Getty Images.

the wishes of Mohandas Gandhi, arguably capitulating to the demands of Hindu and Sikh sectarian groups in Punjab and Bengal. Finally, the British viceroy, Lord Mountbatten, announced and instituted the division as the British prepared to leave power, and many Indians and Pakistanis felt that he abandoned responsibility for the process as it descended into violence. The relative importance of these causal factors are much debated among scholars of South Asia, but one thing clearly emerges from different accounts—namely, the primacy of the modern nation as a resolution for communal tensions that had grown during the colonial period and come to crisis during the decolonization movement. It was thought that modernity in the form of the nation would offer refuge from sectarian violence; instead, that violence reached its peak with the emergence of an independent India bracketed between two parts of Pakistan.

While Partition was catalyzed by these top-down political decisions, it materialized on the ground in local and immediate ways. Violence in the name of the nation found its force in riots, ambushes, and personal betrayals. Ethnic nationalism also gathered symbolic power as sexualized violence, mobilizing gendered narratives of the nation. The concept of woman had been infused as a powerful signifier in the nationalist struggle[12]; during Partition, women became a symbolic site of cultural identity within a violent struggle over cultural nationalism. Rape and mutilation were used by both sides as weapons of war that, among other things, appropriated or destroyed the other community's reproductive vitality. Violence was also directed at masculinity itself; many memoirs record how, during some part of the hostility, men were forced to show their genitals as a way to attest their communal identity (in the South Asian community, it was mostly Muslim men who were circumcised). Moreover, castration was also used as a mutilation. "Spontaneous" and gendered violence was not incidental to other kinds of force but constitutive of Partition and the construction of new states.[13]

The violence that operated under the name of communalism was more complex than simply religious antagonism. Scholars debate the definition of "communalism," though the term, dating back to British categories of rule, is commonly used in India today.[14] David Ludden defines communalism in India as based on the idea that Muslim and Hindus constitute separate, antagonistic communities.[15] Achin Vanaik ascribes the phenomenon to religious sentiments only in part; these, Vanaik argues, combine with nonreligious elements to increase divisions and tensions between religious communities and thus consolidate power.[16] Certainly, communalism gained force through its form as a political movement and it took legitimacy in the shape of nationalism. Etienne Balibar describes how competing ideological formations are ultimately instrumentalized in the service of the nation:

> Incontestably, national ideology involves ideal signifiers (first and foremost, the very name of the nation or "fatherland") on to which may be transferred the sense of the sacred and the affects of love, respect, sacrifice, and fear which have cemented religious communities; but that transfer only takes place because *another type* of community is involved here. The analogy is itself based on a deeper difference. If it were not, it would be impossible to understand why national identity, more or less completely integrating

the forms of religious identity, ends up tending to replace it, and forcing it itself to become "nationalized."[17]

Balibar both distinguishes between national and religious ideologies and blurs their differences. The instrumentalization of religion may take place only because it exists as a separate category. The model that he depicts moves from "difference" to "integrat(ion)" to "replace(ment)"; yet religion is not rendered mute by the process of being appropriated and supplanted. Here, the powerful affects of religious communities (love, respect, sacrifice, and fear) are articulated through the ideology of the nation. Balibar's model can be used to understand the way communal identities inhabited *national* subjectivity during the time of Partition. At that moment, communal identities were subsumed beneath a national identity (as the decision was made for Partition) as religious affiliations spoke through the form of a nation.

Scenes of Partition violence were not simply evidence of a return to "tradition" from "modernity." During Partition in South Asia, communal identities were cast retroactively as original divisions and given primacy. In these cases, ironically, communal identities were formulated at the same time as the nation-states, for written and oral histories describe how local identities, such as those of village or class, often superseded others until that moment of crisis. At that historical moment in a cracking India, all identities were subordinate to national identity as the decision was made to create two states, while religious affiliations simultaneously found voice in the form of a nation.[18] The categories of national and local, secular and communal, were thus articulated through each other. One should note this complexity as one considers the way that Partition discourse has characterized the violence as solely religious antagonism. Furthermore, one would do well to remember that these defining binaries were never absolute, a point readily apparent in the representations of Partition.

Partition's Written and Visual Culture

The archive of letters, fiction, memoirs, and film relating to Partition spans over sixty years and continues to grow. Memoirs provide the most immediate account of the violence. In her autobiographical work, for example, Dr. Zahida Amjad Ali recalls how she traveled from Delhi toward Pakistan in a tense train carriage into which panicked refugees were crowded—their weapons confiscated. She looked out from the train window at a horrific landscape: "Human skulls without flesh were an obvious proof that there had been a brutal massacre. At many places, you could see corpses lying on one another and no one seemed to have any concern."[19] The dreadfulness outside soon entered the compartment in the form of a rampaging mob. The doctor witnessed the attackers searching for Muslim women and children to kill; they brutally stabbed her mother and six-month-old sister, whose presence was betrayed by tiny, jangling anklets.

Official records show that brutalized citizens turned to the state for justice, only to be confronted with the failure to handle the problem at best, or complicity with the violence at worst. A letter from a woman named Mridula Sarabhai to the Department of Railways and Transport in India tells of a Muslim train derailed and attacked on September 23, 1947, near Amritsar. She details how the assistant stationmaster was hesitant to give water to the refugees; the military and public service organizations "seemed to have become partisan" and the medical staff, "half-hearted and disinclined,"[20] did not send for the ambulances. In one particularly moving passage, Sarabhai describes how the military stood by while the attackers, members of a supposed relief society, killed off the remaining refugees after a massacre:

> We had a chance of seeing the working of the Sewa-samiti [Service Society] volunteers. Some of them were removing the dead bodies and throwing them in the railway van. I was surprised because they belonged to the same organization which believed in retaliation. So I watched them and found that they were finishing off half-alive refugees, were going to throw a live child among the dead bodies, which I saved, and were ransacking the compartments looking for property.[21]

Sarabhai was a person without official status who, in writing this letter, turned to state channels that oversaw the administration of the railway, a state-run system that was the visible face of the government of India. Her gesture to hold someone accountable sits in the National Archives of India as a hidden but persistent reminder of both the failure of the state and the persistent vigilance some individuals showed despite that breakdown. Also recorded there is the official response to her letter, a brush-off in which a railway area officer blames the "lack of drinking water" on the "persistent thefts of water taps, usually of brass, by public," and asserts that the doctor "was not aware of the seriousness of the incident."[22] Archives of letters of aggrieved individuals like Mridula Sarabhai show that normal citizens responded to the violence by placing their trust in bureaucratic channels; these letters represent "a thread of commitment to the new nation, and to the newly-forming state,"[23] Urvashi Butalia tells us. They also challenge that the state lived up to its obligations to protect its citizens.

Looking at this immense body of written and visual culture on Partition, it is evident how genre has shaped the intentions and impact of these works. Memoirs, testimonies, and letters provide a view of the experience of migration from the ground up. Fiction has given writers an opportunity to expose hidden histories. Partition-era novels, short stories, plays, and poems act as a literature of witness: They expose the terrifying experiences of massacres, rapes, mutilations, and suicides, as well as the sense of loss and confusion that many experienced as their personal geographies were erased. The works represent "what the body remembers," as the title of Shauna Singh Baldwin's Partition novel phrases it.[24] These written works also detail the disjuncture between the leaders who made these decisions and the ordinary people who put them into effect. Film, especially popular Hindi cinema, has been able to reach an even broader audience in this nation, where diverse languages and frequent illiteracy make visual culture a powerful way to shape a national public.[25] Films that deal with issues concerning Partition have become a powerful medium through which to resolve lingering questions of nationalism.[26]

In addition to variations between genres, the diverse historical conditions of production in different decades since 1947 have given rise to multiple responses to Partition. Stories and novels from the 1950s, including Saadat Hasan Manto's Urdu vignettes, Khuswant Singh's novel *Train to Pakistan*, and Bhisham Sahni's Hindi story "We Have Arrived in Amritsar" ("Amritsar Aa Gaya Hai"), as well as Manmohan Desai's 1960 Hindi film *Chhalia*, were created when the violence was still a recent memory. These works forced audiences in India and Pakistan to confront the murders, rapes, and abductions that were being written out of the official histories as India and Pakistan raced into their respective futures as independent nations. They were cultural representations with social importance for audiences in which many people knew victims, were victims, or, had themselves been perpetrators of violence.

One prominent type of work from this period is the film of national resolution. A representative film, Manmohan Desai's *Chhalia*, attempts to resolve some of the lingering questions of national belonging that followed Partition. Shanti, whose name means "peace," travels securely in a women's carriage from Lahore, Pakistan, to Delhi along with other Hindu and Sikh women who are being repatriated after Partition, a reference to the mandatory exchange of abducted women between nations in the years following the violence. The film opens with an exterior shot of a train racing across the landscape. The speed and shape of the streamlined train suggest India's modern age, and its connection to the nation is established quickly as the camera shifts to the perspective of Shanti, as she looks out the window. "Here comes India, our India," she says to the other women as the camera captures the panoramic gaze from the carriage window, a view that amalgamates the landscape into a national symbol. Later in the film, the happy interior of the women's carriage will be juxtaposed against a scene of an abducted women's "home," a place of despair nearly open to the street that presents both the emotional and spatial counterpart of the train carriage. Over the course of the film, Shanti's possession of India will be lost until national subjectivity is finally recuperated through tradition, not modernity, in a final scene of a religious festival.

Although he elevates the religious, Desai does not challenge the vision of the collective nation as the way forward and the train as its symbol. In another scene, a Pathan (a Muslim) meets a Sikh on a train back to Pakistan; in a strange twist of fate, the Sikh is traveling with the Pathan's missing sister, looking to return her to her family. In this moment, in the aftermath of Partition, the third-class carriage becomes a place of possibility for transcending embedded social relations that caused the brother and sister's original separation. Desai's work is one of national reconciliation after Partition and represents a dominant strain of writing, discussed in chapter 4, that asserted itself during the postcolonial period. For most works that deal directly with Partition, however, the failure of the idea of the modern nation is brought to the fore in their representations—it is these that are dealt with in this chapter.

The impact of Partition has reached into all parts of Indian society, even though, with the exception of Hyderabad, relatively little of the direct violence and displacement touched the South. Kavita Daiya argues that "the 1947 Partition continues to haunt contemporary life in India. This is true not only for discourses that debate the place of religion in India but also for the historical interpretation of justice and minority belonging, and for the tension-ridden struggle over the production of secular national culture in the subcontinent."[27] The haunting is not simply the impact of a past period upon the present moment but an ongoing process, because borders and national identities are still being contested. Partition persists in terms of a continuing discourse with familiar symbolism; it also remains in the sense that such integral concepts as religion, justice, constituency, and secularism, as well as gender, ethnicity, and citizenship are still affected by the experience of violence. Partition has transformed subjectivity; as Suvir Kaul puts it, "what had changed utterly was the familiar relation between self and society."[28]

From the mid-1960s to the 1980s, there were fewer works on Partition, some notable exceptions being Bhisham Sahni's 1973 Hindi novel *Tamas* and Chaman Nahal's 1975 English novel *Azadi*. It was not until the communal violence and the anniversary of independence in the 1980s that one saw a remarkable surge in Partition works.[29] Communalism's uncertain place in present-day India arguably gives rise to this persisting unease and has motivated the contemporary interest in films and fictional and scholarly writings about Partition. More recent creations, like Mukul Kesavan's 1995 novel *Looking through Glass*, Deepa Mehta's 1998 film *Earth*, and Anil Sharma's 2001 Hindi film *Gadar: Ek Prem Katha* focus on the sectarian conflicts of Partition and connect earlier communal violence to the recent rise of religious fundamentalism, both Muslim and Hindu.

Partition remains as a discourse that reshapes a past event. The rhetoric of Partition haunts communal violence between socio-religious groups and disputes over borders—in that sense, the Partition is not over. As the conclusion of this book describes, journalistic accounts of contemporary violence, like the 2007 bombing of the *Samjhauta* Express, or the Friendship Express, that connects India and Pakistan, evoke a history of Partition.[30] In forging these connections, these accounts make sense of the contemporary violence as a *reoccurrence* rather than something also derived from, for example, tensions in this current period of globalization. The Indian media sets Partition as the unstable cornerstone for the construction of India as a nation. Furthermore, it reduces that historic moment to the religious aspects of the violence, leaving aside how the tensions were exacerbated by class difference, mediated by caste distinctions, and executed on the basis of gender.[31] Although religion was not the sole cause of Partition violence, it has become the main signifier of difference in accounts of the period. In contrast, earlier works like *Chhalia* emphasized other aspects of decolonization and nation building. Put simply, the primary way of remembering the violence in current popular culture is as a dispute between communities of faith. By reading the image of the train, this chapter attempts to supplement this understanding with an analysis of the changing meaning of modernity represented by the breakdown during Partition of the colonial—and nationalist—ideal of railway space.

The Train as an Icon of Partition

For all the pieces of written and visual culture detailed previously, the image of the train becomes a way to explore the promises of emerging nations and the failures of modernity. The train is, of course, just one of a number of symbols that recur in Partition works. For example, many literary and filmic works are careful to establish that each side raped, maimed, and killed members of the other community; this notion of retribution appears in this body of work as the image of balancing accounts. Other tropes emphasize the bodily aspects of the experience. Short stories like "The Return" ("Khol-do") by Manto, in which sexual violation becomes a mechanical process remembered by the body of an abducted woman (she automatically opens her legs for her father), reveal how trauma is inscribed on the corporeal. Numerous earlier narratives, both fictional and autobiographical, memorialized cross-religious love as a casualty of the violence; in later works, this romance became a symbolic resolution of the rifts between communities. In short stories, the abandoned house offers a material sign of lost family histories that persist on now-foreign soil. Characters like the insane man and the abducted woman show the transformation of people under the conditions of Partition.[32] These scenes and characters recur in multiple works, creating a kind of shared cultural memory of Partition. As well as being but one of several recurrent images, the train scene reflects individual artistic decisions. For example, the train does not have the nuance in Pamela Rooks's 1998 Hindi film version of *Train to Pakistan* as it does in Singh's novel; in contrast, the serialized, television version of *Tamas*, directed in Hindi by Govind Nihalani in 1987, emphasizes the train more than Sahni's novel. Arguably, however, the train has become the dominant trope for representing the violence of Partition—this despite the fact that refugee trains played a far less important historical role in the East Pakistan Partition.[33]

The train has been the primary icon of Partition because of its emblematic resonance within South Asia. Colonial writers envisioned the railway as a force of cultural change, a model for the kind of technological innovation that would carry India toward modernity. The nationalist perspective was politically different, but even for those who strove for independence, the railway still maintained its symbolic importance. Late nineteenth-century politico-economic theorists fixed on the railway as a sign of the economic exploitation that had been part of colonialism. By the first decades of the twentieth century, Gandhi marked the train as a harbinger of a mechanical culture that he deemed alien and destructive. Yet despite these interpretations—or maybe because of the way they maintained the emblematic status of the railway—the colonial discourse that represented the train as a sign of transformation continued to have a powerful legacy. By 1947, the train symbolized for many the journey into modern nationhood.

The train's particular role as a metaphor for the nation has made it an important site to reflect on India's new status. In literary and visual renderings, the train represents the nation in such diverse media as the postage stamp, the novel, and the itinerary. A circulating system, the railway dynamically transforms geographic space into a simultaneous community. It continually bonds that national space through trade and travel. Further securing its relation to the state, cultural interpretations of the railway carriage as a public space have historically attempted to reproduce the nation by inscribing its ideology, hierarchies, and divisions. The railway produces as well as reveals this logic; in doing so, it acts as an emissary of the nation that promises to enclose all within its security. "Enter! This thing is the work of the Government,"[34] a character calls out to the Tibetan lama in Rudyard Kipling's 1901 *Kim*, and the same sentiment is still being repeated when, during the decolonization struggle, Jawaharlal Nehru calls the railway India's greatest national asset.[35]

The dominant paradigm of the train is that of a space suspended from the intimacy of place and transformed into abstract, symbolic terms that rely on anonymity, a process that parallels national constituency. To those who view the passing train, the vehicle appears as a concrete sign of that abstract collective identity; to the passengers inside, the train represents the nation moving toward its imagined realization. The railway's ability to reconstruct space and time through movement made it a primary space for the constitution of new national identities. The train was an agent of deterritorialization because it transferred its occupants into a new collectivity out of their original local context. In the process, the trains produced an identity extracted from the complexities of location. The collectivity was an anonymous one that placed people in more danger than they might have been in a village where they had longstanding relationships across religious lines.

At the very heart of Western modernity, according to Anthony Giddens, lies a process in which social relations are disembedded.[36] As well as being a symbol of the nation, then, the train during Partition was a central place representing a modernity constituted through mobility. That disembedded, mobile identity was certainly national in character during Partition, for people put their faith in the railway as a metonym for the state. Ironically, though, that modern mobility, that amalgamation within national constituency, also gave rise to increased communalism. Movement reduced people to their communal identities by removing them from homes in which they occupied far more complex selves that included, for example, class and caste identities, family friendships, and economic relationships. The trains themselves came to represent communal identities as the direction of the train signified the identities of the passengers and made them vulnerable to attack. A train traveling east near the border became a signifier of Hindus, and one traveling west a symbol of Muslims. The point here is not so much whether the designation of a "Hindu train" or "Muslim train" was completely accurate (because it sometimes was not), so much as to show the abstraction produced by mobility that enabled the violence to take place. As argued previously, this process of disembedding represented both modernity and the nation; thus, in these works the modern nation has become derationalized, communal, and embodied.

It was not coincidental, then, that during Partition, the train came to signal what was felt to be the failure of modern nationhood. The train represented in material form the promises of secular modernity—and showcased the failure of these ideals of security and freedom. The literature and films of Partition depict a moment which breaks down the ideal of the train carriage as a "rational utopia,"[37] the idealized space of regulation seemingly separated from a chaotic outside. This concept, I have argued, was central to the construction of the railway as modern space in colonial discourse. These works represent the unstable aspects of modernity by challenging the future-orientation of the modern, by showing borders as permeable and national identity as fluid, by presenting images of the uncanny in contrast to the rationality of technology, and by offering an embodied picture of national constitution.

Partition literature uses images of the train to confront the notion of imminent transformation that lies at the heart of modernity's colonial narrative. The train is often depicted as the emblem of a forward-facing modernity, and as the embodiment of a progressive history. Yet South Asian Partition literature set on the train often challenges, if not undermines, the notion of progress. The period of Partition transforms the nature of that temporality; as both India and Pakistan gain national sovereignty, the image of the train journey changes into one of perpetual reversal. The altered timeline of modernity appears in narrative in the form of a train that shuttles back and forth in violence and retribution rather than goes forward: a pendulum rather than a vector.

Cultural works fix on the railway, not simply because it was a modern national symbol but because the train's nature as a mobile space represented the movement that was part of Partition. Historically, the train held an important role for this dividing India; it enacted that division by displacing people across the border, but it also bridged that separation through its very movement back and forth across the lines. Because of this, the train came to represent both the violence of division and the potential reversibility of that separation. Moreover, movement gave the train fluidity so that a train could "belong" to first one community and then to another as it passed over the border. For example, in his autobiography, Shahid Ahmad of the Progressive Writer's Movement records a train journey: "After half an hour the train started as if the dead have had new life. 'Pakistan Zindabad' and 'Quaid-e-Azam Zindabad' slogans started to be raised. We understood that we have now entered the borders of Pakistan."[38] Mobility also lent the train the indeterminacy that symbolized the unclear status of a border zone. S. H. Vatsayan (Ajneya) captures this sense of un-belonging in his Hindi short story "Getting Even," in which a Hindu asks a Sikh where his home is:

> "Used to be in Shekhupura. Now it might as well be here."
> "Here? What do you Mean?"
> "Wherever I happen to be, there's my home! One corner of a
>   railway compartment."[39]

These works reflect the liminal state that was central to a Partition experience in which a home might be "moved" from one nation to another as national borders were redrawn.

Writers and filmmakers have mobilized the train as a symbol of the modern, secular nation during and since Partition to challenge the nature of modernity, secularism, and nationhood; to do this, they transformed the symbol of the train. Their works witness a history and rewrite the cultural meaning of railway space by using the setting of the train to expose modernity's violent side. Partition literature has produced counternarratives of modernity; these counternarratives turn time backwards, transform technology into a body, ascribe the machine with an uncanny presence, and mark the train carriage as a communal space embedded in the local world around it. They transform the train carriage, once a symbol of liberation through mobility, into a place of incarceration where people await their deaths. These counternarratives are produced by the dialectical expression of modernity, emerging from within the myriad form that is the modern while destabilizing its primary narratives of temporality, technology, rationality, and secular nationhood. The following sections look more closely at a select few of these creative works to examine how this process works.

Khushwant Singh's *Train to Pakistan*

In *Train to Pakistan*, the image of the train is used to render shifting local and national identities in symbolic form. Singh, the author of this, the most widely known novel about Partition, set his work in the town of Mano Majra in the Northwest Frontier in the summer of 1947, when millions were forced to move to escape the communal violence. The idealized Mano Majra exists as an "oasis of peace" until relations break down between Sikhs and Muslims there as India moves into independence and Partition. There is relative harmony between villagers of different classes and religions, and Singh represents their commonalities as they encounter an outsider from an urban area. The villagers all revere a sandstone slab that represents the local deity, and they gather in the Sikh temple, where the leader Meet Singh presides but even the imam is welcome. Like many Partition narratives, Singh's novel idealizes pre-1947 life and communal relations.

Yet in Singh's pastoral ideal, it is the passing trains that foster the collective identity. The sounds of the railway have made "Mano Majra very conscious of trains";[40] this consciousness structures the villagers' daily life.

With the sound of the morning train, the mullah begins the call to prayer, and, hearing that, the Hindu priest performs his ablutions. Even the local thieves orient their nightly raids by the timetable of the train. This "railway time" has become entrenched in daily life, giving rise to an integrated local railway consciousness. Just as the passing trains prompt the timetable of religious rituals, statements about the railway become substitutes for other kinds of interactions: "When the goods train steams in," the narrator tells us, the villagers "say to each other, 'There is the goods train.' It is like saying goodnight."[41] In Singh's representation, a railway consciousness becomes embedded in local life, and local identity is articulated in terms of the railway.

In the novel, time acts as an organizing structure to show the intersection between the local and the national; it also calls forth the paradigms of progress embodied by the temporality of the railway. The railway has often been represented as imposing a new temporality associated with modernity, a measured time that structures the social world around it.[42] It orders it in terms of a disembedded, simultaneous time that evokes the nation. In Singh's novel, the railway timetable that organized the villagers' daily life begins to fluctuate as violence comes to Mano Majra:

> Some days it seemed as though the alarm clock had been set for the wrong hour. On others it was as if no one had remembered to wind it. . . . Goods trains had stopped running altogether, so there was no lullaby to lull them to sleep. Instead, ghost trains went past at odd hours between midnight and dawn, disturbing the dreams of Mano Majra.[43]

If "railway time" signifies the nation, something is changing within the order of the nation itself. With the unsettling of the "lullaby" of the trains, the village is waking to its national identity—one that had remained latent, in the dream world of night trains, until now. The narrator marks a progressive degeneration that accompanies this consciousness as something mistaken (set for the wrong hour) or forgotten becomes a thing "disturbing the dreams" of the village.

In transforming the image of the train, Singh disrupts the linearity of time that is central to the notion of modernity. The train, with its perpetual forward motion, functions as an emblem of progress, a concept often rendered in artistic form through the image of the journey. The train is usually a symbol of where it is going: The train's future is ahead, down the tracks. Singh references this orientation through the character of Hakum Chand, a chief inspector who recalls Prime Minister Jawaharlal Nehru's famous line from his speech at the moment of independence: "Long ago we made a tryst with destiny and now the time comes when we shall redeem our pledge, not wholly or in full measure but very substantially."[44] Nehru's metaphor suggests the forward-looking paradigm of modernity, which perceives a future imminent to the present. In the novel, however, the chief inspector looks back instead of forward, remembering a man who killed his wife and children on a halted train to save them from dying of thirst: "He came to his tryst by train."[45] The ghost train, which is a central image in the text, offers the same kind of reference to a prior event: a massacre that has already taken place. As a collective gaze is turned away from the future to look back to an imagined past, this past reemerges in new forms under the historical contingencies of the present. Thus, it is not only the temporality of the train that is altered but the temporality of modernity itself. An imagined communal past is summoned by this technology—in the form of a ghost—rather than a transcendent secular future.

In addition to altering notions of time associated with the modern, Singh's image of the Partition train also challenges the ideal version of the technological by fusing the mechanical to the embodied and communal. Trains have often been anthropomorphized in literature; this trope appears in the well-known Urdu short story by Krishan Chander entitled "Peshawar Express," in which a train that has left Peshawar with a caravan of refugees witnesses their murder and narrates various other horrific events.[46] In *Train to Pakistan*, the train begins to function as a metonym for the communal body; Singh achieves this effect through the image of a body-machine hybrid. As refugees push across the border by train, the trains become merged with the identities of their "cargo." Singh depicts the express train from Lahore crossing the new border to enter India: "Like all trains, it was full. From the roof, legs dangled down the sides onto the doors and windows. The doors and windows were jammed with heads and arms."[47] The author represents the refugee train as a cross between a crowd and a machine. Later in the novel, Singh describes another refugee train as having a "solid crust of human beings."[48] In yet another image, the train stands in place of its passengers as the author displaces the mood of the passengers and engineer onto the train itself:

> All trains coming from Delhi stopped and changed their drivers and guards before moving on to Pakistan. Those coming from Pakistan ran through with their engines screaming with release and relief.[49]

Singh reconceptualizes the image of the train from a value-neutral vehicle to a fraught and embodied social space in the image of a human-machine. Previously a national symbol, the train now symbolizes a communally coded vehicle, a caravan of Muslims traveling into Pakistan or of Sikhs and Hindus into India. It becomes the very bodies of those identities. When the first "death train" arrives over the border, "There was something uneasy about it. It had a ghostly quality."[50] The character of the train has changed from the instrument of reason (the clock) to a body and then to a specter.

In the climax of the novel, the body of the peasant Jugga meets the machine, as he climbs a rope meant to derail the train and cuts it, even as he is hit by the ongoing train, so that the train of refugees might go on to Pakistan. Kavita Daiya presents an insightful reading of this scene, arguing, "It is on [Jugga's] crushed, rural, masculine body that the triumph of secularism—figured as inter-ethnic love—is inscribed."[51] The victory for secularism granted by India's independence was historically problematic. The narrative choice to kill off Jugga certainly highlights the uneven sacrifices made for this triumph, but the accident itself also poses a challenge to this national modernity that is the train's destination. As I argue in the conclusion of this book, the image of the accident presents the confluence of body and machine; this collision undoes a culture of modernity that begins with the separation of the corporeal and the mechanical.[52]

In conclusion, Singh invokes and recodes several narratives of the railway, and in doing so he transforms the representational field of modernity. First, he alters a notion of time. The linear time that is a hallmark of the modern and emblemized by "railway time" becomes something irrational and uncanny. As Singh reverses the reader's gaze backward down the tracks toward the origin of the death train, he shifts temporal orientation from future to immediate past. Singh's train to Pakistan that closes the novel returns the gaze toward the future, but the notion of the tryst with destiny has already been critiqued thoroughly. In the context of Partition, the very idea of this progress is called into question. Second, Singh shifts from a mechanical vision of the train to first an anthropomorphic one and then an uncanny one, altering narratives of technology to offset the rhetoric of colonial modernity. Remo Ceserani describes the uncanny train in the European context as suturing together competing social notions of industrial modernity as both devastating and progressive.[53] Singh creates counternarratives of modernity—the anthropomorphic machine, the uncanny presence of the modern—to alter notions of what modernity means in this particular context of national constitution.

Gadar and Earth

This collapse of a national modernity may also be seen in Anil Sharma's 2001 blockbuster Hindi film *Gadar: Ek Prem Katha* (Uprising: A Love Story) in both the breakdown of the order of the railway space and in the appearance of a ghost train. The film presents two train massacre scenes: the first by Muslims against Hindus and Sikhs in the town of Piplan, which has just become part of Pakistan. A Sikh family attempts to flee to India, only to meet with the violence of a mob after they enter their compartment. The parents are killed and the sisters raped. The second train massacre scene takes place in Amritsar, as the Muslim family of the heroine, Sakina, tries to flee to Pakistan, only to be attacked by a mob of Hindus and Sikhs. They make it to Lahore, but she does not, and after she awakes at night among a mass of corpses on the train platform, she is hounded through a desolate encampment of disaffected refugees by a group of rapists. She is ultimately saved by the Sikh Tara Singh, who stands with a signal light in the middle of the tracks like the train she so desperately needs.

The film uses romance to resolve communal conflict, a common trope in works of Partition. Despite its overt message of equality, the film ultimately elevates the Indian perspective. One may see this in the communal allegiances subtly revealed in the train massacre scenes. In the first scene, the violence is explicit and shot close-up. As viewers, we see a father's throat slit, and the camera focuses, in the final shot inside the train, on the face of a Sikh woman being raped. The bloodied train pulls into the Amritsar station, where Tara Singh reads the Urdu words, "Indians learn from us." The second train massacre scene is less explicit. The camera focuses on those trying to get on the train and quickly cuts between shots. The violence takes place around and behind the focus of the camera.

Thus, although both scenes are those of a train massacre, the scene with the murderous Muslims is given an immediacy—and a primacy because it is first—that the later scene of Hindu and Sikh retribution is not, a representational decision that stirs the audience's emotions against Muslims even as it overtly condemns that sentiment.

The common character in the two sequences is the train. In both scenes, the train's whistle shrieks as it becomes a kind of collective embodiment of the victims that it contains. The machine also represents the desires of the refugee: In both scenes, the camera focuses the wheels of the train straining to move along on its journey but slowed down by the hoard. Both scenes show an aftermath of violence that reproduces the ghostly "death train" image used by Singh. In the first scene, the train pulls quietly into the station with dead bodies positioned in their carriage window seats like passengers on a gruesome journey. The second scene of the Amritsar platform massacre presents a night prospect of slaughtered bodies. Sharma uses the absence of sound to produce a haunting atmosphere. It is isolated sounds—the crunch of Tara's footsteps, the rasp of Sakina's breathing, and a distant call of a train—that return life to the scene.

The image of the ghost train reappears in Deepa Mehta's haunting portrayal of a train massacre in the film *Earth*. A Muslim man, Dil Navaz, waits anxiously at night on a railway platform for his relatives due on a refugee train; when the train arrives, he discovers the horrific sight of massacred bodies. Khushwant Singh, in his novel, had shown a village's collective experience of the death train rather than a single character's; but Mehta renders the politics of Partition in terms of personal transformation that gives rise to communal violence. The opening shot focuses on the face of Dil Navaz, and even when the camera moves back to show the entire platform waiting, no other characters face the camera. As viewers, we are closely tied to this particular character's experience, conveyed masterfully by the subtle acting of Aamir Khan.

Despite the emphasis on individual subjectivity, Mehta picks up on the cultural motif of the death train developed by Singh, using the possibilities offered by the genre of film to develop the experience of the uncanny. The scene is marked by its stillness and devoid of everyday sounds; in place of the noise of a crowded platform, the director uses a soundtrack as a way to interpret the muted scene. The background music is particularly important: its lyrics link the pulsating of the train to an anxious heart waiting in an atmosphere of impending doom.[54] The slow cadence of the music builds, ethereal strains overriding the mechanical noises of the train as the train slides into the station. The train's soft hiss is just discernable behind a song that, in its regular repetition, becomes the viewer's experience of a train. Sound in the scene renders the train eerie, an effect Mehta also achieves through lighting. The night scene is mostly dark, and the incoming train appears initially as a moon of light over the shoulder of Navaz, slipping into the station with the stealth of a ghost. After Navaz becomes aware of the train, he rushes to the door of a compartment. In this shot, the camera is positioned within the interior darkness, and we become aware of the blood on the floor not through sight, but by the sound of a fly and then growing recognition on the character's face. It is only after showing this realization that Mehta turns the camera and lights the scene to show a railway compartment and corridor filled with the bodies of adults and children.

As in Singh's novel, the stillness is highlighted here as Mehta presents a haunting image rather than a frenzied image of violence. Like Manto's "Hospitality Delayed" and Sharma's *Gadar*, Mehta's *Earth* achieves some of its disturbing quality by distorting a normal scene of railway travel. These writers and filmmakers tap into this other narrative stream to render the contradictions inside modernity within this historical context. They revive the tropes of this counternarrative — the uncanny versus rational technology, the anthropomorphic versus the mechanistic — to challenge the dominant narratives of modernity in the context of Partition.

Permeable Boundaries

Works of Partition also use the train's unique construction of space as a way to show the ruptures in a sense of order brought by the violence. As I argued in chapter 1, the spatialization of the railway highlights certain kinds of relationships; this nexus pivots around the paradigm of inside and outside, one of the primary binaries constructing railway space. This split between inside and outside produces what Michel de Certeau calls "a closed and autonomous insularity," a fantasy that becomes important as the train travels through the back door of urban spaces that many of the passengers would never walk through. The critic likens the railway carriage to "a bubble of panoptic and classifying power, a module of imprisonment that makes possible the production of an order, a closed and autonomous insularity — that is what can traverse space and make itself independent of local roots."[55] The space of the railway promises the order of modernity; to be within the regulated ranks of the railway car is to be protected by the state and simultaneously the promise of modernity, a "rational utopia."[56]

The binary of inside and outside stands at the center of modernity's rhetoric of exclusion and is charted in the representational space of the train. The boundaries of the train carriage mark interior from exterior; they also reference and divide national space inside from local space outside. The structure of the railway carriage offers voyeuristic possibilities with its elevated view of the world protected by a metal shell. The division between interior and exterior space of the railway becomes a continual reenactment and reinforcement, of hierarchies already in place. Of course, the train was never disembedded successfully from the localities it traveled through. Although these spaces of inside and outside are marked as separate, the boundaries between them—and the relations between their occupants—are more fluid than they initially appear. One need only think of the anxious relationship between observing traveler and observed native, or between threatening terrorist outside and vulnerable passenger confined in a carriage, to reflect on an anxiety that points to this permeability of boundaries. The carriage might appear to be apart from the land it travels over and the passenger a distant observer of the outside world, yet they are a part of both a national public space and a local space—and subject to both their realities. The violence on the railway during Partition exposes the permeability of boundaries and thus the fallacy of this separation. The image of the moving train as a place in which the interior is literally and metaphorically suspended above the outside local space becomes important in representations of the train as a site of violence during India's Partition; it allows writers and filmmakers to comment on the relationship between immediate and national identities.

Singh's *Train to Pakistan*, Sharma's *Gadar*, and Mehta's *Earth* locate their perspective primarily outside the train, or from within a stopped train. Other Partition narratives focus on the shifting dynamics within the mobile train carriage. Bhisham Sahni's short story "We Have Arrived in Amritsar" ("Amritsar Aa Gaya Hai") presents a view of the fluid landscape of Partition from within the moving train. Diversity marks the interior of the railway car traveling from West Punjab (now Pakistan) toward Delhi in Sahni's short story. The compartment has a mix of passengers, described by the narrator in terms of their ethnicity or language: a Sardar, three Pathan traders, and a Pushto speaker (from Peshawar). The narrator, meanwhile, is of an unknown background, a factor that will position him as an "objective observer" of the events. In the opening of the story, although the passengers have heard about Partition, they ask such questions as whether Muslim leader Mohammad Ali Jinnah will continue to live in Bombay or move to Pakistan. The author clearly wishes to highlight people's ignorance of the changes that Partition had in store.

Like *A Train to Pakistan*, "We Have Arrived in Amritsar" tells the story of a descent into violence. Violence initially appears as an omnipotent aura characterizing an unseen exterior. As the train passes through troubled areas, it uses motion to outstrip its perceived vulnerability.[57] A key aspect of this story is the construction of the "rational utopia" of the railway carriage as a neutral space suspended from the vagaries of the outside.[58] As things deteriorate within the railway car, it becomes evident that the space of the carriage is not inviolable. Despite the passengers' chit-chat, tension lies immediately under the surface of "normal" railway camaraderie. The events are catalyzed by a group of thugs who exacerbate those tensions. Several rowdy Pathan traders make an initial offer of unidentified red meat, a suspect display of generosity on the part of these Muslims that quickly turns into a ritual for the delineation of communal affiliations of those in the compartment. When the man from Peshawar refuses the meat, they taunt him: "Oh Zalim, if you don't want to accept it from our hands, pick it up with your own. By God, this is goat's meat and not of any other animal,"[59] statements which refer to certain Hindu food prohibitions.[60] With this act, the communalization of the railway space has begun.

As the passengers in the train gain a new awareness of the permeability of public space, there comes an increasing sense of vulnerability. Even though the carriage seems isolated when viewed from the interior of the car (particularly when the blinds are pulled down), the train is also part of the outside spaces through which it rapidly travels. The dynamics governing that space also govern the interior. For example, a tangible sign of the violence materializes in the guise of a frantic Hindu man and his family fleeing something outside, perhaps a mob, with his trunk and cot. When the Pathan aims a kick at the man, and instead kicks the man's wife, keeping them outside, the communal tensions "outside" reveals themselves to be within the compartment as well.

A train dramatizes the geography of power in a way a fixed public space cannot, for it is subject to both an interior order and a changing exterior order. In the story, the power dynamic inside the car begins to shift depending on the location of the train; the power balance of the towns through which the train travels is mirrored inside the seemingly detached space: Sahni describes how the Hindu and Sikh passengers tense and the Pathan passengers relax as they learn the ravaged town they have just passed was predominantly Muslim.[61] As the train moves east, the power of the majority changes hands, and the dynamics inside the railway car similarly echo and reinforce those outside of it.

After crossing the border, one Hindu man, previously teased and cowed, crashes an iron bar down on an unknown Muslim man (his religion identified by his idiom "In the Name of Allah"), as the man and his wife try to gain access to the moving train. The mobile geography of power and the particular relationship between interior and exterior space enable this ironic change in the Hindu's character. A beleaguered man suddenly gains authority as they pass over invisible space: He is supported by an imagined nation mapped with national and communal identities designating who has power where. The train carriage, despite the fact that it is set apart as a "neutral" space, represents the status of this outside world.

By setting his story on a moving train, Sahni presents the dynamics of mobile space. His story offers a fluid geography of power, as the relation between interior and exterior space determine the relative power of Muslims, Sikhs, and Hindus. Sahni invokes a dominant trope of the railway, the binary of inside and outside, that symbolizes the tenets of modernity. But like Singh, he also introduces a counternarrative—the anxiety of the permeable boundary that lies at the heart of railway terror—and thus alters the imagination of modernity.

Contemporary Partition Works

The contemporary depictions of the train in South Asian literature and film continue to question the rhetoric of modernity in representing the period of Partition. Recent events have turned attention toward the opposition between the sacred and the secular, prompting writers and filmmakers to rethink the binary between the two. The increase in Partition literature produced in the past two decades has arguably been due to rising concern about communalist violence in contemporary India, including the anti-Sikh riots in 1984 and the violence following the destruction of the Babri Masjid in 1992. This concern has been voiced by both writers in India like Bapsi Sidhwa, whose 1988 novel *Cracking India* (*Ice Candy Man*) was remade into the film *Earth*, and by diasporic writers such as

Shauna Singh Baldwin with her 1999 novel *What the Body Remembers.* The scholarly work of Urvashi Butalia, Ritu Menon, and Kamla Bhasin has helped recover and record women's experiences. These contemporary literary and scholarly texts continue the project of grappling with modern nationhood begun by those produced immediately after Partition.

The railway acts as a stand-in for the modern nation in some of these literary works, even as its representation also opens a space for reexamining what that concept means. Mukul Kesavan's 1995 novel *Looking Through Glass,* for example, uses the symbol of the railway to connect the contemporary moment to the period before Partition. The railway is a conduit between the two times. Kesavan's unamed protagonist hops momentarily off a train from Delhi that stops on a bridge just before Lucknow. Standing on a precarious observation platform, the man attempts to capture on film the image of a man in the river who is looking back at him through a telescope. Pulled between the girders into the river by the weight of his telescopic lens, the protagonist is plunged into 1932. In this scene, Kesavan imaginatively renders the force of a writer's interest in his or her historical subject and throughout the book continues to play with ideas of representation and object. Notably, the protagonist falls backwards in time from—actually through, since he goes between the girders—the train, a symbol of temporal progress.

Now living in the years leading up to independence, the protagonist continues his troubled relationship with the railway. A train offers his first betrayal in what will become a historical period marked by treachery. As he finds the regular *Daily Mail* cancelled by the military crackdown on the Quit India independence movement, he muses, "I didn't once consider the possibility that the train might not reach me back to my own time, that my displacement in time might not be reversible . . . some things are matters of faith and for me the Mail was sacred."[62] The wry sentiment here recalls Singh's representation of a pre-Partition world grounded in the regularity of trains. Returning again to the tracks, the protagonist becomes an unwitting part of a nationalist (and antisectarian) plot to blow up the lines to prevent an intercommunal cricket match arranged by the British. As his companion Asharfi walks up on the ties, the representation evokes the spectral character of the railway:

Asharfi had gone further in the direction of the coming train
and stopped. The train swung into view, its face a black round
set with a glowing eye. The cloud banks had split and the cracks

between them glowed with the radiance of the hidden sun like
still, pink lightening. The clouds shaded into the smoke rising from
the funnel—breath by breath the looming train was puffing out
the sky.[63]

The naturalized and spectralized train in this passage recalls Singh's train
to Pakistan moving along the tracks in the dark. An image immediately
following reinforces the godlike agency assigned to this train, as the narrator calls it a "blinding, searching, moving sun."[64] The photographer-
protagonist becomes the object of the train's gaze in this image; in fact,
the train, which shines in back of the woman who looks "like a heroine in
a suicide scene waiting for directions,"[65] acts as the camera in this passage.
Thus, Kesavan creates a doubled perspective of representation, that on the
part of the narrator and that on the part of the train, an image that recalls
the aforementioned passage with the present-day photographer looking
through his lens at the 1932 man with a telescope. Within the context of a
novel that explores communal identities leading up to Partition, this doubled perspective symbolically depicts the necessity of looking at India's
history from both sides of a historical moment—1947—that became a
dividing line in identity and geography.

Kesavan also uses a railway station to render a complex relationship
between the religious and the secular. In a climatic scene in the novel,
Kesavan envisages a mosque set between the intersecting tracks of the
railway. The protagonist glimpses the strangely situated mosque as he
passes on an overbridge:

It sat precisely between platforms one and two, so conspicuously
out of place that it was almost invisible. It was, in fact, in plain
sight of the overbridge—three lumpy, whitewashed domes, a
little flattened by my point of view, and a tiny courtyard. From my
elevation, I could see the bearded maulana and his congregation,
bending and straightening in prayer.[66]

"Skirling Arabic sounds"[67] of prayer call the narrator's attention to the
mosque in a lull between trains; as a train arrives, the opening words of
prayer combine with the mechanical sounds of the engine, creating an
aurally hybrid space that fuses the sacred and the secular.

With this image of a mosque between railway platforms, the author locates religion within the dominant narrative of modernity, producing a counternarrative of modernity through the metaphor of an interstitial space bound by the rigid structures of development. The mosque is not quite invisible, and the sounds of a sacred ritual escape out to meld with the sounds of technology as the sacred and secular come together within the space of modernity. Kesavan's choice of a railway station recalls the close association between the train and Partition; on a broader level, this setting taps into an even longer association between narratives of the train and modernity. Like the other writers and filmmakers discussed in this chapter, Kesavan chooses these very narratives to rewrite the dominant story of modernity. Kesavan's 1990s novel offers a luminous image of something embedded in much of the mid-twentieth-century Partition literature, namely an invocation of the railway to produce a counternarrative of modernity.

Partition narratives rewrote the story of the train, departing from the colonial ideal of a rational utopia. To do this, they called upon elements of that narrative so central to a colonial rationale for rule. A primary aspect of this colonial account had been the idea of the train as the symbolic nation; one may see this as early as Rudyard Kipling's vision of a diverse set of characters comprising an imagined community in the railway carriage of his novel *Kim*. One of the reasons the train offered itself as a symbol of the nation was the social construction of its space: In the abstracted space of the railway, it seemed, identities were disembedded from their location and offered up as allegorical symbols. The temporal and spatial qualities of the train—the way it sped forward down the track—presented a visual representation of the ideas of progress. The technology represented the ideal separation of the mechanical and corporeal. The train appeared as secular, a place where those religious affiliations were subsumed by the broader order of the state. All these ideas were instrumentalized and altered in the stories of Partition that turned the train into a body, reversed the forward paradigm of modernity, and showed the overlap between the sacred and the secular. Ironically, then, through these counternarratives, the "ultra-synonym of modernity" became a way to challenge the central tenants of India's secular modernity that grew out of the rhetoric of its colonial and nationalist past.

CHAPTER 4

New Destinations:
The Image of the Postcolonial Railway

THE POSTAGE STAMP, an aspect of visual culture mandated by the state and disseminated in the form of a mobile commodity, reflects simultaneously the rhetoric of the state and the cultural iconography around which the identity of a nation coalesces. In India, as elsewhere, this tiny object has often used the train as a symbol of the nation; the railway's primacy derives from the fact that this particular technology helped constitute a synchronic community by circulating mail within a civic space. An Indian postage stamp was issued during the colonial period in 1937 with a picture of King George VI adjacent to the mail train, visually conjoining imperial rule with national mobility. Railway stamps do not represent only mail trains, however. A stamp memorializing the centenary of the first passenger train, issued five years after independence, juxtaposed the old steam locomotive with the new, sleeker engine of 1953, representing progress. A later stamp, issued in 1982, also recalls the colonial past by representing history in the form of a vintage four-wheel rail coach shadowed by an older steam engine. State sovereignty — the name "India" — is inscribed onto the image in both English and Hindi. The picture of the two trains and the national designation pull together two modern concepts into one image, naturalizing a relation between technology and the state and legitimizing contemporary development in terms of a colonial past that rested its authority in mobility.

Movement helped to produce the postcolonial nation in India. This was not because mobility was new to the subcontinent (it was not), but for several related reasons. First, organized movement constituted a powerful rhetoric of modernity: As the logic went, to be mobile was to be modern, and to be modern was to belong to a nation. Second, movement was integral to the nationalist movement, a point perhaps best represented by

Gandhi's unceasing tours of India by rail, but also evident in nationalist writers' focus on the subject of the train. Third, India as a nation had its origins in movement because it was realized in part by the mass migration of Partition. Fourth, mobility helped bring the nation into being through the active construction of space. Finally, as the example of the postage stamp shows, cultural objects secured a correlation between mobility, modernity, and the nation through the power of representation.

The rhetoric of modernity as mobility was surely inherited from the colonial discourse that promoted technology in general and the railway in particular as a means of achieving modern nationhood. Colonial rhetoric had focused on the railway as a way to progress; as a means to secure the colonial state, the Indian railway had always been tied to an emerging polity. Given the centrality of technological development during the colonial period, it is not surprising that after independence, the railway would maintain its key ideological role within India. The train, previously a symbol of colonial rule, became the sign of an independent, industrialized nation.

The national narrative of mobility cannot simply be seen as a carryover from Britain, for it materialized from within India's distinct history. In addition to the legacy of colonial rhetoric, this national identity embodied by the railway also drew on the struggles of the independence movement, including the critiques of economic underdevelopment that had been disseminated by people like Dadabhai Naoroji and Mohandas Gandhi. Moreover, the symbol of the train as nation emerged from the particular history of India that included a massive displacement of peoples. One of the important early debates in the Indian public sphere, namely the relationship between rural and urban constituencies in the new nation, shaped the perceived cultural role of the train. Finally, the train was seen as an instrument in an ongoing negotiation of difference in a state that sought to amalgamate an extraordinary number of diverse ethnicities, religions, castes, classes, and languages.

In the mid-twentieth century, the railway enabled Indians to grasp the nation imaginatively; it did so in official rhetoric as well as in symbolic references, icons, and narratives that constructed national identity through movement. Prime Minister Jawaharlal Nehru, who led the newly independent India into a period focused on the dream of development, advanced a vision of India through the railway. During his term, which lasted from 1947 to 1964, Nehru renewed the commitment to technological advancement that had been the cornerstone of colonial expansion. Nehru aspired to transform traditional India, "to build her new temples of modern times in the form of these engineering wonders."[1]

Those wonders included large-scale projects, such as hydroelectric, flood prevention, and irrigation works. It was the railway, however, which Nehru called India's "greatest national asset,"[2] that arguably maintained an emblematic primacy among these development schemes. Unlike Gandhi, Nehru never saw the machine as a symbol of exploitation; he drew inspiration from the group of nationalist writers like Dadabhai Naoroji and Romesh Dutt that had formulated a politico-economic critique of the railways but remained committed to the ideal of industrialization. Thus, in an article in the *National Herald* in 1939, the man who would become prime minister in less than ten years underscored that he found it "clear that the rapid development of a large-scale machine industry is an urgent need for the country."[3] For the newly independent nation, the national character of the railway became a key rhetorical, strategic, and imaginative aspect defining its independence.

One may recognize this emphasis on nationhood in the administrative practices of the Indian railway. These practices include the bureaucratic organization of the network that became institutionalized as Indian Railways (IR), a state-owned, state-operated institution that is directed by a national board.[4] New construction under Nehru also revealed national priorities. Most of the primary train lines had been built under colonial rule, but the period after independence saw expansion in select areas, especially in those areas concerned with national security. Lines had been severed by Partition, and India needed to reroute lines to strategic locations in Kashmir and Assam. The state also extended lines to build up ports as India took command of its own natural resources.[5] The IR became a means to strive for an ideological goal: economic homogeneity within the nation.[6]

The nation was realized through the active social construction of space as well as through rhetoric and administrative policies. The "permanent way" of tracks charted a national space and the movement of trains upon them continually renewed a constituency of citizens by interconnecting parts of India. The railway also dynamically reconstructed geographic space into a system which circulated both bodies and commodities. As a primary mode of transportation for people as well as goods, the train has been a means for sustaining a national economy that includes those going on long-distance business travel in or out of major cities, as well as those carrying their goods on short trips to a local market. Troops have also often been moved around India by train. The railway has enabled rituals of pilgrimage that constitute an integral aspect of many people's identities (Figure 8).[7] Finally, travelers have used the railway as a way to perceive India as a kind of panorama, reflecting on the nation as they survey it through the window. In this way, the railway during the postcolonial period has come to produce the nation through the economies and practices of movement.

Writers and filmmakers have reflected India's particular history as they used the train to render their own versions of the nation. In the early postcolonial period, R. K. Narayan and Satyajit Ray sought to articulate the connection between rural and urban parts of India as a dynamic relation sutured by the railway. More-contemporary writers, including Anita Nair and Shuma Futehally, have continued to use images of mobility to author new subjectivities within the frame of the modern nation. In their work, the train carriage becomes a moving box that functions as a microcosm of

Figure 8. A Hindu traveler in Mumbai's Central Train Station holds a Ganesh figure as he looks out the train window. Photograph courtesy Sebastian D'Souza/AFP/Getty Images.

society, comprised of people of distinct faiths, different genders, various castes, and diverse classes.

Despite this symbolic ideal of a unified nation, national consolidation has always been problematic in India. The evocative images of Partition and its powerful challenge to the dominant narratives of modernity have not been forgotten, and the ghost train still haunts the image of the railway in contemporary Indian fiction. Even works that do not reference Partition directly in their representations of the railway present other kinds of national fissures, ironically through the same paradigm of mobility used to secure national constituency. Although representations of the railway convey how the nation comes into being through mobility, these depictions produce counternarratives of modernity to show how the setting and image of the railway are used to critique the nation.

In this chapter, I read postcolonial representations of the railway that show the construction of national identity through the train and expose how the nation fails to contain the multiple identities within it. The first part explores various kinds of railway mobility that have come to create—and challenge—the nation. I examine how the presence of the railway fostered new subjectivities as the network made connections between different geographies in the first decades of the postcolonial period. Interpreting the works of R. K. Narayan, Satyajit Ray, and Phanishwar Nath Renu, I look specifically at how these practices of mobility inscribed a relation between the rural and urban that became a defining feature of Indian nationhood. Furthermore, I examine how these writers and filmmakers show an ambivalent mobile subjectivity that defines the early postcolonial nation. The second part explores how railway travel cultivates individual transformation through movement, a process that is paralleled by narration. It also shows how the unique spatialization of the railway carriage offers different writers and filmmakers a paradigm for exploring the borders of the nation and the fault lines within it. The final part turns briefly to the international view of India shown by depictions of the train in literature and cinematic works created outside that nation. For the international tourist, the image of the Indian railway functions much as it did in the colonial period: as a way to mobilize a self set in opposition to an outside constituted by difference. For the diasporic writer, on the other hand, the image of the train allows for reflection on his or her own movements away from an imaginary homeland.

Rural and Urban Subjectivities in the New Nation

Traffic as Consciousness and Social Relation

Although it appears just to move between points in a network, the train actively defines these points as places. For the traveler, a train station gives an identity to a rural location. For the rural subject, the train cultivates a relation between these small places and other points, making a network fully imagined as a nation. The railway appears to compress the nation and allows travelers as well as people who live near the train to envision themselves adjacent to other, different, settings. Even Indians who have never set foot on a train have sometimes actualized their relation to the nation through an encounter with the railway. Literary representations witness this experience so frequently that such scenes of awakening have become a pervasive cultural image. For example, at the end of R. K. Narayan's first novel, *Swami and Friends*, a young boy watches as the train departs with his friend, and he begins to imagine other places connected to it. In works like this, the nation is represented as relations within a larger network, and for points in that system, these connections are deemed the source of a promised change. It is through this notion of imminent transformation that the concept of modernity makes itself felt as something closely related to the nation. This train might be coming or going from the station, or it might pass through the familiar landscape near a home, but in either case, it signals an outside world just over the horizon where the parallel lines converge.

It is quite common to consider the railways as an urban phenomenon, and often people think of railway tracks as leading into rather than out of the city. Indeed, because of its origins in an industrializing Europe, the concept of railway development has always been closely tied to urbanization associated with capitalist development. Writing of nineteenth-century England, Michael Freeman argues that although there was certainly urbanization before the 1830s, the railway played a fundamental role in the cultural shift from a rural identity to an urban one; as he puts it, "the agency of the railway in capitalist urbanization is inescapable."[8]

Yet this relationship to a world beyond is not an inexorable compulsion toward the city. Even in Britain, it was not urbanization but the *relation* between the rural and urban that comprised the experience of modernity mediated by the train. One may turn to Raymond Williams's work *The Country and the City* to theorize this aspect of the modern. Williams has argued that "traffic is not only a technique; it is a form of consciousness and a form of social relations."[9] He highlights the symbolic importance of movement for modernist writers in early twentieth-century Britain, but his words may be applied to the postcolonial Indian context. In his reading of D. H. Lawrence's 1913 novel *Sons and Lovers*, Williams jettisons the separation of rural and urban England and instead shows how Lawrence explores the intersection of the two. Williams counts Lawrence among the writers who "insist on the connections [between rural and urban]. It is mobility, or even the *possibility* of mobility, that highlights the tensions of the self."[10] In this paradigm, the notion of movement is not based on the idea of the city as the *telos*, the ultimate endpoint; rather, the emphasis is placed on the connections themselves as sites to interpret new subjectivities and a broader social order. This relation is ambivalently experienced as what might be called a *subjectivity of traffic* comprised, as Williams puts it, of "a complex interaction and conflict of values."[11] In the postcolonial space where the relation between urban and rural reflects both the experiences of colonialism and post-independence national agendas, this consciousness has been even more discordant.

In 1950s and 1960s India, the railway represented certain kinds of social relations and new kinds of consciousness during a period of national development. In particular, it forged more connections between rural and urban areas and populations, links that reflected Prime Minister Nehru's vision for an integrated India. Nehru focused on state planning as a means for economic growth—industrialization in particular—as the means to achieve that end. Yet the prime minister did not equate industrialization with urbanization, and he maintained that agriculture was the "keystone of our planning . . . the solid foundation on which we have to build."[12] He saw the goal as integration, and he described the first Five-Year Plan as "an attempt to bring the whole picture of India, agricultural, industrial, social, and economic, 'into one framework of thinking.'"[13] The connections between rural and urban areas did not necessarily represent new lines of travel because most of the rail network had been in place since the colonial period and other paths of mobility had preceded the train, but they did mark a shift in people's understanding of themselves, their locations, and their imagined futures within a newly independent nation.

Thus, rather than seeing the train as a symbol of the city, one might instead focus on it as a kind of seam. Railways create a relational space where none existed, linking not only the rural to the urban space but also connecting the city to the country; after all, a train travels in two directions. Areas with small stations and parts of the country where the train passes through on a permanent line are essential parts of the railway world. In Narayan's 1958 novel *The Guide*, for instance, the railway is a vector that changes not only the town and the lives of its residents, but also the lives of travelers who alight there. Passengers get off at the small station looking for an authentic India comprised of ruins, waterfalls, and vistas. Even though they imagine themselves stepping into tradition, the station actually marks a modern locus, the meeting point between urban and rural. Satyajit Ray, in the film *Pather Panchali*, shows the railway line passing through a field as a symbol of imminent transformation for a young boy mesmerized by his first sight of a locomotive. The train represents not simply the destination of the city — although it does so for the boy at a later point — but a more complex, ambivalent kind of subjectivity of traffic that will relate these two worlds.

Early postcolonial writers and filmmakers like Narayan and Ray show young men (and, less often, women) from the villages who are enthralled or transformed by the possibility of movement. That potential might take the form of the urban destination, but it more generally reflects the "form of consciousness" of mobility itself, representing a set of social relations emerging in a period of national development. The fact that these subjects of traffic in these works are predominantly men is significant in the sense that it shows the gendered nature of this consciousness during this period of nation-building. By the 1990s, as the next section shows, literary and cinematic texts show women entering into the thrall of movement, sometimes by means of a gendered railway space — the "ladies coupé," which is a distinctive part of Indian trains. In the 1950s and 1960s, however, most works represent a masculine self emerging through railway mobility. I turn to this body of fictional work more closely here as a way to examine a subjectivity born of the relations of movement during a period of national development.

R. K. Narayan's The Guide

In his novel *The Guide*, R. K. Narayan depicts the town of Malgudi as split into two, literally and metaphorically, by the new railway construction; when the line is laid and the station finished, "The steel tracks gleamed in the sun; the signal posts stood with their red and green stripes and their colorful lamps; and our world was neatly divided into this side of the railway line and that side."[14] The father of the protagonist, Raju, owns two stores, which become the symbols of the two sides of the small town. In the old store, Raju's father sells daily provisions, and his friends from the village linger there to chat. When the railway comes, the father seizes the opportunity to open a store in the new station, only to find that his goods barely stock a quarter of the built-in shelves of the cement-floored building that he finds so strange. His friends, used to gossiping in his village shop, avoid the new place that they find too sophisticated.[15] Narayan represents a change in the social relations of the village, specifically a reorientation toward an outside that is the source of taste as well as commodities. In this depiction, one sees the ambivalence of a traffic consciousness experienced as a conflict of values.

The father does not fit into the railway world, with its strangely artificial spaces and transient mode of being; it only makes him question what he had seen as his accomplishments. Raju, however, fits into this place so well that his own identity becomes conflated with the new mode of movement, as he takes the name Railway Raju.[16] The identification starts early; as the first tracks are laid, Raju, then a child, embraces them, reveling in the way the embankments reshape his landscape by creating new "enchanting" perspectives. He squirrels away the detritus of the railway, "sawn-off metal bits, nuts, and bolts," in a trunk with his mother's saris.[17] As he grows older, the boy capitalizes on the presence of the railway by taking passengers on excursions from the station, but Railway Raju has a more profound relation with the train than simply finding in it a means for extra income. Reflecting on this connection later, he muses:

> The railways got into my blood very early in life. Engines with their tremendous clanging and smoke ensnared my senses. I felt at home on the railway platform, and considered the stationmaster and porter the best company for man, and their railway talk the most enlightened.[18]

Raju depicts the railway as magical and physically seductive on the one hand, and as the site of learning on the other. The station platform literally becomes his new school as he sits between trains sorting and reading the pages of printed matter that he uses to wrap up his goods. Through his exposure to the railway, Raju develops into a person who is unable to settle down and who can no longer meet the demands of his traditional family or even the village.

It would be a mistake, however, to read Raju's restlessness and alienation as the result of becoming too urbanized. Raju takes on a subjectivity of traffic — a life of movement and impermanence that begets the consciousness that Williams describes. The protagonist continues to form and unform throughout the book, becoming what people see: first a guide and then a guru. Narayan is critical of this subjectivity that leaves Raju without commitment, and Raju ends up in jail, without his family and the woman he loves. By the end of the novel, he has become a reluctant spiritual leader, forced by his lies into a much-publicized hunger strike to bring rain to a village. While it is unclear whether Raju dies in the end, what is certain is that Raju is no longer in motion.

Narayan emphasizes Raju's identity, a narrative choice that enhances what might otherwise only be a narrative about development — how the railway altered the social relations of the small town of Malgudi — into an exploration of a subjectivity of traffic. Raju has not become urbanized as much as he has been doubled: split into two by the railway, much like his own town. He remains very much a rural subject, but one who has lost his sense of place through a mobility comprised of both literal movement, as he guides tourists, and metaphorical movement, represented by his constantly changing sense of self.

Satyajit Ray's "Apu Trilogy"

Filmmaker Satyajit Ray's famous "Apu Trilogy" provides another excellent example of the new consciousness and social relations formed by mobility, this time presenting a character who does leave a rural home. The train has a central place in all three films of this trilogy in Bengali, comprised of *Pather Panchali* (Song of the Little Road/Lament of the Path; 1955), *Aparajito* (The Unvanquished; 1956) and *Apur Sansar* (Apu's World; 1959).[19] Indeed, the films offer probably the most famous images of the train in Indian cinema. The sequence of films has often been read as representing movement from rural to urban, or from tradition to modernity. For critics such as Ben Nyce, the train acts as an emblem of this shift, marking the impact of modernity as an urban phenomenon.[20] Yet Ray does not present a linear narrative of development with its endpoint as the urban and industrial; rather, the filmmaker uses the train to represent the production of the ambivalent consciousness and social relations of traffic. To see this, it is worth tracking and differentiating the image of the train in the three films.

In the 1955 film *Pather Panchali*, the train is a symbol of the outside for the small world of the ancestral village and the even-smaller world of the family compound in rural Bengal in the second decade of the twentieth century. More specifically, it represents the possibilities of transformation offered to a family that struggles in poverty — a perpetually working mother, Sarbajaya; her husband, Harihar, a Brahmin priest who finds only occasional work and is often away from the family; the two small children, Durga and Apu; and Indir Thakrun, an elderly relative dependent on their care. The train first appears in the film as a whistle cutting through the darkness as the family sits together at night. The nightly train is already part of their lives. In this way, although the world of the train seems distant from this family home without a single industrial machine, it is arguably an integral part of its domestic world.

The nightly sound of the train acts as a way to summon a conscious reflection on the mother's dissatisfactions. Ray's choice to identify a woman with the train provides an important exception to the predominant identification of men with railway mobility. In one scene, as Sarbajaya and Harihar discuss their economic prospects, the train sounds in the background. The wife then asks her husband about the city of Benares, where he had lived: "I had dreams too," she says, in this sequence of questioning initiated by the noise of a train. Despite its persistence, however, the train is not presented as a kind of submerged symbol of freedom; given that some of the family's troubles are rooted in what might be called modern changes, such as new forms of art, Ray does not offer an easy dichotomy between village life as traditional and oppressive and urban life as modern and liberating. Moreover, the train as a primary motif is counterpoised to images of isolation and death; in this scene, the sound of the night train transforms into the elderly relative Indir's off-camera song, which laments being abandoned by all who have gone before her. Rather than show the train as an emblem of liberating transformation, Ray presents the notion of change as immanent to this world, latent beneath the surface but brought into consciousness — for good and ill — by the train.

The train in *Pather Panchali* is most closely identified with the character of the boy Apu. In this film, Ray sets up a close relation between the train and Apu's subjectivity, which he maintains throughout the three films.

Apu is the one who is willing to name and seek out the possibilities represented by the train. Only the boy makes an overt reference to the train after they all hear its sound, asking his sister Durga if she has ever seen the machine. The sequence in which he and his sister see the train forms the centerpiece of *Pather Panchali*, and it was the initial scene that Ray shot as he tried to secure funding for this, his first film. Looking for a lost calf, the children wander into a field of long grass at the edge of the village; there, they are drawn inexorably toward the new electricity pylons by a humming. The children both in turn place their heads wonderingly against a pole to listen. The mechanical sound alienates them from the familiar natural landscape.

When the train comes close, Ray again places sound first: We hear the train and then see the children frantically looking for the source. The train appears first between the fronds, its steam rising over the top. A fully visible image of the train then shoots across the screen, bisecting the frame of the picture with a horizontal line. This is a loud machine entirely different from anything else in the film; moreover, its velocity and hardness provide a striking contrast to the hypnotizing waves of fluffy white flowers. The train's sense of urgency is mirrored by the small boy who races across the field to meet it. When the train passes him, we initially believe we see it from the perspective of Apu because we have been following his line of sight, but unbeknownst to the viewer until the train races past, Ray has shifted the camera to the other side of the tracks. We see the image of Apu watching from the other side of the train; thus, we are given a picture of the boy literally framed by the train, seen in shuttled fragments between the body of the train and the tracks.

Surajan Ganguly offers a convincing reading of this camera angle that enables us to understand the scene in terms of the impact of the train on the village. He argues that the shift in perspective forces us to view the scene as more than an epiphany; Ray highlights the social and historical place of the train. In the scene, the director "seeks to bring to the fore [the modern's] composite nature, which incorporates issues and experiences that are often mutually incompatible."[21] Although I agree with this point about social relations, I would clarify that the train at this moment is not new so much as it is a persistent symbol of the new; this train probably would have passed by Apu's father at the same age because most of the tracks in Bengal were laid in the last half of the nineteenth century.

In this scene, and specifically in the surprising camera angle that shows Apu through the moving train, the director also symbolizes what the boy has become and will remain throughout the three films: a subject of traffic that is brought to crisis by the conflict of values born in the relation between the rural and urban. Although Ray only hints at this in the first film, by the end of the second film, *Aparajito*, viewers understand that Apu never regains the coherent world that he had before he saw the train.[22] As Apu becomes a fragmented subject of traffic seen between the frames of the train, Ray represents him as split between what he was and what he might become. What the director has set up by the end of *Pather Panchali* is a still-undefined reference to an exterior world and a symbolic stimulus for change. In the subsequent two films, that suggestion will take shape as the connection to the city. Yet at this point, the train is purely magic for the boy, a naturalized reference to a modernity that appears in the hazy form of change, the traces of which are felt in the deepest part of people's lives.

Of the three films, the train plays the most overt role in the second, *Aparajito*, produced in 1956. The opening shot shows the view from a train traveling over a bridge into Benares. As viewers, we see the city framed by the train window, cut between the metal trusses of the bridge. After this shot, trains are completely absent from view in the entire first portion of the film, which immerses us in the sacred aspects of Benares by showing the father's role as a priest. The train reappears after the death of the father, Harihar, in a scene that recalls the sound of the night train in *Pather Panchali*. Sarbajaya pauses on the stairs to watch her son play, presumably musing over her two choices: She and her son may continue to live with a family for whom she works as a servant, or she may travel to join a relative in the village of Mansapota. As the camera focuses a close-up on her face, reflecting myriad unarticulated thoughts, a train screams in the background. It is the call to change that she needs, and her face shows that she has made her decision. The next shot — a low-angle close-up of giant train wheels gathering momentum — gives a sense of dynamism as she sets her plan in motion.

The next view from the interior of the train reverses the path of the opening scene by having the train travel back across the bridge away from the city. This time, we look from the perspective of the passengers — the mother, her elderly relative, and her son, Apu — back at Benares. The city is framed by the blurred trusses of the passing bridge, and one gets a sense of the emotional distance that the train provides to the mother. Critics often read the railway as the antagonist of the mother for reasons explained next, but in fact, throughout the journey the train is closely identified with the interior state of Sarbajaya. Ray represents the passage of space and time by using the panorama from the window: The landscape evolves from barren farms in broad daylight, to mountains at dawn, and then to the lushness of the tropics as another day arrives. The railway provides Sarbajaya with a sense of distance from her husband's death, and as she looks out of the train window, she smiles for the first time in the two films.

In the mother and son's new home in the village of Mansapota, the train has a daily presence, as it did in Nischindipur, the village of *Pather Panchali*, but unlike in that previous film, it is visible from the family home. Through the doorframe of their compound, they can see the railway tracks that form the horizon of their new life. Apu has always been mesmerized by trains, but now the train becomes part of his daily ritual, calling him at regular intervals to watch its passage. In *Pather Panchali*, the train represented an amorphous outside presenting the possibility of change — it does not have the specific meaning of a destination. In *Aparajito*, however, that outside takes form for Apu, and the vague promise embodied by the railway in the earlier film becomes concrete in the route to the city of Calcutta. As Apu tells his mother about the possibility of studying in Calcutta, the train whistles in the background. Later, he walks in the middle of the tracks that represent his life path.

After Apu moves to Calcutta, the train becomes a conduit for movement back and forth between his mother's home and the city where his school is. Although Ray emphasizes the train as an exit strategy for Apu, the railway represents return as well as departure. It also continues to shape rural consciousness; the director shows the life of Sarbajaya defined in tragic ways through the mode of traffic. For the mother, the train has come to remind her of her son, but it represents the way that her son has been pulled away from her. She looks at it longingly as it passes, bemoaning Apu's departure or anticipating his possible return. When she knows that he is coming, she watches for the train before she hurries to prepare for his imminent arrival. As Ganguly puts it, "The passage of the train in long shot — a moving line on the horizon — becomes a symbolic clock hand that determines his going and coming. . . . it evokes for her [Apu's] presence within his absence."[23] Through the train, the rural Sarbajaya is mired in a *relation* with the city of Calcutta; that connection becomes tragic for the mother, as right before her death, she hears the train, sees it cross, and imagines wrongly that her son is finally coming home.

For Apu as well, the world of the train is one of promises as false as the magic ointment that a train hawker peddles to cure all ills. As Apu's train enters Calcutta, its track joins multiple lines that show the many roads converging in this place of promise — too many roads for all the promises to be fulfilled. In the crowded station, Apu is but one of many young men in motion, striving toward a promised destination of success. In this part of *Aparajito*, Ray anticipates the function of the train in the final install-ment of his trilogy, in which the city's prospects, hinted to the boy in the first film and taking shape as urban education for the young man in the second, reach a disappointing fruition for the mature Apu.

In the third film of the trilogy, the 1959 *Apur Sansar*, the train is no lon-ger presented as representing liberation to Apu but as a track binding him to its interminable path. Outside his bedroom window overlooking the train yard, the noises of the trains disturb rather than inspire the young man. As in *Aparajito*, the train is linked to time and the division of daily life, but it now affords him none of the pleasures that such regulation offered in his village home. The train still represents the outside, but here it is the burden, rather than the promise, of the outside world upon his imaginative life. The train also disturbs the tranquility of Apu's domestic world with Aparna, his new wife, who races in from the balcony covering her ears as the train screams.

In this third film, the train remains an integral part of Apu's self despite his disappointments. The railway continues to represent the path of life and the possibility of change, as it did in the other films of the trilogy. In one night scene, Apu walks back with his best friend, Pulu, along the series of tracks. They talk of Apu's dreams and his aspirations to write a novel. Even after Apu marries and seeks to develop his small world with Aparna, the train still defines him. In one beautiful shot, his two worlds merge; after Aparna fills a brazier on the balcony, its white smoke rises to meet the steam of the train in the background, bringing together the home and the world.

The train returns in a defining scene after Apu learns of Aparna's death during childbirth. A low-angle shot of the tracks shows an oncom-ing train. As the director cuts to a close-up of Apu's face, we understand that he is contemplating throwing himself on the tracks. Ray focuses on

Apu's expression as the train wails in the background. The scene mirrors the earlier one in *Aparajito* when Sarbajaya decides to make a radical change and take her son to the village. Yet unlike in that scene, the train no longer beckons with new prospects in most of this third installment; it now primarily represents a force upon a life. The train whistle mesmerized Apu as a child and called him as an adolescent; it now compels him as a young man. Ray moves the camera from Apu's face to the sky with a trail of steam in the corner, before shifting it down to a violent scene of a pig run over by the train. For most of the rest of the film, Apu turns to nature for solace, traveling to the ocean, the mountains, and the forest. To get there, however, he must take the train. Thus, Ray resolves the films with an ambivalent relationship to a rhetoric of modernity that, in the guise of this technology, offers the seductive and compulsory "song of the road" that forms the title of the first film of the trilogy.

In his "Apu Trilogy," Ray depicts the early twentieth century, but his film reflects the preoccupation with transformation of the 1950s, when he made the films. His first film, coming midway between Nehru's first and second Five-Year Plans, reflects India's moment of development. Ray's story shows a family that exists on the edges of the railway, changed by the lines that run through it but also becoming part of that railway's world. While this is as true for Sarabjaya as it is for Apu, as she too heeds the call of the train, it is through Apu that Ray fully develops traffic as a form of consciousness. Apu's compulsion to move at first inspires and then encumbers. The young man, who tries to escape his troubles on the very train that represents the life that he wishes to flee, ultimately finds himself trapped within his subjectivity of traffic.

Phanishwar Nath Renu's "The Fragrance of a Primitive Night"

In 1967, eight years after *Apur Sansar*, the Bihari writer Phanishwar Nath Renu returned to the vision of the rural subject of traffic, offering a voice of protest emerging from the rural sector that held a central ideological position in Nehru's national reform program. The railway station forms a nexus between an impoverished rural location and the broader nation in Renu's Hindi short story, "The Fragrance of a Primitive Night." Like Raju in Narayan's *The Guide* and Apu in Ray's trilogy, Karma, the story's twelve-year-old protagonist, is a subject of traffic; mobility shapes his consciousness and the social relations around him. Renu shows the character as a prisoner of this subjectivity, rendering the compulsory aspects of this form of modernity. Karma was discovered as a baby in a wood crate on a goods train from Assam, "Without any tag, without any label. Unclaimed property!"[24] By equating Karma with transport goods, Renu emphasizes the character's dispossession inside the system of capitalist commodity circulation enabled by the railway. Karma does not belong to any place, and even his assumed name, which is simply represented with the code "K," leaves him "without any label." He has no home and works for his food by helping a series of station agents who are themselves but temporary relief workers at rural railway stations.

Like Raju in *The Guide*, Karma tries to embrace the transience of his situation: "where my body happens to be, that's where my home is,"[25] he says. As the story's main theme underscores, however, he is ultimately unhappy in this mode of traffic. The contradictions of his existence are underscored in a nightmare, which forms a focal point of the story, in which he is glued to a track and then torn apart by an oncoming train.[26] The nightmare makes clear how Karma feels interminably bound to the railway, much like Apu in the final film of Ray's trilogy, *Apur Sansar*. In the climax of the story, Karma comes to realize that his railway home is really no home at all, and he jumps down from the train to stay in one place. Karma represents the modality of movement that is the dream of modernity, but like Raju in Narayan's story and Apu in Ray's films, he longs for the stability of place. Renu ultimately validates the constant over the mobile; yet his position is not simply nostalgia for lost rural origins. Renu's story echoes those of Narayan and Ray in the sense that they all present a figure that exists uneasily within the consciousness and social relations of traffic that characterizes this period of national development.[27]

Artistic works produced in the decades following independence represent an India under transformation, compelled by narratives of development that delineate relations between the urban and the rural. Both modernity and the train have usually been seen as urban rather than rural phenomena, but the mobile train represents the dynamic relation between these spaces. The geographical and imaginative connections established by the railway — connections between the rural and the urban or between both types of places and the nation — force us to rethink the landscape of modernity. The place down the line beckons as a destination: The passengers in Narayan's novel seek the antiquity and naturalness that they associate with the rural, while Apu in Ray's film trilogy seeks the promised transformation of the city. Yet however important the place of origin or destination, it is the line between them that mobilizes the paradigm of modernity. The subjectivity of traffic promotes an uneasy consciousness for characters like Raju in *The Guide*, Apu in *Apu Sansar*, or Karma in Renu's "The Fragrance of a Primitive Night," and the new social relations that it engenders destroy families, render former friendships irrelevant, and alter economies. Yet the traffic also activates the "forever forming, forever unforming, / Continuous coming, continuous going" described by Rabindranath Tagore in his Bengali poem "Railway Station."[28] This sense of creation and undoing makes this mobile modernity as compelling as it is troubled.

Mobile Identities and Narratives of Nation

Railway mobility constituted the nation through the social construction of space. The tourist came to know India through train travel; in the process, the railway journey shaped the India that was consumed by the national and international tourist. In the 1930s, a series of IR "Visit India" posters represented the nation for an audience of potential consumers abroad. These IR posters did not usually represent the train graphically; instead, they stylized ancient India—the Taj Mahal, Ellora, Budh Gaya (Bodhgaya)—in the distinct aesthetic of the modernist railway poster, so as to appeal to the tastes of a cosmopolitan viewership. As these posters characterized an India that may be apprehended through train travel, they became part of a broader symbolic field relating mobility to the nation. For the national audience, such a cultural referent also appeared in the practice of the all-India route, which highlighted this symbolic relation between traveling on the train and realizing a national identity. With the slogan, "Discover India, Discover Yourself," the Department of Tourism promoted train travel as something simultaneously transformative to the self and the conception of the nation.

In Indian representations of the railway, subjectivity, mobility, and narration are aligned. The allegiance appears in three ways. First, movement presents itself as a metaphor for a tale that seemingly compels the reader forward. Second, the unique construction of space in the railway carriage promotes the possibility of storytelling. It is a space both solitary and collective; it contains an audience comprised of suddenly intimate strangers. The train carriage also seems suspended from the world around it, allowing for reflection upon that outside world. Finally, the motion of the train itself takes on a distinctive phenomenological character that inspires imagination and memory. This last characteristic is sometimes represented as the magic of the train, as it is for Saleem in the train in Salman Rushdie's *Midnight's Children* who, "in the quinquesyllabic monotony of the wheels . . . heard the secret word: abracadabra abracadabra abracadabra sang the wheels as they bore us back-to-Bom."[29]

The trip across, or sometimes even crisscrossing, the land represents the nation as something to be imagined symbolically through movement. Postcolonial literature and film represent this. The overland passage of a famous actor in Satyajit Ray's *Nayak* provides a means to reflect on India's changing relation to art. As an unhappy young woman journeys south to the tip of India in Anita Nair's *Ladies Coupé*, or as the elderly railway wife in Anita Rau Badami's novel *Tamarind Mem* finally gets to ride the lines that her husband commanded in his life, these characters grasp India as their right and bring it imaginatively into being as a coherent whole. A line from Vikram Chandra's 1997 short story "Shanti," in the collection *Love and Longing in Bombay*, beautifully renders this process of an India brought into being through the railway. In this tale, a young woman's stories of train travel chart a dynamic new nation for a lovestruck young man: "Shiv listened to the tales of the trains, and imagined the tracks arrowing across the enormous plains to the north, and to the south across the rocky plateau, and hairpin turns over vertiginous ridges, and through black deserts."[30] Although postcolonial representations of the Indian railway frequently present a nation emerging through the process of mobility, they just as often use narratives set in the railway space as a means to critique the nation by showing the fault lines of this construction in the striations of gender, communal identity, and class.

Director Satyajit Ray returned to the setting of the train with his 1966 Bengali-language film *Nayak*. Nearly the entire film is set on a train, and the film juxtaposes two technological transformations associated with modernity—the railway and film—using the setting of the train to examine how film as an industry has reshaped notions of art, especially acting, and created a new national public that identifies art with celebrity. It is such a community that is represented on the train, as Ray uses the unique social construction of railway space to present a microcosm of Indian society. In this way, the railway, so central to Ray's earlier work, continues to offer the director a way to investigate a nation undergoing transformation while placing his own work within the nexus of mobility and narrative.

As it does so often in narratives, in *Nayak*, the experience of the train prompts the telling of a tale to a stranger. A famous actor, Arindam, travels by train to receive an award after he embarrassed himself by fighting publicly over a married woman. In the dining car, he meets a demure journalist named Aditi and tells her his story, describing his rise to fame, his betrayals, and the beginning of his affair with that woman. The neutral space of the dining carriage allows the two passengers, traveling in different classes, to meet, and it fosters an openness that would be impossible in nearly any other setting. Arindam and Aditi overcome their different backgrounds and moral codes to strike up a friendship, although in keeping with the realism of his work, Ray stops short of fully developing a romance that could never survive in the world outside the train. Instead, the train journey engenders another kind of intimacy nurtured by confession.

The setting of the train allows Ray to expose the delicate nature of the complex category of a national public. As he travels on the train, Arindam is forced into contact with that public upon whom he depends as a popular movie actor. Each person on the train is concerned primarily with his or her own life — a father and mother travel with their sick child, the husband of a couple tries to peddle his advertising to an unscrupulous man (offering his wife as a way to sweeten the deal), a famous elderly writer avoids contact with decadent youth, and Aditi journeys to the capital to sell subscriptions to her women's magazine. The various passengers are starstruck by the famous actor to various degrees, but despite their curiosity and appeals for autographs, they maintain a distance between their own lives and his decadent life. They comment critically among themselves about his behavior and maintain their semiprivate family space within the railway compartments. Thus, the train becomes a way for Ray to show the limits of public intimacy. In keeping with this, the train passengers ultimately go their own way at the end of the journey despite their fast friendships, a metaphor for the way that an audience lives a life separate from the actors they idealize. The fragility and limits of this public upon whom he depends leads Arindam nearly to suicide (this scene is discussed further in the conclusion of this book). In the film's final scene, by the station where the main characters disembark, the larger world comes back and interrupts the intimacy developed between Arindam and Aditi.

In several scenes on the train, Ray uses the windowpane, a "slender blade"[31] between inside and outside, to juxtapose the private and the public. In the process, he relates the private, namely memory and confession, to the wider context of the nation. In one memorable scene, Arindam and Aditi sit in the dining car before a window as the train pulls into Burdwan station en route to their destination (Figure 9). As the fans outside recognize Arindam and begin banging on the window, the camera faces the crowd as if from the perspective of a passenger across the aisle watching the man and woman interrupted in an intimate conversation. The scene deals ostensibly with the cultural differences between the modest Aditi and the cosmopolitan Arindam: She is unnerved as she is put on display, while the actor is familiar with being the object of scrutiny. But the scene also provokes the viewer to contemplate the relationship between audience and subject. Like Arindam and Aditi, we as viewers are confronted with a gaze *into* the train, a perspective that challenges the panoramic perception so central to both the train and filmic narrative. The spectators' gaze mirrors our own; there are two outside audiences looking at this story, the

Figure 9. A scene from Satyajit Ray's film Nayak *showing a perspective out the window of a train carriage. From the Aida Sofyan Collection of the Satyajit Ray Center, University of California, Santa Cruz.*

ones on the platform and ourselves. We are forced to see ourselves inside the film in relation to this national public. In this scene, Ray cultivates the relation between inside and outside, a relation distinctive of railway space, as a means to link the railway narrative to the nation at large. The opposition between within and without becomes a paradigm through which the railway narrative interprets the limitations of the nation.

In postcolonial works, such political commentary might be overt, but more often it is represented through the transformation of the self. For the individual, movement becomes a way to see the subjectivities and social relations that constitute his or her life. As has been mentioned, in earlier postcolonial literature and film from the 1950s and 1960s, such as the Narayan and Renu stories discussed previously, it is often young men who are mobile, with Satyajit Ray's character Sarbajaya as a notable exception. Representative works from the 1970s and 1980s, such as the popular films discussed in chapter 5, however, show railway space as an ambivalent space for women — one that offers the chance to supersede social strictures through public space but also a threatening one, a dangerous site of potential violation. Although this characterization of railway space persists, for a group of more recent writers who use the train as a setting, the railway presents mobility for women as well as men.

Women and Mobility

Several contemporary women writers place the chronicles of women on the railway as a way to depict change brought on through their movement out of the home: revolutions of self represented by mobility. They also use the train to show changing relationships to family, new sexual possibilities, and the politics of caste, class, and gender inside a new India that emerged in the 1990s. For these feminist writers, movement allows women emancipation through narration. In the 2001 novel *Ladies Coupé*, Anita Nair depicts the railway carriage as a place for women to express untold stories and the journey as a metaphor for moving on. The protagonist, Akhila, originally takes the train as an escape, but it becomes the way for her to recognize her life through storytelling and finally to resolve her desires for her lover — and for bodily pleasure in general. For the widow of a railway officer in Anita Rau Badami's novel *Tamarind Mem*, the experience of traveling on the train allows her to finally make sense of her life through the stories that she tells other women and through the journey itself. In Shuma Futehally's *Reaching Bombay Central*, a woman is granted the space and time to narrate her own story as she takes a long journey across India.

From *Ladies Coupé's* opening pages, in which the smell of the platform fills Akhila with fantasies of departure, the railway journey in Anita Nair's novel is presented as a means of liberation. Akhila dreams "[o]f being part of such a wave that pours into compartments and settles on seats, stowing baggage and clutching tickets. Of sitting with her back to her world, with her eyes looking ahead. Of leaving. Of running away. Of pulling out."[32] The passage alludes to the culture associated with train travel, for it is not only the possibility of movement that attracts Akhila; Nair evokes the seductive future orientation closely associated with the concept of modernity, a negation of the past represented by her forward-facing seat. The novelist also shows how the railway beckons as a way to become part of an anonymous public.

This anonymity is a characteristic of public space that in Indian representations of the railway both repels women as being unsafe or unseemly and attracts them as a way to loosen the social strictures of the home. Indeed, Akhila is a character who has never married, who has instead taken care of her family after her father's death and given up on romance for their sake. She is "[h]ungry for life and experience. Aching to connect,"[33] and the train's ladies coupé fulfills both desires in two ways. First, through mutual storytelling, Akhila is able to bond with other women in her compartment and expand her vision of life. Together in the ladies coupé, these women interpret their lives by relating them.

The second way that Akhila experiences life and connects with others on the train is through contact with other bodies — especially but not only through sexual contact. Representations of the Indian train portray a bodily and domestic character; although this image may be traced back to the negative depictions of the colonial period, this ascribed character is reclaimed in contemporary writings and films. In Nair's work, there is "Jasmine wound in the hair, sweat and hair-oil, talcum powder and stale food, moist gunny bags and the raw green-tinged reek of bamboo baskets."[34] Akhila's relationship to the crowds that characterize Indian trains is ambivalent. On the one hand, she fears the "swell of passengers [that] surged forward as the train drew to a halt";[35] on the other hand, the bodily aspect of the station connects her to her own sexually unfulfilled body. Nair offers a radical view of a woman enjoying the physical proximity with other bodies that is so prevalent in Indian trains, for Akhila first awakens sexually to the persistent touch of an unseen man aboard a crowded commuter train. Although this act traditionally would be presented as a cause of outrage, the experience opens her to a sensation that she enjoys. Later, Akila meets a younger man, who in time becomes her lover, in the first-class compartment of a regular suburban train. The train is part of Akhila's sexual experimentation, not just because it is a conduit to illicit and culturally inappropriate opportunities but because it arouses her physically with its vibrations and visual panoramas. In the ladies coupé, Akhila will come to legitimize that sexuality through narrative, while the train itself fosters that arousal as it "pitched and heaved through the night."[36]

As well as presenting railway space as a place of narrative and a site for bodily stimulation, Nair suggests that the train's motion itself becomes socially transformative. The particular relationship granted by the train between inside and outside converts Akhila's chaotic world into a visual representation, "a gallery of nightscapes, each framed by the window."[37] Indeed, at numerous points in the novel, Nair gives montages of still-life portraits, rendering the passing countryside, the cityscape, and the platform in fragmented sentences. The static landscape set against the mobility of the train is a splintered world with its external continuity severed and its relations mobilized only by the train. Akhila finds this broken-up world liberating because it is free from the social relations that she has found so stifling.

Anita Rau Badami, in her 1996 novel *Tamarind Mem*, depicts an older woman named Saroja, the widow of a railway officer, who takes to the rails when she is finally freed from her domestic duties by the departure of her grown children. When Saroja took her first railway journey with her new husband, she found the railway compartment a kind of prison, a noisy space where the husband secured the compartment to keep people out and reprimanded Saroja for touching the window bars. In contrast to this, Badami shows Saroja's later solitary railway travel in the women-only compartment as a process of personal empowerment through mobility. Saroja moves around India, and through narration, as she relates her history to the other women. For Saroja, these trains also present the route to her full national subjectivity. The empowerment comes through contact with new people and the sensory experiences of places that she visits. The connection to a national body comes even more viscerally, operating on a bodily level through shared physical contact mediated by the trains. At one point, for example, Saroja rests her head on a window grille and ponders: "Beggars have touched these windows, spit from a thousand mouths has dried on them, they carry the germs of millions who have travelled before me."[38] Just as Akhila reveled in her bodily contact with strangers, Saroja embraces this anonymous contact with the masses of people because it frees her from the isolation demanded by her husband and represented in their first train ride. Both writers represent the train as liberating because of its movement and because this public space allows women out of what is represented as a constrained private space, connecting them to other bodies.

In Shuma Futehally's novel *Reaching Bombay Central*, a woman also undergoes a transformation on a train journey, this time to Bombay. As in Nair's work, mobility gives rise to a sense of liberation for the protagonist, Ayesha. "Just at the moment she was sheltered from her home on the one hand and her chore on the other hand," Futehally writes, "she was free of everything."[39] This freedom has its cost. Futehally's novel, like Ray's film *Nayak*, meditates on the limits of the easy friendships of the train. Ayesha's husband faces jail after compromising his job by issuing illegal licenses as a favor to an old classmate, and she is traveling so she can appeal to one of her relatives, a well-connected police officer. Shamed by her task, she is unable to tell her fellow passengers her story, for "telling would go on and on, it would narrow into endless, thread-like tributaries."[40] As Ayesha reflects on her life of lies, this life "where nothing is real,"[41] she is actually challenging the realness of the world of the train, a place of narration where people may be whoever they want to be.

The borders inside the imagined community of the railway carriage are there to reinforce differences of gender, caste, race, and religion. Colonial discourse encoded particular signs of difference, such as gender and class, into the very structures of the train carriage even as it idealized the train as a means to overcome differences within India. Similarly, the Indian railway as a space offers in its ideal a microcosm of the nation in which difference might be acknowledged while subsumed to a secular order. Works like *Reaching Bombay Central* offer a very different picture of how these differences are negotiated. Like Nair, Futehally is attuned to the struggles of women inside public spaces. Ayesha finds herself unable to fill her water bottle at the crowded tap at the station, an experience repeated on her last few trips, and must appeal to a man for help. Futehally's work also carefully charts delicate communal and religious lines in India present within the social microcosm of the railway. As Ayesha introduces herself to her fellow passengers, she is aware of the "flicker of a pause"[42] as they recognize her Muslim name; this moment represents a life in which this religious identity defines her family's existence in India. In the train carriage, passengers approximate the regulations of their daily lives, and the author shows how the simplest religious observances, like the ordering of vegetarian and nonvegetarian meals, map lines of difference within the train.

Futehally especially reveals how class defines the lives of those within the railway — after all, for some the railway is not a space of leisurely travel but a place of labor. In two similar scenes that bracket the book at the beginning and end, a "coolie," or porter, solicits money on top of the agreed-upon compensation from the passenger whose bags he has carried. Futehally shows the inhabitants of the compartment beleaguered by these demands as they board the train. The passengers are represented as at war with these "belligerent" handlers, who extract additional money from inexperienced travelers, as well as with the railway attendant, who takes their lunch menu robotically and "unrepentantly" leaves, and with the unofficial sweeper boy, who "begins to sweep more because no one has succeeded in stopping him" and forces himself into the compartment that passengers employ.[43] Futehally does not invite the reader to identify with these anonymous workers, for it is not her goal to expose the exploitation represented by the class structures of the railway; what she does show, however, is a subtle class war taking place in the railway.

Offering a critical view of the nation, Futehally challenges the broader practices of corruption that permeate Indian society in the form of favors and bribes. As readers, we see this world partly through Ayesha's own story about her husband who gets caught up in that culture as it shapes the political arena, but also in Ayesha's own surroundings. The train acts as a microcosm of that larger, corrupt space. Even the decisions about who sits where in the train are choreographed through a system of "*bakhsheesh*," or bribe money, passing hands.

Thus, even as postcolonial Indian writers depict the train as a paradigm for the nation, they also show the substrata that challenge that order. The determining boundary of inside and outside is shown to be permeable. Unofficial practices, like bribery, coincide with highly bureaucratized official ones, like the labeled reservations posted on the outsides of carriages. These representations suggest, then, that India constitutes a myriad of micrological orders that challenge its master narrative. That idea and its implications are considered further in the conclusion to this book.

In Futehally's novel, the unofficial economies of the railway are certainly not celebrated. Moreover, although the work is critical of India, the image of the train ultimately strengthens the idea of the nation. When one character comments to the other members of the compartment that India is going the wrong way, another tells her: "See, it is like this train. It is not always facing Bombay. Just now, in the dark, we cannot even see where we are going. But we know that in the end we are reaching Bombay Central. It is like that."[44] Just as Jawaharlal Nehru cast the nation as the final destination for a journey to decolonization, so too do these travelers understand their own experience of travel — a journey that brings them to resolve their problems — as a metaphor for the rightness of the nation.

A Broader Culture of Mobility

All these writers, whom I refer to as postcolonial writers, work from within India, but as one moves outside India to the international tourist and the diasporic Indian, one also finds India portrayed through the train. Paul Theroux is perhaps the most internationally influential of these authors. He has shown India as a nation through railway travel in works like 1975's *The Great Railway Bazaar*, 1985's *The Imperial Way*, and 2008's *Ghost Train to the Eastern Star*. For Theroux, as a foreign visitor, riding the Indian train is a generative experience. He describes how much train travel energizes his imagination and offers him the seclusion to order and write his thoughts: "I traveled easily in two directions, along the level rails while Asia flashed changes at the window, and at the interior rim of a private world of memory and language."[45] His India is made up of an assortment of characters — mostly other passengers, but also those who work on the railway, those who sleep in the stations, and those who perform their daily ablutions squatting down along the tracks. Theroux's work thus exposes the same kinds of micrological orders of society as Futehally's work does. Despite his clear-eyed gaze upon these subjects of traffic, one sees the legacy of colonial travel writing in Theroux's work, for the carriage wall divides the autobiographical narrator more sharply from the India around him than it does any of the Indian characters represented in postcolonial fiction. Those figures, like Akhila or Ayesha, are unable to keep the distance that Theroux's autobiographical narrator so enjoys in his work, even given the class lines that distinguish them from the world of the slums outside. Thus, Theroux's travel narratives present a different kind of possession; it is not the collective ownership and responsibility of the national subject but rather the objectively amused gaze of the traveler who comes to "know" India through mobility.

The popularity of Wes Anderson's 2007 film *Darjeeling Limited* shows the enduring fascination with Indian trains as a place of spiritual renewal for the Euro-American traveler. Although given a new vividness by cinema, Anderson's film about three brothers who travel through India in search of their mother and healing after their father's death revives many of the colonial motifs of the Indian railway. The story about reflection depends on a location understood as culturally and visually different — this train could not, for example, traverse upstate New York. At the same time, the train carriage is deemed separate from the world outside it. Their first-class compartment is also divided from the carriage where the Indians travel together in an open compartment. A shot of one brother walking through that third-class compartment provides one of the only scenes of fellow Indian travelers, for the only other Indians on the train are those who serve the men. Much like in nineteenth-century images, the Indian train in *Darjeeling Limited* provides a place for a traveler to a foreign space to work through his or her place in the world; also like those representations, Anderson's Indian train represents the illogic ascribed to India — in an unlikely occurrence, the train "takes a wrong turn" in the night. Anderson highlights the motif of storytelling; one brother shares his autobiographical writing with the others, and the film consciously reflects on its own fictionality through the direction, set, plot, and cinematography. In pairing railway travel and the theme of narration, Anderson returns us to the solitary reader described in the opening of chapter 1, for whom India — and the self — unfolds as if in a story.

Works of the global diaspora also look back to the train to evoke the nation as homeland. One sees this in the extraordinary collection of the online Indian Railway Fan Club, which includes more than 6,500 members worldwide. This site includes an immense amount of material — including visual art, historical information (including archives gratefully accessed for this book), memoirs, and technical details. The labyrinth of pages amasses to a virtual structure remarkable for its obsessive attention to a single, albeit fascinating, object: the Indian train. The sheer quantity of contributions by individuals from around the world suggests a way that the train provides a bond with India for those both in the country and outside of it. Such a bond is also evident in popular literary and filmic representations of the diaspora — even those produced in India. In Aditya Chopra's 1995 film *Dilwale Dulhania Le Jayenge*, the father recalls India as a train journey, specifically as a view of a passing landscape of girls gathering marigolds in the Punjab. Here, the train journey represents a homeland remembered nostalgically; more specifically, the panoramic gaze out the window becomes itself a symbol for remembering India.

Diasporic literature that uses the image of the train recaptures the fraught nature of the early postcolonial subject of traffic depicted by Narayan, Ray, and Renu. Here, the train is often the first stage in a more extended experience of mobility that takes a person across the seas. That mobility is frequently experienced ambivalently as the loss of identity. In Kiran Desai's novel *The Inheritance of Loss*, the train creates a relationship between the local, the national, and the global.[46] In a scene early in the novel, an older judge recalls the formative train journey that he took as a young man:

> Father and son had rattled forth all through the morning and afternoon, the immensity of the landscape within which Jemu had unknowingly lived impressing itself upon himself. The very fact that they were sitting in the train, the speed of it, rendered his world trivial, indicated through each window evidence of emptiness that stood eager to claim an unguarded heart. He felt a piercing fear, not for his future, but for his past, for the foolish faith with which he had lived in Piphit.[47]

Ironically, mobility *places* Jemu, locates his previous self even as that self is already superseded by his departure. Whereas some might embrace this cosmopolitanism, Jemu experiences it as loss. Travel forces him to jettison his past, not because he has left Phiphit, but because the experience transforms his old home into the emptiness outside the railway carriage. Desai gives us a very different image of travel and cosmopolitanism than the colonial archetype of mobility as conquest. She reverses the colonial narrative with a train that leads to England's heart of darkness for the young student, who will arrive to the loneliness anticipated by his train trip. The modality of travel creates anxiety; the displacement, temporal and spatial arrangements, and spectatorship associated with mobility confront Jemu with loss. Yet this emptiness is also seductive because it seemingly allows him to shed his identity.

The image of the railway helped both fashion and test the postcolonial nation. In the decades following independence, new national subjectivities emerged in the relation between the rural and the urban. The railway connected lives through a network of tracks and set those lives in motion. Writers and filmmakers like R. K. Narayan, Satyajit Ray, and Phanishwar Nath Renu show this compelling experience as giving rise both to liberation and constraint for the trafficking subject. For the traveler, freedom finds its paradigm in the movement of the train. Postcolonial writers show how the space inside the carriage fosters narration, a process that, for women travelers in particular, becomes a means of transforming the self. They represent how the train also becomes a scene of difference, a symbolic place that reveals the structures of the nation even as it promises to overcome them. Looking back from abroad, diasporic writers rethink the mobility of the railway as part of their own real or imagined journeys out of India. It is through this mobility that they place the past, locate a previous self, and thus create what diasporic writer Rushdie calls an "India of the mind."[48]

CHAPTER 5

Bollywood on the Train

O NE OF THE MOST pervasive symbols in Indian film is the train. This is true in both so-called art film and in popular cinema. Chapter 4 looked at the way art film director Satyajit Ray uses exterior and interior scenes of the train in the "Apu Trilogy" to explore the relations between the rural and the urban as India entered a period of national development programs. It also considered Ray's scenes of a traveling train carriage in *Nayak* as a way to examine the changing nature of the public sphere in India. However, it is in the popular Hindi, or "Bollywood," films, produced in Mumbai (formerly Bombay), that the train gathers momentum as a cultural symbol. Bimal Roy, for example, employed the setting and shrieking sounds of the train carriage to suggest the mental wanderings and anguish of his lovelorn protagonist in *Devdas* (1955). From the melodramas of the 1960s and 1970s like *Mere Huzoor* (directed by Vinood Kumar; 1968) and *Pakeezah* (directed by Kamal Amrohi; 1971), to thrillers like *Sholay* (directed by Romesh Sippy; 1975) and *The Burning Train* (directed by Ravi Chopra; 1980), to the blockbusters of the 1990s, *Dilwale Dulhania Le Jayenge* (directed by Aditya Chopra; 1995) and *Dil Se* (directed by Mani Ratnam; 1998), to the 2007 global release of *The Train* (directed by Hasnain Hyderabadwala and Raksha Mistry; 2007) and *Jab We Met* (directed by Imtiaz Ali; 2007), Bollywood is fascinated by trains.

Filmmakers use the space of the train to expose the fraught relations of love and desire in India's modernity. This is particularly true in the cinematic romance genre. Love stories in popular Indian cinema rely on broader cultural understandings of modern space. In using the train as both setting and symbol, these films represent the gendered nature of such spaces by relating the public space of the railway to the private space of the home. They construct a notion of modernity in which men and women are given different versions of what it means to be modern. Furthermore, filmmakers present the phenomenological experience of the train—its rhythmic sounds, panoramic views, and cadenced vibrations—as a way to reflect the dynamics of desire. Malika Arora dances erotically atop a train to its mechanical beat to Farah Khan's award-winning choreography in the sequence "Chaiyya Chaiyya" in *Dil Se* (1998); more demurely, Sharmila Tagore's character stares sideways out the train window at her love-object in *Aradhana* (directed by Shakti Samanta; 1969). In these popular Hindi films, the train becomes the means to transgress social conventions. Even as it mirrors social order, the train offers itself as a way to move across society's lines through a version of modernity presented in the guise of mobility.

Gendered Public Space

Masculinity and the Cinematic Train

Although this chapter concerns itself primarily with melodrama and the constructions of femininity, it is worth pausing to describe the way the train is used to depict certain notions of masculinity in the action genre of popular Hindi cinema. In the 1970s and especially in the early 1980s, films like Ramesh Sippy's *Sholay*, Ravi Chopra's *The Burning Train*, and Manmohan Desai's *Coolie*, used the setting of the railway as a way to depict the nation in crisis during and following Indira Gandhi's prime ministry.[1] Appropriating the technological narratives that elevated mobility, speed, mechanical power, and invention, they offered a way forward that was invested heavily in colonial and nationalist rhetorics of modernity. This was a gendered resolution, in the sense that the same technology seen as progressive also provided a space in which men could cultivate relationships with each other and prove their prowess through mastery of the machine.

Hindi action films borrow from the Western, gangster, and war films in which, Lalitha Gopalan argues, "[v]iolence structur[es] the bonds between men."[2] Ramesh Sippy's film *Sholay*, known as the classic "angry young man" film in reference to the character of the protagonist, played by Amitabh Bachchan, places the train in a prominent role. In an extended flashback in the early part of the film, a former officer narrates how two petty thieves, his prisoners, once came to his rescue on a train besieged by horseback bandits. The train in *Sholay* certainly cements the reference to the Western, offering the familiar trope of a shootout between train passengers and outlaws. The men take possession of the train, especially by jumping on and running across its roof, and ultimately solidify their control by entering the steam engine carriage. In *Sholay*, the train functions as the site for homosocial bonding, and it appears as an exclusively masculine space.

Another action film of the same period, Chopra's *The Burning Train*, also represents the railway as a place to foster male relations and prove masculine prowess through the technological innovations associated with modernity. In an opening scene, three boys walk along the railway tracks, each boasting that he will construct the fastest train when he grows up. The story that follows, in which one boy grows up to design India's first Super Express train but neglects his family, another boy becomes perverted by disappointment, and the third slips into depression, offers a cautionary message about the price paid for such obsessions. Yet despite several gestures elevating traditional values such as family and religion, the film ultimately celebrates speed, a phenomenon that Stephen Kern has identified as bringing out both the aspirations and dark side of modernity.[3]

Like many other works set on the train, both literary and cinematic, *The Burning Train* uses railway space as a tableau to show national diversity. Among the passengers who board the new train are a military man, a Hindu *pandit* (Brahman scholar), a Muslim man, a female entertainer, and a group of schoolchildren from a Catholic school. This representation draws together disparate aspects of Indian culture into a shared space, evoking the geographic arena of the national homeland. Much of the plot involves the interactions of the passengers, who find themselves on a shared journey. When the train is sabotaged by a bomb and later engulfed in fire, the burning train suggests a nation on a course to destruction. Chopra's film, like many other action films produced in the same era, should be understood as a product of the socio-political climate of urgency, violence, and civic unrest.

Like *Sholay*, *The Burning Train* forges a resolution through the command of the machine, especially the engine but also the entire body of the train. Two male characters run back and forth across the roof and scale the outside of the rushing train; a third man, the designer of the train, climbs a rope between two speeding trains. The goal is to take control of the engine—historically, an almost exclusively masculine space. In the process of commanding the train, the two men bond with each other and with the designer of the train to overcome the devious designs of another man.

Thus, the train space fosters that homosocial bond within a larger narrative of the railway as nation; the film tells us that the nation must progress though a particular form of manhood redeemed by modernity.

In Manmohan Desai's 1983 film *Coolie*, the masculine world of the train is divided into two parts: the corrupt railway bureaucrats appear to control the train, while the "coolies," or porters, maintain actual physical and logistical rights to the railway space. Desai vividly portrays the maleness and power of the porters in opening scenes that show an incoming train. The camera remains stationary, emphasizing the athletic bodies of the men with a slow-motion shot of the porters, who push up from a squat and toss away their Beedi cigarettes before they run along the platform. The porters line the track as they wait for their fares, presenting a human barricade between the train and platform. In one scene, a key confrontation, the protagonist, played by Amitabh Bachchan, jumps onto the top of the train from the overpass, claiming the train space as his own. The men's possession of the train and platform reinforces the general theme that the working man finds agency in the power of his labor; after the son of a railway official attacks a man, a strike immobilizes the traveling public. Critics have interpreted Desai's film as part of the larger group of films that challenged authority during the time of the Emergency, a period of state repression under Prime Minister Indira Gandhi from 1975 to 1977, by showing the state as violent, unjust, and ineffectual.[4] The film reclaims the train, owned and operated by the state, as something that belongs to the working man. At stake here in the image of the train is both class-consciousness and a notion of masculinity aligned with the power of the machine.[5]

Men in popular Hindi cinema possess the railway in a way women rarely do; indeed, even in fiction, the train is a dominantly male symbol, generally used by male authors to represent male characters.[6] The train scene in the action genre of contemporary Indian cinema inculcates the men with a larger narrative of progress as mobility. Lalitha Gopalan discusses the repeated use of the train scene in these films: "In all these instances, railway tracks and moving trains emerge as indelible parts of the post-colonial fabric where movement through landscape promises change and progress."[7] The train becomes a space where masculinity is constituted within a certain narrative of modernity, and, in turn, compels that version of the modern through the affective force of gender. In looking at representations of the public space of the railway, then, it is necessary first to understand it as constructed primarily as a masculine space, and then to consider how women enter and reframe that arena to produce a different, more ambivalent mobile modernity.

Women and Railway Space

Cinematic representations that place women in the space of the railway are part of a broader cultural discourse about women in public spaces that dates back to the train's origins in the mid-nineteenth century. This body of texts includes official colonial writings, travel narratives, and articles in Indian newspapers. British proponents of the railway saw the train as liberating women from a traditional way of being. The entrance of women to the train was seen as an important part of the colonial project, which would enact a modern transformation by changing the social customs around women. William Muir, lieutenant governor of the North West Provinces, saw it as imperative to encourage female travelers, noting: "It is not perhaps too much to say that nothing would contribute more than this to the general enlightenment of the people and to the eventual introduction of a more civilized and rational treatment of the female sex in India."[8] Other writings make clear that it was not enough for Indian women to witness the wonders of the train; modernity was to be fully achieved by mobility of both sexes. Writing the introduction to Bholanatha Chunder's 1869 travel narrative, English writer J. Talboys Wheeler celebrated the turn against what he saw as superstition through increased movement, "as all the wealthier classes, and especially the females, avail themselves very considerably of the safe and speedy mode of traveling by the Rail."[9]

Although Europeans embraced the idea of women on the train as a symbolic step forward, many Indians had a very different reaction to the notion because in India, public space was (and is) gendered through a series of social regulations. Unlike Wheeler, Bholanatha Chunder, who was otherwise enthusiastic about Indians using the train, presented a more ambivalent perspective on the subject of women passengers. Describing one of his own train journeys, he wrote:

> Our patience would have given way under the strain put to it, were there not faces to peep from behind the purdahs of ekkas—faces of females whom the rash innovator, Rail, had drawn out from the seclusion of their zenanas, to throw them upon the rude gaze of the public.[10]

Although Chunder's comment overtly celebrates the opportunity to see the faces of the female travelers, he groups his own glance with the "rude gaze of the public." Moreover he attributes this violation to the "rash innovator" of the rail. For Chunder, the technology that he saw as the greatest memorial of an enlightened nation was a gift that undermined deep cultural norms that regulated women's mobility.

The social restrictions on women's mobility were seen as a way to preserve women's reputation for chastity by keeping them from even visual contact with men outside their family. Writing about the Middle East, Sarah Graham-Brown ascribes similar restrictions to a fear of free expression of female desire: "Segregation of space and control over the visibility of women were forms of patriarchal control which emphasized the need to channel and contain women's sexual power."[11] Life in gender-segregated space should not be seen as simply something forced upon Indian women, however, for *purdah*—a term referring to the secluded inner rooms of the *zenana* reserved for women—lies at the heart of cultural notions of domestic space and is viewed by many women as a way to preserve spiritual as well as sexual purity. Moreover, these restrictions are often a means to establish class status socially. Historically, Hindu as well as Muslim women of the upper class were subject to the circumscriptions on personal space represented by *purdah* and the covered palanquin carriage carried by attendants.

Early discussions about female travelers conceptualized a highly regulated space for the protection of women's bodies and reputations. In 1869, Indian men and colonial railway officials engaged in correspondence on the issue. The Indian representatives worried about the exposure of women to the gazes of strange men, including railway officials, fretted over the further possibility that those men would be of a different caste or class, and finally asserted the need for women to have access to the protection of male relatives. They wondered how women would enter the carriage from the screened palanquin in which they had traveled to the station. The writers strategized about new problems that emerged with the collective form of traveling: how, for example, each woman would have access to the men in her family while remaining invisible to all strangers. In response, the East Indian railway proposed several changes to the European model of the train, including a first-class female compartment accessible by palanquin, third- or intermediate-class carriages with compartments at each end divided by Venetian blinds and designed for families, a third-class, exclusively female carriage (from which prostitutes would be barred), and women's waiting rooms next to stations. In 1870, the *zenana* carriage was introduced, an antecedent of the contemporary women's carriage today, sometimes called the ladies coupé, which has no British counterpart.[12]

The women's train carriage might have been seen as simply a more technologically advanced version of the palanquin carried over land or the *purdah* vehicle pulled by bullocks; yet it assumed a different cultural significance in the colonial culture and ultimately prescribed new identities for Indian women that were not the liberating ones imagined in the colonial discourse. Entrance to the public space of the railway marked Indian women as vulnerable on the one hand and as sexually available on the other. For women who could not afford the *purdah* carriages, the railway measures had the unexpected effect of shading their reputations. Laura Bear argues that "[t]he travel in the public spaces of the railways un insulated by the *zenana* carriage and unprotected by male companions was a hazardous prospect for women of limited means."[13] The way that the train marked lower-class women who could not afford the *zenana* ticket made them more vulnerable than they would have been because they were exposed and therefore perceived to be sexually available. By the 1890s, the railway was a place filled with "railway outrages," or incidents of harassment. Lower-caste and lower-class women, identified as such by their tickets, were verbally hassled, physically assaulted—and sometimes even raped—in the train, the waiting rooms, and the platforms. Even for women who traveled alongside their husbands, children, or male relatives, train journeys were fraught with potential danger.[14]

Nor did railway travel liberate women of the upper class from gender restrictions so much as open them to its more harsh enforcement in the form of systematic harassment. The "outrages" itemized in the late nineteenth-century Indian press were certainly more pervasive for women with third-class tickets, but they were not confined to that group. Bear cites an example from 1895 when a Eurasian ticket collector at Lahore station forced three Indian women out of an intermediate-class carriage to allow Eurasian women to travel alone. The train left the women at the station to face unwanted attention on the open platform.[15] For all classes of Indian women travelers well into the twentieth century, entrance to the public space of the railway meant the possibility of being read as fair game for sexual overtures that could range from unwanted visual attention to outright violence.

Women's entrance into the public space of the railway in the nineteenth century thus placed them in a tenuous position, both in terms of their safety and in terms of their reputations. This nineteenth-century idea of the railway as a space that marks the female traveler as sexually available finds its legacy in Indian filmic representations of women on railway platforms or in the train. The train appears as a dangerous place for women in Shakti Samanta's 1970 Hindi film *Kati Patang*. In one scene, Madhu, the main character, sits on the railway platform silently contemplating a passing train and reflecting on her recent troubles. Offscreen but presumably on the same platform, a man calls out to her with a crude sexual proposition. He recognizes her as a woman who recently created an uproar in town by jilting her fiancé at their wedding and characterizes such a woman as sexually available. To some extent, the film attributes the harassment to her storied past: Madhu had escaped her wedding to join her love interest, only to find him in bed with another woman. Nevertheless, I argue that the gendered history of railway travel allows Madhu to be seen as a promiscuous woman by her fellow passenger simply because of where she is sitting. The public space of the railway becomes for the woman a place of misinterpretation and vulnerability. In no other place throughout the film is Madhu subject to public violation, even when her past is revealed. The film tells us that *any* woman traveling alone is vulnerable because she may be seen as sexually available.[16]

As the nature of space in Indian society was transformed through modernization, women became a kind of front line for maintaining certain patriarchal and class social orders. At the same time, the railway allowed women more opportunities for mobility, and, in certain ways, extended their freedoms. They were finally, as J. Talboys Wheeler predicted, able to move about the region or even the country with more ease, an opportunity many of them used to take holy pilgrimages.[17]

The image of women in the train in contemporary popular Hindi cinema must be seen as culturally ambivalent, suggesting exposure and vulnerability on the one hand, and the freedom to challenge the social order through the process of mobility on the other. By the 1960s, a new discourse had emerged about women in popular cinematic romances set on trains. The romantic films produced since that decade reference the moral discourse that decried the "railway outrage," but also embrace the public space of the train as a site for the expression of private desire. This desire might be a male desire imposed on a woman in the form of an unwanted gaze, a proposition, or the threat or realization of physical contact; more often, however, in the genre of romance, the train is presented as a place for the origins or expression of reciprocal desire. Put simply, in Indian cinema, people fall in love on the train.

Romance on the Train

The image of the train has been consistently used to represent sexual desire. In the American context, the final scene of Alfred Hitchcock's *North by Northwest* shows a train entering a tunnel as the advertising executive Thornhill pulls his lover, Eve, onto the upper berth. The phenomenological experience of the train—its vibrations, its panoramic view, its rhythmic cadence—has been offered as either the cause of erotic stimulation or as a symbolic reference for bodily sensations. The train carriage, which allows for close proximity to new or old friends, has been a common setting for real or imagined sex in many different films, one of the most recent being *Darjeeling Limited* (directed by Wes Anderson; 2007) in which an American traveler successfully propositions an Indian attendant in the bathroom. Thus, it is not surprising that Indian cinema, which has a history of displacing representations of desire onto bodily experiences other than sex (a couple caught in a rain shower, the heroine on the swing imagining the hero), would use the train to convey physical longing.

As well as a symbol of sexual desire, the railway has been a common setting for romance. Once again, the structure of the carriage space lends itself to narratives about meetings. The movement of the train suggests a relationship hurtling into an unknown future. The motif is used crossculturally to show the beginnings of a relationship, such as in the American film *Before Sunrise* (directed by Richard Linklater; 1995). The railway love story is depicted in Indian popular cinema as a way to negotiate new forms of love that transgress old social structures. Karen Gabriel describes the Bollywood love story as "a genre that attends to and negotiates questions of gender, sexuality and desire directly";[18] the function of the train in these films is to provide a plausible setting in which those elements may be explored within a delimited, temporary public space.

Given the history of gender relations on the train discussed previously, it is not surprising that in popular Hindi cinema, men are the ones who most often express sexual desire on the train. In Vinood Kumar's 1968 *Mere Huzoor*, the train scene plays with the tension between the public and private space of the train and undermines the distinction between chastity and desire. In the scene, a young woman, Sultanat, is accompanied to the door of the train by her uncle—a way of denoting her "purity," because as has been discussed, a female traveler who arrives at the train alone is viewed as potentially a prostitute. She is in a burqa with full-length black robes and a veil showing only her eyes through transparent chiffon. The veil forms a mobile expression of the private space of *purdah* within the public arena; nevertheless, as a woman in the public space, she is immediately open to a man's advances. The train jolts as Sultanat boards, and she is caught and held for a moment by a young man named Akhtar, a stranger to her. She subsequently joins Akhtar and another man in an otherwise empty carriage. Once she sits, Akhtar looks at Sultanat's exposed hands before he ogles her sandaled feet. Unexpectedly, she lifts her veil to read, exposing her face to the two male passengers.[19] Mesmerized even more by her face than her feet, Akhtar pronounces her "beautiful."

As Sultanat turns, demurely wide-eyed, she is shocked as a pornographic magazine, with an otherwise nude blonde holding a towel to her breasts on the cover, drops to the floor. Once again, the train is represented as a place for the exposure and sexualization of women. The magazine actually belongs to the other male passenger, a significant fact that places Akhtar back into the bounds of propriety. Together, the two men facilitate Akhtar's long come-on to Sultanat, although Akhtar never addresses her directly in the song he sings about meeting a beautiful woman whom he asks to take off her veil. Akhtar's song invokes an Urdu poetic tradition expressing longing, tempering and legitimating what might otherwise be perceived as a "railway outrage." Sultanat has literally already taken off her veil, although she faces the window, and the train space has also made her public and thus, in a certain way, available.

Although in this film the setting of the train primarily allows for the expression of male desire, the train itself is complicit in female desire. Sultanat initially acts outraged at Akhtar's advances, but at two points, she is shown to be seduced by the train itself. In two nearly identical shots, the camera focuses on the speeding track going underneath the train and then the passing landscape. In the first shot, the camera then cuts to an exterior view of Sultanat looking rapturously out the window, her head rocking to the vibrations of the train. Shortly after, the director again uses the exact same sequence, but this time, after a view of running tracks and a panoramic view, he shows Sultanat as she sways to the movement of the train with her eyes closed and a slight smile playing on her face. Director Kumar allows Sultanat to be seduced by the train when she cannot be openly seduced by the man who travels along with her—at least, she cannot do that and still maintain her chastity, which is a defining attribute for an Indian female protagonist.

In *Mere Huzoor,* the train marks and advances the start of a romantic relationship that would not have occurred within family and social structures. Sultanat is a doctor's daughter from the city; Akhtar is from a rural area and has been without a job for two years. The train allows for them to be on equal footing temporarily. They become, in the words of Akhtar's song, "fellow travelers." Sultanat Sinha ultimately falls in love with Akhtar and his poetic musicality, and she marries him rather than the far-more-prosperous Nawab Salim, whom she meets through her social circles. In addition to providing a site for the expression of female desire, romances on the train challenge social structures based on class or family that restrict access to potential mates. In other words, many of the leading couples in cinematic romances such as this one would never have met if not for a chance encounter on the train because they inhabit different social worlds.

Traditionally in Indian society, the family has a primary role in determining who can marry, or even which couples can meet. Marriage is often viewed as a way for a family to increase its social or economic status, forge new connections, or protect its assets. Karen Gabriel writes of the Indian joint family system, in which a single family includes many extended members living together, that

> Marriage is viewed primarily as a means of enhancing social, economic and sexual capital, that is marriage as a matter of appeasing neighbours, and relatives, acquiring social connections, procuring free domestic labour to supplement/replace the ageing mother's capacity for work, enrichment through dowry, continuance of (patri)lineage and protection of property (not monogamy) through legalized and regular sexual partnership.[20]

Not surprisingly, then, the plots of popular Indian films often center on family relationships, challenging or recuperating the family's role in determining the social structures that regulate desire.[21]

The train scenes act as ways to motivate conflict or change through the introduction of a lover who is unsanctioned—at first, at least—by the family. In *Mere Huzoor*, the relationship does not work out well, and Akhtar ultimately pursues another woman while Sultanant and her child turn to the social and economic protection of Nawab Salim. Similarly, Avtar Krishna Kaul's 1973 Hindi film *27 Down* also provides a tragic ending to a railway romance in which a young ticket collector falls in love with a passenger. Their relationship develops on the train as they journey together, but when they step off the train, their romance is quashed by the pressures of their respective families.

In most films representing a railway romance, however, the love relationship does survive, but only after passing back through the private space. In these cinematic romances, the train becomes not so much a space of violation as a kind of opening for a socially transgressive relationship that will ultimately be redeemed through a family-sanctioned marriage. Kamal Amrohi's 1972 *Pakeezah*, one of a subgenre of Hindi films known as "courtesan films," which is set in a Muslim community in the northern city of Lucknow at the turn of the twentieth century, provides a good example. The film presents the railway carriage as a fraught space where both a man and a woman might transgress familial traditions regulating desire and romance. A late traveler, Salim, enters a private train compartment, only to find it occupied by two women sleeping in opposite beds. As he sits down next to one of the women, her hennaed foot slips out from between the covers and her toe erotically taps his leg with each sway of the fast-moving train. The sleeping woman, named Sahibjaan, has *Ghungroo* bells strapped to her ankles — the sign of her dancing profession — that clink to the rocking rhythm of the train as she sleeps. Sahibjaan is a court dancer like her mother, who had run away to a legitimate marriage only to be rejected by the groom's family because she was in a profession associated with prostitution. Sahibjaan never sees her admirer, but when she wakes at the station in morning, she finds a note tucked in between her toes. Signed "fellow traveler," the note tells her never to put her beautiful feet on the floor. The love story that begins reconciles the potential violation of a sleeping woman traveler being observed by a strange man, making this not a "railway outrage," but the beginning of salvation for a *pakeezah*, or "pure one."

The incident on the train becomes a life-changing event, and that moment and its significance is recalled later by the train itself. Sahibjaan comes to treasure the note, interpreting it as a message that she is meant for a more respectable life. She understands that to put her feet on the floor as a dancer is in some ways to dishonor herself: The actual practice of dancing for a group of men leads her closer and closer to selling her body, but even if she never were to prostitute herself, she would always be seen as impure. Throughout the film, the sound of the train's whistle pierces the private sanctuary where the dancers stay, and the camera focuses on Sahibjaan looking pensively off into space when she hears it, presumably thinking on the possibility of a different life. That life is symbolized by the unknown man, Salim, who had left the note and whom she later meets; that different path is also represented by the train, as Sahibjaan gazes longingly out her window at departing trains. In fact, at one point in the film, she describes the life-changing moment in which she encountered her fantasy lover in terms of the railway: "A train leaves its path and passes through my heart." Thus, *Pakeezah* registers female longings for alternative possibilities and offers a symbol of it in the form of the train.

Even as director Amrohi makes the courageous choice to represent female desire, he does not validate it as sufficient to lead Sahibjaan to a better life. Gabriel writes of female agency in Bollywood film:

> Agency and choice as universal rights on the one hand and as source of the power of gender on the other, generate representation and narrative tensions that may often be laid to rest only by the rehabilitation of feminine agency into (possibly reformed) patriarchies.[22]

It is difficult to say that Sahibjaan gains agency as she sleeps and awakens to find herself celebrated by a voyeuristic fellow traveler in the form of a note between her toes, but she takes that experience and uses it to imagine a new identity. The resolution of the film, however, reclaims that agency and places it firmly back in patriarchal control.

Sahibjaan's desire, place, and character must finally be sanctioned by the patriarchs of her family, especially by the uncle who threw out her mother and father. Luckily, her love choice, Salim, happens to be the son of that uncle, or her first cousin. The film thus presents a tension between the possibilities of public space and the necessity of private — especially familial — authority. Gabriel argues that the Indian cinematic love story renders ambivalent binaries between tradition and modernity that alternately use transgression and resolution to "[explore] changes of individual subjectivities to enable transformations of the *notion and imagination* of community, without challenging specific communities themselves"[23] (italics in the original). In the Indian cinematic romance, the representation of the train as a place that presents the opportunity to meet across social and gender boundaries, and therefore challenge social conventions, operates in the narrative as a way to reinforce traditional social values. These include those based on blood, class, and familial authority. The illicit relationship in *Pakeezah* between the strangers on the train is ultimately legitimated by blood (she is the daughter of his uncle), by religious blessing (her parents were officially married), and by family-sanction (his uncle gives the union his blessing). However, the film does not simply reproduce social values. *Pakeezah*, like Manmohan Desai's 1960 film *Chhalia* (discussed in chapter 3), makes a moral argument for embracing a woman who has been tainted by circumstance;[24] these films use melodrama to do the work of social reform. In challenging and then restoring the structure of Indian communities, works like *Pakeezah* might also be, as Gabriel suggests, changing their audience's vision of who might belong to that community. To do so, they use the medium of the public space of the train.

In Aditya Chopra's 1995 film *Dilwale Dulhania Le Jayenge*, commonly called *DDLJ*, the Indian community is reimagined by the inclusion of diasporic subjects, and once again the train plays a key role in enabling desire. *DDLJ* has been one of the most popular Bollywood films to date among Indians on both the subcontinent and abroad. Although the lead characters, Simran and Raj, are both second-generation Indians living in London, the film deals more with Indian rather than British themes; as Jenny Sharpe puts it, "*DDLJ* does not attempt to reproduce the reality of the British Indian experience so much as to transplant a typically Indian family to a foreign locale."[25] Raj and Simran are from different classes and have radically different morals—he is a rich playboy, while she is the obedient and demure daughter of a convenience store owner—and for this reason, at the beginning of the film they have never met. At the end of the college school year, each one plans to join a group of friends leaving London by train to take a European holiday. When they are both late and running to catch the train, Raj pulls Simran into an empty compartment of the departing train, only to find that they are locked apart from their sets of friends. They are forced for part of the trip into the intimacy of sharing a train compartment oddly devoid of seats. Like Sultanant in *Mere Huzoor*, Simran tries to read a book as an unknown man comes on to her, but Raj is far less subtle than Akhtar, who politely sang a love poem to his fellow passenger. The love story undermines the potential creepiness of Raj's aggressive pursuit by making him a playful, witty character and hinting at the possibility that desire is secretly mutual. The initial encounter on the train outside the bounds of her family sets Simran on the path of finally realizing her desire. First, it allows her close access to a man who is not a relative. Second, the train transports her to another location away from home where she can finally express her desire.

As in *Pakeezah*, however, in *DDLJ* the family must ultimately sanction the union, as the public space gives way to the private. As I have argued, Bollywood films dramatize the conflict between desire, especially but not exclusively female desire, and familial social structures. Tejaswini Ganti argues that since the rise of the Hindu right in the mid-1990s, Bollywood audiences have witnessed a more conservative cinema that expresses family values in which "compliant lovers willing to sacrifice love for family honor has become norm."[26] Luckily, after heated opposition, Simran finally finds space for her preferences within her family structure as her father finally comes to accept Raj. That might suggest a patriarchy that is reformed enough to allow Simran to make her own choices if not for the fact that Raj proves his worthiness by subsuming himself to the patriarchal order. In the climax of the film, he chooses to abandon his love because he cannot gain her father's approval, but luckily he is saved by a late-coming blessing. With the ending, the film places the diasporic Indian within a traditional, domestic Indian community guided by patriarchs. Here, the diaspora does not challenge the traditional values of society; rather, it only reinvigorates them. In *DDLJ*, the train plays a stimulating, if oppositional, role in this process, as the film narrates the expression, sublimation, and finally compromise of female desire that is first made possible by the entrance of a woman into the public space of the train.

This movement, from the transgressive opening provided by the train to the family—and socially sanctioned marriage—appears in several other Hindi films, including two released in 2007: Imtiaz Ali's *Jab We Met* and Mani Ratnam's *Guru*. In other films, the train is not so much a meeting point as a place for the hero and heroine to express their desires. The roof of the train can provide the scene for this freedom. In the disco-era film *Zamaane Ko Dikhana Hai* (directed by Nazir Hussain; 1981), the heroine might have boogied with the hero on the open dance floor, but it is only on top of one of India's famous small "toy trains" that she gives in and admits her love.

Danger on the Train

It should be clear that Indian cinema presents an ambivalent relationship to the kinds of desire and love enabled in the public space of the train. The train provides a site for questioning the social restrictions placed upon love and offers a countersite for romance that falls outside the bounds of family sanction. However, most Bollywood films ultimately shift the site back to the family home, often ritualizing this social sanction in the extended scene of the wedding.[27] One may conclude, then, that the train—or any public space—is still not considered a "proper" context to foster a relationship. Popular Hindi films show this by using another prominent motif of the railway: the image of the train as a place of danger.

The notion of the train as a dangerous place is an idea that dates back to the railway's origins in the Victorian period. Nicholas Daly considers the sensational railway drama in his book *Literature, Technology, and Modernity, 1860–2000*. He argues that playwrights of the mid-nineteenth century gave voice to cultural anxieties about the new mode of transportation. Numerous melodramas included scenes of characters dramatically rescued from an oncoming train. Daly argues that the plays incorporated and refashioned a new industrial modernity.[28] Wolfgang Schivelbusch describes fears of accidents saturating early representations of the railway in his book *The Railway Journey: Trains and Travel in the 19th Century*, and Ian Carter devotes a chapter of his book *Railways and Culture in Britain: The Epitome of Modernity* to "Crime on the Line."[29] Thus, the depiction of the railway as a dangerous place, like its representation as a place of love and desire, has a long cultural history referenced and made particular by popular Hindi cinema.

Mani Ratnam's 1998 blockbuster *Dil Se* offers a view of the train as simultaneously a romantic place of possibility and a dangerous place where you never know who you will meet. Early on in *Dil Se*, the key scene that introduces the two main characters takes place on a railway platform. Amarkant Varma meets Meghna on the windswept, deserted nighttime platform of a rural station. Meghna is huddled on a corner bench under a shawl, and Amar first speaks companionably to her as if she were a man, assuming that a woman would not be traveling alone. When the wind blows off her covering, Amar assumes a posture of respect and apologizes, but he continues to approach her, telling her she is beautiful. Meghna is clearly made uncomfortable by the attention; the scene stresses both her modesty and his infatuation, but it also recalls some of the early discussions about women traveling alone. In Amar's mind, Meghna is available to his flirtations precisely because she is a solo woman traveler. She is swept away from that possibility into propriety as her male companions arrive and escort her into the train.[30]

The most fantastic train scene in the film—and arguably in Indian cinema—is a song-and-dance sequence that immediately follows Meghna's departure[31] (Figure 10). Jyotika Virdi writes of the musical sequence in Bollywood cinema, "In Hindi cinema, songs perform various functions within the narrative; a song can be marshaled to advance the story at a rhapsodic juncture within the narrative or to convey moods—love, passion, separation, longing—or the lyrics may simply be part of the extra-diegetic music overlaid upon a montage sequence summarizing the narrative."[32] In *Dil Se*, the camera cuts from an image of Amar in the nighttime rain looking longingly after Meghna's departing train to a fantasy scene of an unnamed woman (Malika Arora) stretching sensuously in the morning light. As the camera backs up, it becomes clear that she is on top of a train, traveling with

Figure 10. A promotional still from Mani Ratnam's 1998 film Dil Se *shows the famous dance scene on top of the train. Courtesy BFI Stills.*

other migrant laborers in the rooftop space associated with the Indian train. As Arora's character moves into a dance, the song "Chaiyya Chaiyya" reproduces the mechanical tempo of the train. Her hips gyrate like the pistons on the engine, as other laborers fuse folk dance within a technological space and musicality by moving in squares around the perimeter of the train, stomping their feet and waving their arms in rhythm to the train. The director uses the light and dark of passages through tunnels to create and diffuse intimacy between the unknown woman and Amar. Yet the sensual energy between them is contained by class differences and by the public space that delimits fleeting encounters. Although Amar's encounter with the fantasy woman is far more erotic than that with Meghna, both meetings are structured by possibilities offered by the cultural associations of railway space.

The railway encounter hints at, or even encourages, the possibility of a tryst outside the bounds of social decorum, but the same anonymity that allows for those meetings also gives a sense of anxiety. That is not the case in the "Chaiyya, Chaiyya" dance scene, which remains in the realm of dance-sequence fantasy, but that disquiet is there when Amar and Meghna meet on the platform. Amar asks her to tell him where she was born or a relative's name, as he tries to place her within acceptable structures of social orientation. He jokes lamely that he is carrying a bomb. In fact, in the film, it will ultimately be she who is carrying a bomb, for she turns out to be a terrorist working for a separatist group. The train can put you next to a lover or a terrorist, and *Dil Se* plays on these two possibilities by placing them together. The railway appears only in the beginning, but it sets up the potential for the confluence of desire and danger that constitutes the film's primary theme.

That anxiety about the train as a place of both love and peril reappears in Hyderabadwala and Mistry's 2007 film *The Train*, an international production heavily marketed to a global audience. Set in Bangkok, the film opens with a view of a train crossing over a highway and then cuts to a view of a crowded station; the images then speed up to abstracted, rapid-cut shots signaling that we have moved from a view of the train to a view from the train. The opening shows both the centrality of the commuter train to the city life and places us inside its world. In the film, the railway world is filled with upwardly mobile people, especially Indians. Vishal Dixit, a graphic designer somewhat unhappy in his marriage, meets a beautiful woman on the train. After they meet several more times on the morning commuter line, they begin an affair; it is only after he has given her all his money that he finds out she is a con artist working with her boyfriend.

In *The Train*, the railway is a place of anonymity and sexual permissiveness that allows for possibility of an illicit affair. It is a place where you might lose all your money as well as your heart to the alluring stranger. The film contrasts this space with the family home, where Vishal and his wife try to work out their differences, and ultimately deems the domestic more valuable than the public, represented as the space of a striving, young, upper middle class. Thus, the film identifies with traditional rather than capitalist values of upward mobility.

Bollywood films increasingly idealize the growing urban cosmopolitan class of professionals, both in India and in diasporic communities in places like Bangkok, Melbourne, London, and New York. Heroes and heroines are often studying law or getting their MBA, or they might be high-level business people, like Vishal in *The Train*. The films frame these identities through the depiction of public spaces, such as the commuter train, which act as a site for the expression of desire—aspirations for money, for success, for sex, and especially for love. Yet in an industry dominated by traditional values, popular Hindi cinema holds fast to the notion that the family should ultimately broker desire. Public desire is thus given an ambivalent quality in contemporary film, especially for female characters, for which spaces like the train continue to represent both emancipation and restraint. In the older films, this ambivalence marked worries about the emergence of women into the public spaces that represented modernity, concerns that date back to the nineteenth century. Those anxieties about gender shifts are still very much present, but the films of the 1990s and this decade increasingly have represented concerns about the effects of a globalizing India on the morals of both men and women. Somewhat surprisingly, given the fact that the railway is a fairly old technology, the train has played a significant symbolic role in articulating concerns about globalization, both in film and in the broader cultural context. The conclusion of this book, which discusses terrorism, shows how the railway has become an emblem—and target—for those who wish to challenge India's economic liberalization and cosmopolitan identity.

Terrorism and the Railway

*The trains are the great social laboratory of [Mumbai]. And today,
they became a charnel-house.*

Suketu Mehta, "Indian Bomb Attacks: Analysis,"
Washington Post, July 11, 2006

TOKYO 3/20. Madrid 3/11. London: 7/7. Some of the most significant terrorist incidents in recent years have occurred on a train, including the 1995 Tokyo gas attack, the 2004 Madrid bombings, and the 2005 London Underground explosions. In a country that commonly refers to its railway as its lifeline,[1] the number of railway-related bombing fatalities in India has totaled more than 500 in the past ten years alone. The most recent violence took place in Mumbai's main railway station, Chhatrapati Shivaji Terminus (formerly the Victoria Terminus), where gunmen shot randomly at travelers as part of coordinated bloodshed in the city. Two years before, Mumbai's commuter rail was the site of extreme violence, with bombs exploding on July 11, 2006, on one of the busiest rail lines in the world. Colonial and nationalist writers promoted the railway as a moving box in which cultural, racial, and historical differences could be enclosed within a civic, secular, and public order. Photographs taken at the scene of Mumbai's 2006 bombing show platforms covered in debris and gashed carriages exposing interiors to the open air (Figure 11). The strange scene of trains turned inside out seems to signal some kind of endpoint. Has modernity, emblemized by the train, reached its terminus, or is this violence just another expression of the modern? This book has argued that one may interpret the prevalent image of the railway in India to show how modernity's commitment to mobility has consigned it to a reconfiguration that is partially its undoing. This chapter reads the symbolic aspects of terror as they intersect with that real and imaginative history of the Indian railway to argue that what we are seeing are actually the inherent contradictions of modernity expressed in the form of violence.

Figure 11. Commuters wait for a train at Mahim railway station in Mumbai a day after bombs exploded on the railway lines. Photograph courtesy Indranil Mukherjee/AFP/ Getty Images.

Narratives of Terror / Counternarratives of Modernity

The image of the airplane in the sky was forever changed by the acts of 9/11, as Ian McEwan suggests in his novel *Saturday*: "Everyone agrees," he writes, "airliners look different in the sky these days, predatory or doomed."[2] To understand terror, one must think through its imaginative component, how terror is at once something in the world with material effects and something comprised of representation and interpretation. One must include both these elements because the real and the fantastic are so closely intertwined in the discourse of terrorism, distinguished not as opposites but as different ways to represent relations to the world.[3] In interviews about the 2006 Mumbai bombings, several people "recognized" the bombings as (re)enactments of different fictional films. As Vyjayanthi Rao points out in her article on Bombay's 1993 "Black Friday" bombing, this slippage represents how particularly in *this* city defined by its cinematic identity, narratives around the bombing and perpetrators are "cinematic in the sense that cinema provided the imaginary for constructing plausible social scenarios around the unusual personas involved in the bombings."[4] Whether filmic depictions were indeed the inspiration for the bombers, observers of this violence certainly understood the factual and the fictional in terms of each other. As the actual bombings begin to inspire fictional accounts, like Nishikant Kamat's 2008 Hindi film *Mumbai Meri Jaan*, they too become part of that imaginative world that charts what terror means to an Indian constituency—and to an international society at large.

After accounting for the representational and interpretive aspects of terror and considering how they constitute a community, one might then look at the way that collective imagination converges on an object. Roland Barthes's theory of the rhetoric of the symbol explains how an image may naturalize a symbolic message by disguising the dense *un*natural structures and processes of representation embedded in that object.[5] "In every society," Barthes argues, "various techniques are developed intended to *fix* the floating chain of signifieds in such a way as to counter the terror of uncertain signs" (italics in the original).[6] The iconic object comes to stand in for a complex amalgamation of sometimes competing referents. This process displaces causality from social agents and processes to the object, so that in the consensual community ("everyone agrees") that McEwan summons in the previous quotation, the airplane, rather than the perpetrators of violence, looks "predatory," and the airplane, rather than the victims, seems "doomed."

The airplane has an important place in a contemporary global cultural consciousness as a locus of terror; so too has the car, as Mike Davis contends in his book on the history of the car bomb.[7] The train, however, has historically been the most pervasive symbol of terror, given the sheer number of representations. The railway's primary and enduring role as an emblem of modernity arguably gives rise to this preponderance. The coincidence presents an opportunity for interpretation: By looking at the train as an object of terror, one may expose that complex assortment of meanings embedded in the machine that has historically represented modernity. In the process, one may recognize the contradictory impulses at work in notions of the modern. Before going on to explore that symbolic history, it is useful to clarify some terms.

The notion of "terror" has been invoked so often in contemporary global politics that the term, as Elleke Boehmer argues, "has been emptied of meaning as never before."[8] Thus, when speaking of terror, one must necessarily offer a working definition at the onset, especially when that notion is paired with the term "terrorism," as it is in this chapter. Often the two ideas are distinguished, with terror*ism* suggesting an organizational structure made of people (terror*ists*) engaged in violence toward social and political ends. Terror, on the other hand, is used more frequently to suggest psychical experience.[9] Going against this separation, the discussion in this chapter interprets terror as both a material and cultural phenomenon; the term indicates acts of physical violence, but its power rests on its ability to have significance in a broader social arena.

Rather than analyze the motivations of perpetrators or attempt to map networks, this chapter explores the symbolic effects of terror; in particular, it looks at violence on South Asian trains as part of a fabric of representation that binds a relationship to a modernity that constitutes national or global communities. In describing this material and cultural phenomenon, I begin with types of terror that are at once individual and collective: the murder and the suicide. I then move on to the experience of the crash. Only then do I consider the aspect now most often associated with terror—the practice of engaging in violence for a social or political cause, which is often called "terrorism." I consider violence made in the name of social and political purposes within this broader field as a way to show how these acts and their interpretation contribute to a cultural phenomenon that articulates modernity in contradictory ways.

By connecting what is often deemed terrorism to terror, I am using the railway to link forms of experience and imagination that are at once individual and collective, social and political, cultural and factual. The goal is not to obscure the materiality of violent acts and their terrible consequences. Instead, this approach emphasizes an understanding of this representational aspect—rather than only, for example, a statistical account—because terror gathers meaning through social signification and interpretation. I argue that terror comes to converge on select emblems (in this case, the railway) for reasons that have to do with our vexed relationship to modernity. I show how that happens in the case of the railway. I then turn, as a way of concluding the arguments of this book, to consider why the Indian railway has taken on that particular role.

Murders, Suicides, and Accidents

Terror has always been part of the symbolic history of trains, in India and elsewhere. Aspects of this culture transcend national borders and distinct historical experiences; thus, it is instructive to move between contemporary South Asian contexts and earlier periods in European and U.S. railway history, keeping in mind some of the distinct meanings generated by the context. The icon of the railway belongs to a collective, transnational cultural consciousness that has long cast the railway as the scene or agent in nightmarish scenarios. In 1861, following the discovery of a body on the train at the Paris terminus—a chief justice who had shared his compartment with a stranger, with dire consequences—passengers throughout Europe feared potential murder at the hands of their fellow travelers. The enclosed compartments from which one could exit only when the train was at the station essentially locked travelers in with each other during the journey. Sensational accounts in the press offered lurid illustrations of victims discovered sprawled over velvet cushions in blood-splattered compartments.[10] A variation of this thrilling scenario showed the victim who disappeared from the train. Popular fiction and film highlighted the impact of these two scenarios on an American and European cultural consciousness—one need only think of Agatha Christie's 1934 novel *Murder on the Orient Express* or Alfred Hitchcock's 1938 film *The Lady Vanishes*.

These terrible visions of violent death draw on the particular spatial and temporal characteristics of the railway to justify anxieties, as well as on its mechanical and sensory qualities. Compartmentalization, which gives rise to both isolation and intimacy, is one such typical point. On a more visceral level, the combination of mechanical sounds and velocity impel fantasies of potential violence. A piece in an 1863 London newspaper gave the following account of railway travel: "The loudest screams are swallowed up by the roar of the rapidly revolving wheels, and murder, or violence worse than murder, may go on to the accompaniment of a train flying along at sixty miles an hour."[11] The scene anticipates the cinematic imagery prevalent in Hindi features like 1980's *The Burning Train*, with its hijacked train en route to derailment, or in the 2008 film on the Mumbai bombings, *Mumbai, Meri Jaan* (discussed in more detail later in this chapter), both of which use the sound and speed of a train to suggest an inherent violence within the vehicle. At play in such imagery is both the strangeness of the train, "a world whose alien nature is dramatized through its 'inhuman' languages (semaphore, telegraph alarms, lights, and whistles),"[12] and its familiarity, which is depicted through the common trope of personification. To illustrate this plainly, consider how a train appears to scream on behalf of its passengers.

Even people on the ground are not safe. Sometimes a simple meeting on a train leads to terror away from the train, as it famously does in Hitchcock's 1951 *Strangers on a Train*, or in the 2007 Bollywood film *The Train*, a Hindi remake of the 2005 American film *Derailed*, in which a seductress entraps an unhappily married man into violence and blackmail. The threat of being run over while bound to the train tracks preoccupied a transnational cultural imagination from the mid-nineteenth century onwards. British melodramas from the 1860s replayed this as a rescue scene, fulfilling, Nicholas Daly argues, the wish to overcome machinery while giving it primacy as a cultural representation.[13]

For the suicide, the machine is deemed the final arbitrator. It is thus for Carker in Charles Dickens's *Dombey and Sons*, and for Anna Karenina at the close of Leo Tolstoy's 1877 novel by that name. As in European literature, in Indian literature and film, the train suicide beckons as a way out for unhappy characters such as in Rohinton Mistry's novel *A Fine Balance*.[14] In Vikram Chandra's short story "Shanti," the protagonist, Shiv, is distraught by his twin brother's death; standing on the platform as a train arrives, "he waited for the two events to come together, the busily grinding three-thirty from Lucknow and himself."[15]

The way of the train is seen as a culturally coded path in many Indian works. Like Anna Karenina, the ill-fated courtesan Sahibjaan in the 1972 Hindi film *Pakeezah* fantasizes about this resolution to her unhappy life. Apu, too, in the third film of Satyajit Ray's Bengali "Apu Trilogy," appears to consider throwing himself in front of the train. In India, the meaning of the train is overdetermined by legacies of colonial rule, including programs of reform meant to transform Indian culture; thus, suicide by means of the train presents an ideologically coded narrative resolution, a way of subsuming oneself to the secular, public space promoted by a colonial rhetoric of modernity. The fact that those two films do not choose to send their heroes to their deaths under the wheels denies that kind of answer and instead opts for a private resolution; Sahibjaan gets married, and Apu retrieves his son. In both representations, traditional Indian cultural identity—interpreted as familial obligation—is preserved against a possible catastrophic alternative of being overcome by a dangerous modernity.

In another Satyajit Ray film, *Nayak*, the train also seduces the main character, Arindam, into near-suicide. He leans out of an open door on the train, mesmerized by the gleam of a single rail in the dark. The camera focuses on the track for an extended period, and as viewers, we are left to reflect on what it means to Arindam. The notion that he contemplates suicide is reinforced by the fact that the young woman Aditi, who arrives later, insists that he return to his carriage before she leaves. But the single line also seems to suggest a line of fate, a life moving interminably into a darkened future. In this film, which I argued in chapter 4 presents critically modern changes in art, Ray presents a compulsory modernity through the imagined meeting of body and machine.

The macabre picture of the railway suicide shows the other side of the desire to overcome machinery, for it is a form of giving way to the power of the machine. Nicholas Daly argues that a culture of modernity, ostensibly predicated on the separation of bodies and machines, instead rehearses their meeting in murder, suicide, or representations of terror on or around the train.[16] These scenes inculcate the audience or reader within a railway consciousness by merging body and machine in the "collision of the flesh and steel."[17] This compulsion is vividly portrayed in Chandra's story "Shanti," as Shiv fantasizes being overcome by the machine: "He jerked his head back, felt the huge weight of the engine, its heat, and began his step forward, seeing the black curve of the metal above him, slashed in half by the slanting sun, the rivets through the iron, and then he staggered back, pulled himself back, an arm over his head."[18] The union, in this example imagined rather than actualized, destabilizes a notion of modernity premised on the binary between human and machine. The machine and body in this fantasy are conjoined, as Shiv feels the weight and heat, and paralleled, as the black curve of metal above him visually duplicates the arm over his head. Chandra transfers what would be violence on the body onto a machine that is slashed and pierced by iron.

This convergence appears dramatically in the portrayal of the crash: the impact of two trains fatefully rerouted onto the same line or a derailment that sends the carriages "telescop[ing] into each other."[19] In The Namesake, Jhumpa Lahiri uses the railway accident as a central motif to represent how the course of a life may be dislodged from its path and flung into a new context. Before the crash, one of the main characters, Ashoke, identifies with the machine, feeling the steam engine puff "reassuringly, powerfully," and the movement of wheels "deep in his chest."[20] The splitting of the train in the crash thus represents a life torn asunder.

By aligning the accident with a scene of reading, Lahiri presents a more general comment about the interrelation between modernity, technology, and alienation. Ashoke is reading Nicolai Gogol's short story

"The Overcoat," glancing occasionally "through the open window at the inky Bengal night, at the vague shapes of palm trees and the simplest of homes,"[21] when his train derails. Reading and train travel have long been paired in life and art, not simply because reading offers a way to pass the time, but because the phenomenological experience of looking out the window colludes with the interpretive experience of reading.[22] Thus, as the real landscape dissolves into the panorama of "vague shapes," the literary landscape acquires an even more compelling force. Gogol's "The Overcoat" gives Ashoke a vision of "all that was irrational, all that was inevitable about the world,"[23] even as the crash that shatters his legs and life forces him to embody that illogic.

The terror of the industrial disaster lies, in part, in the obfuscation and emergence of the train's implicit danger. Ernst Bloch described how the first railways were perceived as demonic, but now it is different: "Only the accident still reminds us of it sometimes, with the crash of collision, the roar of explosion, the cries of maimed people—a production that knows no civilized schedule."[24] One reason that the train crash begets fantasies of terror is that its initial shock to the senses, experienced as the "annihilation of space and time," is subsumed fairly quickly by normalcy. The now-routine experience of train travel bears traces of the original disruption that occurred when the railway was first introduced and now appears only in moments of crisis; railway travel has become normalized, in other words, and the crash interrupts that process and reminds the travelers of the machine's ever-present possibility of violence.[25] As Lynne Kirby puts it: "The instability of the railroad lies first of all in the very experience of mobility, of a passenger's being at once immobile and in rapid transit, lulled to sleep and yet capable of being shocked awake."[26] Kirby's use of maternal and mechanical language, "lulled" and "shocked," only further demonstrates the deep dualities within the cultural symbol of the railway that intensify the contradictory experience of the crash.

The horror produced by a railway derailment and crash may also be ascribed to the nature of a technological accident, in which, rather than coming from an external natural or divine source, the destruction emerges from the inside as the railway, through its velocity, pressure, tension, heat, and other mechanical forces, destroys itself.[27] The image is an old one; an 1844 encyclopedia describes how "[the railway's] very power, once halted or turned from its proper objective, is transformed into a terrible agent of destruction."[28] In mid-nineteenth-century India, the railway was described as a "car of fire" that could potentially shorten life.[29] These fantasies of violence emanate from the phenomenology of train travel itself, which begets a "sensation of violence and potential destruction" as the passenger becomes part of a weapon, "a projectile shot through space and time."[30] The early colonial traveler saw this passivity as a positive thing: "There is a blessed tranquility in feeling that one has handed over for a while,"[31] the narrator of an early twentieth-century memoir states, speaking at once of the rail journey and of empire in general. The notion of "handing over" meant that the traveler is subject to the machine—and even complicit with it. Part of the terror, then, is the traveler's own involvement in the destruction; the anxiety is produced by a sense of passivity in this process. Trapped in a machine hurtling over a fixed course—and then off that course—one is faced with one's profound lack of power.

That sense of passivity extends to an experience of modernity in general. This book has argued that the railway is a metonym for modernity, and by investigating that relationship, one may interpret the contradictions within the concept of the modern. The rhetoric of modernization positions modernity as both tool and master, in the sense that the modern becomes a material way as well as an ideological mandate. But as the railway becomes a scene and agent of destruction, the legitimacy of that modernity is called into question. The conflict appears early in the British context, as well as in recurring scenes of near-death on the railway tracks that show an ongoing negotiation with industrial modernity.[32] Like the cultural imaginary produced in the 1860s, in which "the impact of the machine, or industrial modernity more generally, on the human is a source of trepidation, or even terror,"[33] the contemporary machine seems poised to tear open not just itself but the very fabric of modern society.

One may see this threat within modernity by looking at the pervasive documentation of the train crash, an image so compelling that a cultural aesthetic has grown up around it. In *The Namesake*, Ashoke re-experiences the crash through the photograph that his family saves from the newspaper, an image that shows the train "smashed to shards, piled jaggedly against the sky, security guards sitting on the unclaimed belongings."[34] The scene belongs to a recognizable visual genre. At the beginning of the late nineteenth century, images of railway crashes circulated in American culture in postcards, photographs, popular illustrations, and films.[35] The mass-produced contemporary prints of historic train crashes, like that of the famous accident at the Gare Montparnasse in 1895 in which the engine lies suspended from the fragmented wall of the upper story of the station, attest to the continued cultural currency of this kind of image. Viewers of these prints of the crash derive aesthetic pleasure from a distressing vision of violence in material form. The commodity spectacle mediates this binary, for it returns the crash back into the rational order by making it something that may be purchased.

This visual culture existed in colonial India as well, where it was part of a documentary effort that also included such images as those of construction. Yet the engraving or photograph of the Indian train crash arguably had its own particular meaning separate from other accidents in India and distinct from the images of European train accidents. In Europe, the visual image of a train crash made clear the potential for the industrialism to collapse upon itself; in the colonial context, the scene of the technological accident underscored how the colonial project might be destroyed through its own ambitions. A 1908 *Illustrated London News* image (Figure 12) frames the collision of two engines near Ludhiana, a city in the Punjab. Some of the motifs in this image are familiar from other images of railway crashes around the world: The violence implicit in the depicted damage displaces notions of a secure technological form. The image is compelling for its incongruities: The heaviness of the wreckage is conveyed by the sheer size of a structure that dwarfs the men standing in front of it, yet the metal folds as though it is a delicate material rather than heavy iron. The anomalousness of a scene of two engines tilted up to the sky is further emphasized by the still-intact lines of the telegraph running before them, which contrast the splintered tracks below. The giant wheels that ran on the parallel tracks now hang disconnected in the air. The image also marks conflicting cultural relationships to the train, locating the curious Indians, even a man who is likely a railway worker, as observers of the train (and accident) that is the property of the Europeans who stand guard by the train, some assessing the damage and some looking warily at the curious onlookers. The sign marking the North Western Railway (NWR) is displaced by the accident, visually suggesting the breakdown of a key colonial strategic line that ran between 1886 and 1947 independence. The perspective of the picture behind the Indians makes this image about the Indians' relationship to the train as much as it is documentation about the event itself.

*Figure 12. A 1908 image of two engines after collision near Ludhiana, India. Courtesy of Mary Evans Picture Library/*Illustrated London News *Ltd.*

Imagined Communities of Terror

To examine how the unstable scene of modernity represented by the railway becomes the real and imaginative site for violence in the national and global arena, I turn now to the construction of social and political communities through terror. The imagery of the murder, the suicide, and the crash, so closely connected to the symbolic history of the railway, is part of a broader arena of terror, a field that includes social and political violence. This kind of violence is the most familiar face of terror in the contemporary moment, perhaps because it is apprehended by the largest constituency. Car bombs, train bombs, and other forms of violence, Mike Davis observes, are loud "advertisements for a cause, leader, or abstract principle (including Terror itself)."[36] They are a kind of announcement to a broader community, often using the forum of public space. But to understand how an imagined community is created through this violence, one must shift focus from what the "terrorist" intends to the way that a collectivity interprets and is thus constituted through terror.

Geoffrey Harpham describes terror in terms of cultural effects within the field of social signification and interpretation:

> Terror is a feature of the symbolic order, the vast mesh of
> representations and narratives both official and unofficial, public
> and private, in which a culture works out its sense of itself. It affects
> that dynamic but relatively stable set of implicit parameters that
> establish a group's sense of the actual and the possible and create
> a loose but definite sense of collective identity. Terror may or may
> not be itself symbolic, but its effects are registered in the symbolic
> domain.[37]

Harpham conjoins in the same symbolic network acts of violence, responses to those deeds, and the anticipation of further actions. As a number of theorists on terrorism have argued, those reactions include state security measures, media reports, and a broader culture of fear. The move to consider the effects of terror emphasizes the role that interpretation, as opposed to intention, has in terrorism. Terror has a reader as well as a writer; the community of readers makes terror "work," in the sense that the response becomes the means as well as the ends. Of course, as with any interpretive process, the potential for meaning slipping between "writer" and "reader" is always there. What is being argued for here is not a one-to-one correlation between intention and act, but a constant reinterpretation of the event that is transformed by political exigencies, perspective biases, and historiographic revisions. The focus falls here on what J. Zulaika and W. Douglass call terrorism as "rhetorical product, i.e., quintessential to its strategy and efficacy are the anticipated reactions to and interpretations of, certain concrete acts of political violence."[38]

By looking at terror as a cultural effect, I am challenging the notion that what are called terrorist acts are radically different from revolutionary ones as well as the idea that terrorism falls outside the purview of the symbolic. Peter Heehs, in his collection on nationalism, terrorism, and communalism in the Indian context, separates contemporary "gratuitous violence and crime" from their predecessors in the national movement "activated by a sincere desire for freedom."[39] Such a division, though ethically important, relies upon a focus on the motivations of perpetrators rather than upon the response in a wide cultural field. In this discussion, I am reinserting terror into a broader system of meaning. There is some debate within cultural theories of terror as to whether the violence may even be conceptualized within a representational field. Jean Baudrillard argues that terrorism, unlike revolutionary acts, pushes violence out of the symbolic sphere.[40] He interprets the act itself, rather than the fabric of society so tightly woven around it. Such an approach does not allow us to see how communities such as the nation or a global constituency might form out of terror. The following section explores some of these imagined communities of terror that congeal around such acts of violence as sabotage, bombing, and random shootings in the railway.

Early Railway Terror

Indian railway workers and their supporters were the first in India to target the train; in doing so, they affected the dynamics of both colonial and nationalist communities. In a 1976 essay on "Early Railwaymen in India," Dipesh Chakrabarty details an early kind of train wrecking in the nineteenth century that was, from the perspective of colonial officials, mostly based in personal grievance over such measures as dismissal. He describes an emerging class for which train wrecking lay in the middle ground between crime and protest.[41] By the late nineteenth century, this insurgent group became a protonationalist one unified in dissent over labor conditions. Workers built the lines under onerous conditions that included extreme and dangerous settings, low pay, and unsanitary living conditions beset by disease.[42] Indians protested these conditions of labor and travel both in print and in action, as they took aim at the railway and railway management. In the late nineteenth and early twentieth centuries, current and former railway workers, many of whom were living in villages along the tracks, engaged in train wrecking as a form of guerrilla insurgency; David Arnold describes how saboteurs removed rails and plates or placed obstructions on the line.[43]

Indian passengers also suffered discrimination and were forced to travel in segregated, lower-grade carriages without proper sanitation facilities.[44] Mohandas Gandhi made the condition of third-class passengers an object of international public scrutiny by traveling throughout India in that class. Others had a less pacifistic response. Public hostility towards the railways and the treatment of third-class passengers reached its pitch by the 1920s, and in 1921, the railways were besieged by vandalism, looting, stoning, and derailment, and were the site of assaults on Europeans.[45]

The peaceful and violent protests against the railway helped constitute an emerging nationalist movement, as political leaders formed tenuous common cause with labor leaders opposing the race-based discrimination of the colonial system. Ironically, anti-British sentiment had found its most profound symbol in the very entity that the British had celebrated as a vehicle for emancipation—the train. Although nonviolent campaigns like that of Gandhi against the train in South Africa have received more scholarly and popular attention for their role as part of developing nationalist movements, violent acts also forged those groups. Radical nationalist movements, such as the Maniktala Secret Society, "India's first organized terrorist group with a clear political aim,"[46] engineered derailments. "A small band of young and inexperienced dreamers," recalls leader Barin Ghosh (Barindrakumar Ghosh), laid a mine under the train carrying the lieutenant governor of Bengal, Sir Andrew Fraser, in an unsuccessful 1907 assassination attempt. As part of another group, teenage suicide bomber Pritilata Waddedar blew up the Pahartali Railway Officers' Club in the port town of Chattagram on September 24, 1932, in an attack against British rule and then swallowed a cyanide pill when she was about to be caught.[47]

Writing from the opposite side of political sympathies as Barin Ghosh, British novelist John Masters animated the plot of his 1954 novel *Bhowani Junction* with the specter of railway sabotage by nationalist sympathizers. Masters's novel and the 1956 film version directed by Greg Cukor highlight the troubled position of the Anglo-Indian community in relation to these attacks. As the introduction to this book argued, the Anglo-Indian community was nearly synonymous with the railway itself, not simply because many Anglo-Indians lived near and worked on the trains, but because they developed a distinct identity through those practices. They carved out a space for themselves in India through the structures of the railway. Masters's character Victoria feels the tug of sympathy for the nationalist movement as she comes to identify increasingly as Indian, but for her to take a radical position against the railway would be to undermine her own family's livelihood, because a derailment potentially would injure her driver father.

Postcolonial Terror

As India's nation was forged by means of violence, modernity was articulated as something at once constructive and destructive. This internal contradiction had emerged in the imagery of the train as part of the broader devastation ascribed to modernity within an international context. By the twentieth century, a dread weighed on an international cultural consciousness, one that in the wake of two world wars represented an emerging subjectivity that saw terror as a collective global problem. Terror appeared to be part of a modern condition that characterized national and international arenas. The vision of prisoners en route to Nazi concentration camps, Todd Presner writes, haunted the modern railway consciousness as "an embodied, transitional space emblematic of both the emancipatory hopes and the destructive nightmares of an epoch."[48]

Although Indians were certainly affected by the two world wars, both at home and abroad, the nightmares of modernity gained physical form during the period just before and right after the 1947 division of the British colony into East and West Pakistan and India. After independence, train-related violence helped define the new nation through terror in troubling ways. Refugee trains carrying some of the estimated 15 million people on the move during the Partition period became the site of sectarian violence. The migrants sought safety on the train because it presented a secular, state-sanctioned space that would ideally secure an otherwise dangerous journey across the border. Rather than fulfilling this promise, the train instead became a symbolic target for terror, as trains marked as "Hindu trains" or "Muslim trains" became objects embodying the enemy. Hindus were the victims of rape, torture, and mass murder as the trains passed through Muslim areas, and vice versa in Hindu areas. The perpetrators were sending a message of retribution to the other community.

One may read into the terror of Partition cultural shifts as new nations were defined through violent means: India as Hindu, Pakistan as Muslim. The violence during Partition forced people into communal and national constituencies that might well have been superseded by local, class, or caste identities. In that way, the terror of the Partition period inscribed "that dynamic but relatively stable set of implicit parameters that establish a group's sense of the actual and the possible."[49] Yet terror does not simply bind people together; the phenomenon opens up conflicts that are already extant in the movable bounds of a collective identity that stabilizes modernity. Although sectarian violence might have secured a version of a national imagined community during Partition, for example, it also deepened cracks in the collective.

Railways were the preeminent image of progress because they proffered a means to achieve mobility. They brought nations together, even helped them into being, by facilitating the circulation of people and goods that tied together those imagined communities. Yet from their very origins in Europe, the railways also represented destruction as they tore holes through cities and transformed the countryside in environmentally and socially deleterious ways. In the twentieth century, the European railway became a way to reinforce a fascist nationalism and to enable mass deportations.[50] In this way, the railway represented the deep ambivalences within modernity.

Images of the uncanny had been used in the European context as a way to mediate competing social notions of industrial modernity as both devastating and progressive.[51] The literature of Partition seized upon one Victorian trope in particular, the image of the ghost train that appeared in works like Charles Dickens's "The Signalman," connecting fear of the new technology to older supernatural terrors, as Ian Carter argues in his book on railways and culture in Britain.[52] Within the South Asian context, writers reinvented the image of the uncanny train because it offered a way to invert a notion of modernity represented by nationhood and emblemized by the technological aspirations of nationalist leaders like Jawaharlal Nehru. The ghost train emerged in mid-twentieth-century South Asian literary works like Saadat Hasan Manto's Urdu vignettes and Khushwant Singh's *Train to Pakistan*, and at the turn of the twenty-first century continued to show up in works like Deepa Mehta's film *Earth* and Anil Sharma's Hindi film *Gadar*. Like the image of the death trains of Nazi Germany that forever changed representations of the train in Europe, the legacy of violence on Partition trains has been so powerful that the image of silent trains that arrived filled with bodies arguably haunts any contemporary South Asian image of the train. This is especially true of depictions of communal violence on or around the train.

The specter of Partition violence arguably helped catalyze the horrific incidents that followed the 2002 fire on the *Sabarmati* Express near Godhra, a town in Gujarat with a nearly equal number of Hindus and Muslims that includes many Partition refugees from what is now Pakistan. On February 27 of that year, a train was carrying Hindu activists on their way back from a gathering in Ayodhya, where a sixteenth-century mosque had been burnt to the ground in 1992, prompting riots across India. According to early rumors and news reports, a violent Muslim mob threw a firebomb near the Godhra station and locked the carriage doors to prevent passengers from escaping the flames; however, one later government inquiry attributed the fire to an accident, perhaps a cooking stove. The cause is still a politically charged debate.[53] At least fifty-nine people were burned to death as they tried to escape the train. Rioters throughout Gujarat responded with violence that left approximately 1,000 people (mostly Muslims) dead. New national and regional identities were certainly involved, and one might well connect the hostility to such local and contemporary events as the rise of the Bharatiya Janata Party (BJP) in Gujarat and the uncertain status of a town comprised of nearly half Muslims. Yet arguably the image of a death train also must have conjured powerful communal sentiments, a spectral violence, which fed the riots.

Another bombing evoked these ghosts of the past. On February 19, 2007, bombers attacked the *Samjhauta*, or Friendship, Express, the only train link between India and Pakistan, killing sixty-eight. Many observers saw the violence as symbolic, aimed at severing the tenuous link between the nations in the midst of scheduled peace talks. The prominent newspaper *Hindu* connected the *Samjhauta* bombing to the massacres during Partition,[54] and for many, the deaths on a train to Pakistan must also have brought back memories bound in a collective consciousness.

Partition was not only about communal identity, but also about sovereign territory. In the postcolonial period, terrorism on the train has continued to send "loud"[55] messages that consolidate the nation under certain terms, marking ethnic and geographic borders as well as communal identities. When on December 31, 1996, two bombs detonated under the tracks of a train in the northeastern state of Assam, killing dozens of holiday travelers, the Bodoland Liberation Tigers Force (BLTF), a separatist group, claimed responsibility. According to its statement, BLTF felt compelled to "snap the link between (the) northeast and (the) rest of the country" by attacking the rail.[56] Bombings by groups contesting national boundaries have been among the most common in India's history, and one can see from the BLTF's language that the rail line presents both a literal and metaphorical target for groups endeavoring to redefine national territory. Because terror works by consolidating communities in their responses to acts of violence, the bombings have both entrenched a sense of the nation and displayed its fault lines.

Global Terror

Railway terror in South Asia creates an imagined national community, but it also has a global audience that is part of its collective identity. The crash that forms a central motif in *The Namesake* was possibly the work of unnamed terrorists. The point is a small one in Lahiri's novel, which is mostly about a Bengali diasporic identity, but even from its relatively minor narrative position (or perhaps because of it), terror inserts a wedge that cracks the vision of a coherent nation—the object of longing for the immigrant characters. From the margins of Lahiri's narrative appear invisible characters living in South Asia for whom selfhood might be lost not through displacement but through the sovereignty of the Indian state; these agents unlock the bolts on the symbol of that state and derail the life of an ordinary Indian boy reading a book on a night train. The close connection between the diaspora and railway terrorism in South Asia appears in less subtle ways in the media, as well as in diasporic fiction like that of Lahiri. For example, one British newspaper referenced the recent decision to reinvestigate the incident and ensuing violence in Godhra with a headline that emphasized the reaction of British-Indian Muslims rather than those in South Asia, "UK's Indian Muslims welcome Indian top court ruling on riots."[57]

It might surprise some that global visions of terror have converged on a technology that is over two centuries old, but national symbols have not been dissolved by globalization. Rather, these emblems have gained new meaning and importance as signifiers of new economies. Sometimes it is a city and not the nation as a whole that embodies this identity, for example Tokyo, Madrid, London, New York, and Mumbai. The urban commuter train in particular has come to represent a certain kind of modern identity that is part of a globalizing world. The centrality of the commuter lines to Mumbai's identity as a city weighed in the critical importance of that city's 2006 bombings. On July 11 of that year, eight bombs detonated at evening rush hour in that Indian city within a ten-minute period in various stations, killing nearly 200 people and wounding 700 more.[58] Mouzzam Khan, an editor of a suburban newspaper, described the severed line as "the main artery of Bombay's circulation system."[59] The Western Line is the busiest train in India, carrying 2.6 million people along a 60-kilometer (approximately 37-mile) distance.[60] The bombing is believed to be the work of the Pakistan-based Kashmiri group Lashkar-e-Toiba and the Students' Islamic Movement of India.[61] Although both groups are officially banned by their respective governments, once again, a collective cultural consciousness linked the violence to the historic antagonism between the two nations. This time, however, the violence on the train also took its place inside a global narrative of terror linked by a geographic network of centers of capital.

Because the city is a metropolitan locus for globalization, the social relations synthesized in what Suketu Mehta calls the "great social laboratory"[62] of the commuter trains are simultaneously local and global. Thus, the violence on the Mumbai commuter trains was significant on multiple spatial registers: urban, national, international (India/Pakistan), and global. The bombs all were planted in first-class carriages that carried stockbrokers and diamond traders, both Hindu and Muslim, for which the entrance fee cost ten times as much as for the far-more-crowded third class. As journalist Doug Saunders, reporting for the Canadian *Globe and Mail*, puts it: "These, despite appearances, are not the wretched of the earth; the people who take Mumbai's Western Line are among the world's winners."[63] The targeting of a specific class recalled the days when Pritilata Waddedar walked into the segregated Chattagram railway club to blow it up. Noting the class basis of the violence, some contemporary observers ascribed the Mumbai bombings to those antagonistic to the changing character of the city as it becomes a key site in globalization. Saunders reflects:

> Whoever set off Tuesday's bombs knew exactly what they were hitting. India's huge spurt of economic and social growth, which has propelled it from being a recipient of foreign aid into an aid donor, is in large part driven by the huge middle class that has emerged along the Western Line—a middle class that has shifted

from the old fabric industries that made Bombay famous to the
information-age economies of the new Mumbai . . . It was a surgical
blow to the very heart of the Indian economic miracle.[64]

The symbolic aim at the finance capital recalls other targets, such as the
World Trade Center towers on 9/11 and the Madrid bombings on one of
Europe's most advanced rail systems.

Now, despite its origins in the industrial revolution, the train has
become a means of reaching a global audience. Even as terror constitutes
a global audience through the shared icon of the modern, the experience challenges modernity from within. Writing of the 9/11 terrorists,
Baudrillard says, "they have assimilated everything of modernity and
globalism, without changing their goal, which is to destroy that power."[65]
As in the case of many of the bombings associated with radical cultural
movements, the accused bombers in the Mumbai case ironically came
from the same professional class as the victims: Those charged include an
engineer, a journalist, a computer software professional, and a doctor.[66]
On the Western Line of Mumbai, the difference between killer and killed
lay not only in class, racial, or communal identity, as has been the case
in early violent encounters, but in differing allegiances to the larger structures of modernity represented for both by the vehicle that carried them.

In 2008 the Hindi film *Mumbai, Meri Jaan* came out about the Mumbai
bombings that took place two years earlier. Director Nishikant Kamat's
work marked the first widely distributed fictional representation of these
events that transformed the city and garnered the attention of a Western
world already on edge about terrorism. The film drew its name, which
means "Mumbai, my darling," from an old song of the same name about
Bombay (Mumbai's original name), and both the film and the song may
be seen as a kind of love letter to the city. In works like Salman Rushdie's
Midnight's Children and Suketu Mehta's *Maximum City*, Mumbai (or
Bombay, as it remains for Rushdie) stands in for a particular kind of India,
an India that is both cosmopolitan and corrupt. That is also how it is presented in Kamat's film, which uses the bombing as a way to force open a
discussion about the city and about the nature of India's globalizing self.

Kamat's view of the new Mumbai is not a positive one; this is tough
love, not nostalgia or the rueful love of Rushdie's "imaginary homelands."[67]
Mumbai is presented as a city where, as one alienated police officer
struggling against departmental corruption puts it: "Everyone does the

opposite of what he should be doing." It is a city where the constable is found guilty of raping a girl, and officers take bribes to keep some establishments open even during the curfew following the bombings. Governmental hospitals are ill-equipped to serve the wounded, and the political reforms presented, such as a ban on plastic bags, seem out of touch with the exigencies of the lower classes.

Mumbai, Meri Jaan indicts economic and cultural aspects of a new globalizing city and nation as well as its political corruption. India's aspirations to be a superpower are shown to be an empty shell of conspicuous consumption and excess leisure, represented by a spoiled young man who drives over his BlackBerry as he skids his luxury car away in a fit of pique. The terror that is shown to surround the city even before the bombing—terror linked to communalism—brings out some of the worst of this new self. Mumbai is shown as a place of persistent—indeed increasing—communal tensions, represented by a young Hindu man, Suresh, for whom the bombing fuels nascent hatred into a vague affiliation with Nazism and an obsessive belief that a young Muslim man at his tea shop is a terrorist. The media feeds off the violence that comes out of such hatred; in the film, as in the real-life coverage of the bombing, the tabloid news exploits people's suffering by making a spectacle of dead and injured passengers and intruding on grieving people in search of a compelling journalistic angle. As the ironic slogan of the featured channel puts it, this is "the Truth that You want to hear."

These visions of a globalizing Mumbai are presented against the backdrop of India's aspirations for independence and development. The image of the train sutures this connection in the film. The first shot opens in darkness, with Nehru's famous speech on national independence; as the prime minister intones, "At the stroke of midnight, while the world sleeps, India will awake to the light of freedom," a fluttering flag is shown gradually illuminating. Although the film is named for Mumbai, it is clearly a work about India as a nation-state. This connection is cemented in the sequence during the opening credits, which presents a narrative of development through industry and infrastructure: monuments, the central library, motorcars, trams, trains, steamships, airplanes, and industrialization. The black-and-white footage that gives way to color also offers a history of Mumbai; the city, in turn, is made a synecdoche for India's diversity through a wide range of scenes from Mumbai's varied political, religious, and cultural past. Much of the footage features the railway station, and if

Mumbai is the part standing in for the whole of India, the Chhatrapati Shivaji Terminus, formerly the Victoria Terminus, becomes a metonym for a colonial India remade into a national symbol.

The opening scenes representing the city and the nation's development are recalled visually in the footage of the bombing. The explosion is shown in an exterior shot with a stationary camera on the ground looking at the fast-moving train, as if from the perspective of a bystander. Even before the bomb goes off, the focus on the mechanical aspects of the train, which screams and races forward as if it were itself at risk, instills a sense of anxiety in the viewer. As soon as the bomb explodes, the film holds the camera still, freezing on a series of black-and-white images while the soundtrack intermittently halts the sound of the moving train. These photographs—of a railway clock stopped at 6:23, of a flock of birds leaving a tree, of trains speeding along tracks—make a visual connection to the opening images, relating the bombing to that early national and urban history of development rendered in black-and-white. The photographs also begin to turn the live scene into an archive, which is the way terror will be disseminated through the news media. In this way, the film links the scene of the bombing to its interpretation.

The cinematic representation challenges movement, a primary trope of development, in four ways. First, the train's movement is interrupted visually by the stills. Second, the machine's rhythmic noise is cut off by silence. In both these ways, the movement of the film—a shuttling of frames that should represent a changing picture—is fixed on a single static image. Third, the extended image of a clock with no visible moving parts challenges the notion of progress. The clock and temporality have long been associated with the railway, which was seen as collapsing space into the time of a journey, establishing universal time through the structure of the timetable, promoting a vision of simultaneity between places, and embodying the concept of temporal progression. In *Mumbai Meri Jaan*, time itself appears arrested by the bombing. As with the crash that "occur[s] in 'machine time,' not in human time,"[68] the railway bombing seems to remove agency from the human and assign it to the machine. This is, of course, the very same machine that represented the promise of progress. Finally, the film renders the real-life memorial to the bombing, in which pedestrians and traffic halted for two minutes; this commemoration replicated the way that the bombs themselves obstructed the circulation of the city, as Vyjayanthi Rao argues in an essay on this day known as "Black

Friday."[69] Through these images of stasis, the film opens up modernity by challenging its paradigm of movement.

As the carriage itself is destroyed, modernity is symbolically over-turned, and the film uses the image of the accident—an image familiar to a global audience from pictures in the national and international press—to represent how the very framework of modernity has been ripped asunder. Michel de Certeau describes the integrity of the train carriage, in which the binary of inside and outside is maintained in the "insular bubble of panoptic and classifying power, a module of imprisonment that makes possible the production of an order, a closed and autonomous insularity—that is what can traverse space and make itself independent of local roots."[70] In *Mumbai Meri Jaan*, one extended scene of the wreckage frames the shot through the enormous holes torn through the side and roof of the train carriage. The shot visually structures the suffering through the fragmented whole of the former train as we focus on the bloody scene of wounded people and hear the sound of cries from survivors. The scene is a visual counterpart to the main plot of the film, which shows how the fabric of the society is also torn apart by a culture of terror that is experienced symboli-cally though technological objects like the scooter or the train. This mod-ern nationalism that emerges through terror is certainly shown negatively as begetting communal violence, a point made through one of the story lines about a Hindu man with increasingly fascist tendencies. Yet terror is also celebrated as a tool of the oppressed, as a coffee-*wallah* (a Hindi term designating occupation) manipulates the mass hysteria around the bombings with false warning calls that empty the malls of the rich. In *Mumbai Meri Jaan*, this terror, which is part of an increasingly familiar global iconography, also allows for a radical restructuring of power within the national community.

Mumbai's central railway station presents the most recent scene of real-world terror. In November 2008, gunmen opened fire in the Chhatrapati Shivaji Terminus, shooting randomly and killing fifty-eight at that location alone. As in the case of the 9/11 attacks in the United States, the targets of terrorist attacks like the Oberoi, the Taj, and Cafe Leopold were heavily symbolic, representing not just Western influence and the presence of Western tourists, but also a certain kind of Indian wealth in the new Mumbai. No site of violence was more symbolically overde-termined than the station that once bore the name of India's colonizing Queen Victoria and now memorializes a Maharashtrian leader elevated by the Hindu nationalist party Shiv Sena. The Chhatrapati Shivaji Terminus presented a public space in which to send a "loud message"; as a kind of spatial gateway connecting the traffic of the railway to that of the city, it also represents a kind of rational order that is the promise of modernity.[71] Three images from the station circulate in the press about that attack. One series of pictures show the young Ajmal Amir Kasab wandering with an assault rifle under the Victorian Gothic Revival architecture. Sebastian D'Souza's photographs document how the gunman passed through the porous spaces of the station, onto the platforms and in and out of trains. Another representation presented on video and by oral testimonies recalls the station announcer calmly directing passengers to safety.[72] These visual and verbal images destabilize and then restore the notion of the railway station as a place of order. The third image, of a travel area scattered with the bodies of the dead, undermines the premise of the station as a place of mobility, showing in its place a disturbingly static space.

As terror inscribes different constituencies like the colonial state, the nation, the city, or the global public, it also changes the meaning of those communities and challenges their sovereignty. In doing so, the phenomenon defines modernity in unstable ways. The sudden interruption that takes place with a murder, suicide, crash, or bombing presents a cultural preoccupation with destruction produced simultaneously with the narrative of development. Even as the image of terror on the train has turned cultural metaphor of the railway into a representation of modern fear, the cultural metaphor of the train has played a role constituting terror. In the next section, I consider why the train in particular becomes a locus for terror, reading it as both a textual symbol and an actively constructed social space.

Mobile Modernity

Why does the train—the Indian train in particular—take on this role as a mediating object of the symbolic aspects of terror? Two possible reasons lie in the unique construction of railway space. First, the space of the train invites a distinctive relation between the private and the public. In the space of the train, the everyday meets the ideology of public space; although the train represents the nation or the state, it is also an inhabited space. Terrorism exposes the constitutive presence of the private in the public space. A second reason lays in the porous nature of the railway space. The same openness that signifies the possibility of freedom also represents the potential for destruction.

David Harvey describes public space as contested, a place where the boundary between public and private is porous.[73] In the bombing of the *Samjhauta* Express, the train was a landmark connection symbolizing a new era of potential improved relations between India and Pakistan, but the frequent passengers' reasons for being on the train were usually more often personal than political. The prominent newspaper *Hindu* described the more than 1 million passengers who have used India-Pakistan rail service since it opened in 2004 as "in the main poor and lower-middle-class Muslims from families divided by the India-Pakistan border, but also Pakistani and Indian Hindus, groups of Sikh pilgrims, and a colourful array of part-time traffickers and traders who profit from the two countries' often-absurd trade regulations."[74] Terrorists attacked people from both countries, of both faiths, who had shared the dream of peaceful mobility. The commuters who were killed or injured in the Mumbai bombings were simply going about their daily business when the explosions exposed the lines that connected their seemingly contained lives to a much broader cultural geography. As Alex Houen argues, one of the most terrifying aspects of terror is its quotidian nature, its "capacity to disrupt the security of everydayness."[75] Terror exposes the relation between public meanings and private lives that defines the contradictory character of railway space. After all the riotous images of murder, suicide, massacres, and crashes, the final image of terror on the train is the abandoned suitcase sitting next to the commuter innocently reading the morning paper.

As a permeable and mobile space, the railway enables challenges and alterations to communities even as it helps foster them. Perhaps it is for this reason that the train makes such a likely space for the material expressions of terror, where the "dynamic but relatively stable set of implicit parameters that establish a group's sense of the actual and the possible and create a loose but definite sense of collective identity"[76] are remade. A train, which moves slowly at times, stops regularly, and has many entrances and exits, is more permeable than an airplane, which is hermetically sealed during flight. In India, people move on and off the train even while it is in motion—both paying passengers and fare dodgers jump on and off slow-moving trains. Passengers on crowded commuter lines cling to the outside of the train as they ride. Representations of the Indian railway characterize this openness as a cultural hallmark. Salman

Rushdie depicts the inflow of nonreserved or ticketless passengers into reserved spaces, presenting them as a kind of unruly corporeal force:

> And always, in all the trains in this story, there were these voices and these fists banging and pleading; in the Frontier Mail to Bombay and in all the expresses of the years; and it was always frightening, until at last I was the one on the outside, hanging on for dear life, and begging, "Hey, maharaj! Let me in, great sir."[77]

Within the permeable spaces represented by the train, positions may change and fortunes ultimately move. The permeable space is even more evident on the platforms, which open to the lines as well as to the entrance or station through which passengers proceed.

Railway officials have always attempted to regulate this porous nature of the train through procedures and spatial boundaries. When colonial officials in the 1860s feared potentially subversive assembly on the platform, they instituted entry passes. These passes compelled third-class ticketholders—a class in which 96 percent of Indians traveled—to stay off the platform in the open air or to congregate in waiting sheds until close to the time on their tickets.[78] Today, the government-run Indian Railways (IR) has taken other measures to control the entrances and exits of the carriages, including barred windows and padlocked doors. These procedures have contributed to the horrific outcome of violence; witnesses who rushed to the scene after the 2007 Samjhauta bombing will never forget watching children scrambling to get out of the burning carriage, trapped in their place of death.[79] After the 2006 Mumbai blasts, the Federal Railway Ministry attempted to ban nonpassengers from the platform. Closed-circuit televisions monitor the space, and metal detectors and bomb dogs patrol both the platform and carriages.[80]

The railway is a space that articulates a regularizing order, and this is in part why it lends itself to particular configurations of colonial, national, local, and global constituency. However, the unique nature of Indian railway space has allowed for challenges to dominant narratives that depend upon this ideal of the "rational utopia."[81] Micrological orders destabilize the order of this public space, enabling alterations. Railway space in India is a place for both the mobile and the itinerant—for those socially on the move and those with nowhere left to go. The open spaces of the station, platforms, and carriages that seem chaotic have a kind of symphonic order based in social practice. People in queues will rest as those before and after them save their places; a red-coated porter quickly moves to secure his fare's place on a train; snack-*wallahs* move efficiently from window to window to make the most of a short stopover; a passenger lingers with a *chai* (tea) on the side of his train, swinging back aboard the now-moving train with enviable precision just as the cement platform drops from under his feet; and women carry vegetables to prepare their evening meals on the journey home. Even for the nontravelers who make up the inner city of the railway station, the space offers invisible subeconomies and even educational opportunities. The editor of a suburban newspaper described the vendors who traveled on the Mumbai Western Line selling food, drink, toiletries, and trinkets as the pulse that keeps the city going.[82] In the state of Orissa, there are fourteen Train Platform Schools for the children who live in concrete cul-de-sacs and work for pennies in the station.[83] The Indian railway platform space is multitudinous, but it has its own structures.

Many writers and filmmakers, both Indian and non-Indian, have found the image of the Indian railway platform and its subeconomies compelling in its sheer excess. Traditionally, the railway station becomes a portal to (or from) another world; in the process, it gains its own imaginative character. European writers traditionally imagined the train and the railway station as a space of reflection on movement itself and a "spatial gateway"[84] that provides a transition to a different kind of place. Postcolonial writers show how the Indian railway stations have an excess and a disorder to them that challenges that ideal; in Nair's *Ladies Coupé*, the protagonist muses that all Indian platforms look alike: "The garbage bins stuffed with litter. The cigarette butts. A crumpled plastic coffee cup. A chocolate wrapper. A banana peel. The pink and green plastic bags caught between the railway tracks, ballooning with the breeze, deflating in stillness. The once white but now silvery-grey stakes fencing the station in."[85] For some writers, such as Rushdie in *Midnight's Children*, this chaos becomes its own form of magic:

> A relay runner at the end of his lap, [Doctor Aziz] stood wreathed in smoke and comic-book vendors and the confusion of peacock-feather fans and hot snacks and the whole lethargic hullabaloo of squatting porters and plaster animals on trolleys as the train picked up speed and headed for the capital city, accelerating into the next lap of the race.[86]

Colonial writers saw Indians misusing the railway space by inhabiting it with their daily rituals and bodily presence; one sees in a representation like that of Rushdie an impulse to claim that aspect as a distinctive cultural quality of the Indian trains. The traveler here joins the multitudinous space, displacing his movement onto the train.

Danny Boyle captures this permeable space and subeconomy in his Oscar-winning 2009 film *Slumdog Millionaire*, in which the Indian railway features prominently. In one scene, the two young brothers escape the threat of maiming by leaping on a departing train and traveling around on its rooftop. The fact that the boys are on the roof reinforces a sense of sovereignty, for they are free from even the structures of paid, confined travel.[87] The scene of the boys traveling on top also grasps a cultural ideal—the roof of a train is recognizably Indian, the dominion of an underclass like the migrant laborers memorably shown dancing on top of a train in the popular Hindi film *Dil Se*, the fantasy space of soaring love in Hindi romance films like *Zamaane Ko Dikhana Hai* (directed by Nazir Hussain; 1981), and the last resort for the refugees in Khuswant Singh's *Train to Pakistan*. In the experience of the boys traveling around India, *Slumdog Millionaire* renders the nation through the panoramic vista of travel; the boys grasp their own nation as they travel out from their microcosm in Mumbai and through different kinds of geographies. Although the exhilarating music of Sri Lankan–British singer M.I.A. provides a catharsis for the tension produced during the boy's captivity, the experience of riding on trains also shows the relative disempowerment of this kind of rail travel. The boys belong to that subeconomy that sells trinkets to passengers and steals to survive (a national parallel to the more global narrator in M.I.A.'s song, who "got visas in my name"). They must stay awake in order not to fall off the train, and when they are finally caught, their journey must come to an end.

The mobility represented by the train does not end when the boys are thrown off, however, for the train moves on the margins of many of the frames, skirting scenes of poverty and exploitation. In *Slumdog Millionaire*, the railway spaces that the audience sees are dirty and crowded, and they have a kind of gritty realism that represents class as much as culture. The permeable space allows for movement in and out of the spaces of privilege and poverty as the tracks suture together the two worlds. The main railway station in particular represents such a site. The hero comes out of the slums to rendezvous at the "VT" with the heroine who emerges from her gated compound: He waits at the Chhatrapati Shivaji Terminus (often still called the "VT" or Victoria Terminus) at 5 p.m. (railway time) each day. As I argued in chapter 5, the railway space is a place where people may step momentarily outside their social structures and where illicit love may flourish. At the film's resolution, the lovers meet on the porous spaces of this platform, with trains moving back and forth. Boyle, who also directed the film *Trainspotting*, moves the transnational metaphor of the railway from Scotland to India by representing all railway stations as places of transformation. Yet he adds a new kind of class consciousness to that image in this Indian context by showing the bottom of this famous colonial and national icon, the Victoria Terminus, rather than its vast hall or majestic exterior. Just as the tunnels open to tracks that cut through the life of the slum, this underside of the building with its gothic arches opens out to the "slumdog" world. The same porousness that gives rise to imaginary possibility in Doyle's *Slumdog Millionaire* also allowed for the terror that surrounded the Chhatrapati Shivaji Terminus in November 2008.

The Indian Railway as Cultural Metaphor

This chapter has grappled with the way terror as a cultural process converges on the image of the train, both in texts and in the real world. The discussion of this phenomenon has crossed back and forth over the imaginative history of the Indian railway that has been the focus of this book. I have argued that representations of the Indian train offer a means of seeing how competing cultural influences meet inside today's global mobile spaces, formulating a modernity overdetermined by its colonial and national histories. The Indian railway's particular history as an inherited legacy pushed to the fore contradictions embedded in a colonial modernity. This book does not argue for an essential cultural distinction that separates Indian trains from European or U.S. ones; rather, it inventories a series of conjunctures coming out of a particular history and represented in dynamic cultural and spatial forms. It reads these forms to reveal how mobility, a hallmark of modernity, has reconfigured the modern in unstable ways.

Since the colonial period in India, the railway has been idealized as a "rational utopia"[88]—a moving box in which differences of race, class, religion, or gender could be amalgamated under a civic, secular, and public order. Beginning in 1853, officials, writers, and visual artists used the rhetoric of the train to elaborate aspects of colonial rule. They posited machines "as the most reliable measure of humankind,"[89] turning a particular history of industrial technological development into a universal standard for calculating cultural merit. Colonial writers and artists summoned the image of the train to justify the colonial presence; in the process, they pitted the train against aspects of Indian culture, including Hindu structures of caste and practices regulating the mobility of women. Colonial discourse made the space of the train into an arena for cultural reform, arguing that Indians would become emancipated through access to the railway.

Even as colonial writers and artists sought to bring Indians into the railway world, they produced other descriptions and images that contradicted this impulse. Travel writers denigrated Indians for challenging the secularization of railway space by performing religious rituals and for domesticating it by traveling with large families, carrying cooking implements, and washing clothes in the public taps. Beneath these representations lay a fear that Indians, far from becoming assimilated through the public space, would instead change the very nature of that space. The character of the English men and women who traveled through India was seemingly at risk, for as memoirs and images show, unbuttoned Europeans were doing unseemly things in Indian train carriages, actions that were "a little out of place in general society."[90]

Narratives that established the railway as a means of enlightenment established binary divisions between European and Indian, or public and private. Yet these same narratives also undid these boundaries. Colonial writers and artists ritualized the scene of Indians first apprehending the train as a process based in superstition: In their representations, enlightenment worked not through logic but through the sublime. Moreover, although they used the narrative of the railway to promote the ideal of universality, writers and artists secured notions of difference, especially cultural difference, into the colonial discourse.

Literary and visual texts worked to mediate the contradictions between rational universalism and cultural particularity. Writers like Rudyard Kipling and Flora Annie Steel attempted to contain aspects of India—the religious, the domestic, and the bodily—that destabilized the narrative of the "rational utopia."[91] In their work, however, modernity in the form of this technology only became a staging ground for tensions between homogeneity and difference. By writing difference into the railway with what I have called counternarratives of modernity, Kipling and Steel opened the door of the moving box, representing a colonial modernity in conflict with itself. Far from being a rational utopia, this modernity was private as well as public, religious as well as secular, corporeal as well as mechanical, and Indian as well as European.

Colonial writers like Kipling and Steel might have presented those contradictions in their writing, but they never mobilized them to challenge colonial rule. However, from the late nineteenth century until the 1930s, Indian nationalists, their liberal British sympathizers, and Indian spiritualists did confront the terms and even the existence of colonialism by focusing on the very same emblem that had justified that rule. They seized that image of the train to challenge the culture of colonialism, producing another counternarrative of modernity. One group of social critics produced "an insurgent grammar of political economy"[92] that decried the way that the train had been used in India. Political leaders like Dadabhai Naoroji and writers like engineer Sir Arthur Cotton detailed the uneven terms of railway investment, the role of the railway in famine and environmental devastation, the discriminatory practices against Indians in railway employment, and the humiliating conditions for them during train travel. In the process, these social critics transformed the symbol of the railway from one of liberation to one of enslavement, extortion, bereavement, and humiliation. They challenged the idea that machines were the measure of civilization and instead offered a different calibration of success for the colonial enterprise. Their writings shifted the focus away from a development discourse based in economic growth or cultural assimilation and instead placed the emphasis on the human impact of the railway. This group defied the very premise of colonial railway discourse by showing that mobility was not the same as emancipation.

Another group made up of Indian spiritual leaders drew inspiration from the writings of these social critics, but instead of producing a political economic critique, they turned to the moral authority of Hindu tradition to challenge the economic and political aspects of the railway. Writers like Swami Vivekananda (Narendranath Datta), Aurobindo Ghose, Mohandas Gandhi, and Rabindranath Tagore saw the railway as representing a mechanized way of being that was culturally alien and morally corrupt. They exalted nature over the machine in their writings. Like the social critics, the spiritualists transformed the symbolic meaning of the railway, describing it as a symbol of sin and an emblem of slavery. This group produced an important historical narrative of modernity: a critical vision of the modern that was rooted in religion but grounded in a secular historical materialist critique of technological development. Although they contested European colonial culture, the spiritualists wrote from within the discourse of modernity, producing not a traditional vision but a counternarrative that cast modernity's inherent tensions into relief.

During the period of Partition around India's 1947 independence, those tensions took on a violent form as trains filled with refugees were attacked in sectarian violence. Once again, one might view those conflicts through the cultural metaphor of the railway. Since the colonial period, the "machine ensemble"[93] of carriage and tracks has presented a material emblem of the Indian nation as it has helped constitute that nation through the movement of goods and people. Furthermore, in its ideal, the railway space offers an order based on strict binaries between interior and exterior. Refugee trains were seen as part of a state space that would supersede the violence and communal identities that appeared to be local. However, the train merely reflected the conflicts taking place in the larger nation, in which religious affiliations gained primacy even as secular nationalists fought for India and Pakistan. The train became a place of communal identification (and thus death), as a train to Pakistan and all who were in it were marked as Muslim, and one to India similarly seen as Hindu.

Just as Indians in the early twentieth century had changed the image of the train from its colonial origins, Partition writers transformed the "rational utopia" into an uncanny image of a death train. They highlighted the permeable boundaries of the train that exposed the falsity of the binaries between interior and exterior. They showed how the violence undid the clocks of modernity and reoriented a collective gaze toward an imagined communal past. In the process of creating these counternarratives of modernity, these writers rethought modernity in ways that exposed its violent contradictions and in ways that anticipated the contemporary terror described in this chapter.

The train has continued to present dominant narratives of the secular nation even after the period of Partition demonstrated the paradoxes of that construction. Postcolonial writers and artists in the 1950s and 1960s used the image of the train to articulate rural and urban identities inside a nation undergoing modernization programs. Such representations were presented not only in written and visual texts, but also through the dynamics of space. The image of the train became a way to show the complexities of rural as well as urban identities within a period of national development. For writers and filmmakers like R. K. Narayan, Satyajit Ray, and

Phanishwar Nath Renu, the railway became emblematic of a relationship between rural areas and cities. They elaborated the connections between both places and the nation, exposing the differentiated landscape of modernity. These writers and filmmakers depicted mobility as a form of consciousness, delineating a subjectivity of traffic that was both empowering and alienating.

Filmmakers in the 1970s and 1980s used popular Hindi cinema to represent the way that conceptions of modernity in India brought conflicting images of women in the public space. Colonial writers had promoted the idea of women riding on the train as a means of emancipating Indians from tradition through the increased mobility of women. To a certain extent, their program was successful, but the movement of women into this kind of public space had unexpected consequences. In the late nineteenth century, Indian women traveling on the railway were marked as sexually available and were victims of harassment ranging from verbal innuendo to outright rape. Twentieth-century popular Hindi films have represented the legacy of those patriarchal notions that gave rise to violence by showing scenes of women taunted on the platform or propositioned in the carriage. These same films have also reproduced these ideas, because they rarely present such overtures critically; in fact, they even often rehabilitate what might be deemed harassment using a narrative of romance—the man who traps a woman in the train carriage with his advances becomes her love interest. Despite their questionable politics, these Bollywood films present the train as a place where women might express desire outside of family-bound social structures. In doing so, they show how railway space has indeed been liberating to women in unexpected ways.

Colonial discourse promoted the railway as a way to achieve modernity; in this moving box, cultural, racial, and historical differences would be amalgamated into a civic, secular, and public order. Although the train did continue to symbolize the secular space of the nation, it also became a place where differences were exposed. This book has provided site-based, historical readings of modernity that show that in India, the imagination of mobile space became a way of articulating conflicting visions of nation, gender, religion, or class that constitute the modern. It turned finally to a scene prominent in the contemporary media and pertinent to contemporary global consciousness: Terrorism on the train highlights the contradictory character of this modern space as a place where identity emerges and modernity's binaries are challenged on symbolic ground.

Tracking Modernity has explored the cultural metaphor of the railway as a primary emblem of India's modernity by looking at the ways that this symbol has reinforced and undermined dominant narratives of the modern. It interprets as part of the same metaphor material practices and discursive operations, arguing that the social relations of labor and practices of travel offer a counterpart to a body of railway literature that includes literary and visual culture as well as official documents. Although the cultural metaphor of the railway functioned in India to secure dominant versions of modernity like the ideal of a technological, secular, and public order, one may find in both textual images and in spatial geographies alternative narratives that counter those dominant visions. This book has shown that the broader symbolic order of the train mobilized narratives to uncertain ends; one may read moments of that indeterminacy to expose the conflicting narratives that constitute modernity.

Acknowledgments

I AM GRATEFUL TO THE many Carnegie Mellon students who have inspired me in our conversations about modernity and postcolonial studies. Some of these students worked directly on this book; my thanks to David Cerniglia, Teresa Pershing, and Lauren Sealy for valuable research assistance. Nate Atkinson provided outstanding editorial help; Ross MacConnell pushed me to clarify my prose and sharpen my thinking with his meticulous edits. Jeff Hinkelman helped me track down the films for this book. Thora Brylowe and Elizabeth Heffelfinger offered boundless intellectual and emotional support.

I could not have imagined a more supportive group of colleagues than the Literary and Cultural Studies group at Carnegie Mellon: Kathy Newman, Jeff Williams, Jon Klancher, David Shumway, Peggy Knapp, Richard Purcell, and Kristina Straub read parts of the manuscript, helped me write my book proposal, and gave me unending respect and enthusiasm. I am also grateful to other faculty members of the departments of English at Carnegie Mellon University and Kenyon College for their interest and encouragement. Andreea Ritivoi merits particular credit for reading my work with her characteristic enthusiasm and rigor; Danielle Wetzel also always gave gracious, smart advice. My former colleague Michael Witmore deserves special recognition as well, for his consistently intense engagement with my work taught me to trust my own intellectual ambition at a critical time.

My support at Carnegie Mellon has also been institutional: I am grateful to former English department head David Kaufer, current head Chris Neuwirth, and Dean John Lehoczky for funding and otherwise validating this work. The Falk Grant for the Development of Faculty provided monies for travel to India and the United Kingdom; a generous grant from the Berkman family enabled me to acquire the images in this book.

Outside my university, Susan Stanford Friedman, Laura Chrisman, Amitava Kumar, Sangeeta Ray, Amardeep Singh, Ceren Ozselcuk, and

Goldie Osuri have been champions of my work. They have inspired me with their own writings and with their conscientious citizenship within the academic community. Ian Kerr generously read and commented on the full manuscript, giving me the gift of his extraordinary knowledge about Indian railways. My anonymous readers at the University of Minnesota Press helped me shape this book, inspiring me as much with their criticism as their words of praise. My editor, Richard Morrison, and the rest of the editorial board at the University of Minnesota Press made the publication of this book possible at a key moment in my career; the editorial and production staff at the University of Minnesota Press and diacriTech have helped bring this work to fruition. Susan McClung deserves special thanks for her careful copyediting. My thanks also go to Dave Prout for excellent work on the index.

This book grew out of a piece of my dissertation. My advisor, R. Radhakrishanan, has continued to be a source of generosity and generative thought. I also offer thanks to my other committee members at the University of Massachusetts Amherst—Laura Doyle, Stephen Clingman, and Patrick Mensah—who shaped me as a young scholar. Henry Louis Gates gave me great advice early on about writing. Philip Kozel read my work countless times and has consistently been there to answer my urgent scholarly questions.

Thanks to my mother, Ida, to my brothers Matthew, Eric, and Mark, and to my sisters Luiza and Jean for their continuing support for my career. I am especially grateful to my brother Newton, his wife, Renee, and their children, Morgan and Jordan, for opening their house to me on my trips to London. Thanks also to *mashi* Bhasin for her hospitality in Delhi. My father is remembered here for his support and for first introducing me to the Indian train that inspired him on his trips home from college.

For several years on a daily basis, my husband, Roy, has given me the emotional and logistical support to complete this book; for this, he deserves gratitude—and a vacation. Finally, I thank my daughter Bianca, with her ever-present joy, and the little one, Julian, who was still a work in progress when I wrote this, for generously sharing their mama's time.

Notes

Preface

1. D'Souza, "A gunman walks through the Chatrapathi Sivaji [sic] Terminal railway station in Mumbai, India," Wednesday, November 26, 2008. (AP Photo/ *Mumbai Mirror*, Sebastian D'Souza; #5.)

2. *Slumdog Millionaire* premiered in August 2008 at the Telluride film festival in Colorado and had a limited release in the United States in November 2008 before its general release in January 2009 in the United Kingdom and later in the United States; it won the Oscar for Best Picture in 2009.

3. Hobsbawm, *Industry and Empire*, 89.

4. Tagore, "Railway Station," 114.

5. The geographical space designated by the term "India" shifts in this book depending on the historical period described. The analysis of the colonial period refers to the broader area of South Asia that is now part of Pakistan and Bangladesh. Discussions of postcolonial space are focused on post-Partition India. Contested regions are specified as such.

6. Thorner, *Investment in Empire*, 45.

7. Ibid., 47.

8. Headrick, *The Tools of Empire*, 182.

9. Davis, Wilburn, and Robinson, *Railway Imperialism*, 3.

10. See Kerr, "On the Move: Circulating Labor in Pre-Colonial, Colonial, and Post-Colonial India," 85–109.

11. L. Marx, *The Machine in the Garden*, 192.

12. See Deloche, *Transport and Communications in India Prior to Steam Locomotion.*

13. Davidson, *The Railways of India*, 1.

14. Markovits, Pouchepadass, and Subrahmanyam, Introduction to *Society and Circulation*, 18.

15. Paterson, "The Paterson Diaries," 23 November 1770.

16. See Meyer, "Labour Circulation between Sri Lanka and South India in Historical Perspective."

17. Visram, *Asians in Britain: 400 Years of History*, 52–53.

18. See Bury, "Novel Spaces, Transitional Moments."

19. Kerr, "On the Move," 89.

20. See C. Bayly, *Empire and Information.*

21. Marcovitz, Pouchepadass, and Subrahmanyam, Introduction to *Society and Circulation*, 8.

22. Kerr, "On the Move," 100, 92.

23. Goswami, *Producing India*, 108.

24. De Certeau, *The Practice of Everyday Life*, 110.

25. Clifford, *Routes*, 26.

26. See, for example, Pratt, *Imperial Eyes*; Behdad, *Belated Travelers*, Grewal, *Home and Harem*; Kaplan, *Questions of Travel*; Simpson, *Trafficking Subjects.*

27. Davis, *Late Victorian Holocausts*, 317.

28. T. Roy, *The Economic History of India*, 13–14.

29. Kaplan, *Questions of Travel*, 3.

30. See Kerr, *Building the Railways of the Raj*, especially chapter 4.

31. Clifford, *Routes*, 3.

32. *The Great Indian Railway*, directed by William Livingston.

33. For an anthology sampling some of this writing, see Bond, *The Penguin Book of Indian Railway Stories*. For visual images of the colonial railway, see Satow and Desmond, *Railways of the Raj*; Ellis, *Railway Art.*

34. Works are originally in English unless otherwise noted. English translations are occasionally used in the discussion, with the translator noted in the citation when available. These translations provided here shape interpretations of the prose, style, content, and even politics of the original works, but they are included here in the belief that they convey important representations of the Indian railway to a readership in English.

Introduction

1. Habermas, *The Philosophical Discourse of Modernity*, 16.

2. Lazarus, *Nationalism and Cultural Practice in the Postcolonial World*, 18.

3. Foucault, "What Is Enlightenment?" 39.

4. Tomlinson, *Globalization and Culture*, 34.

5. Taylor, "Modern Social Imaginaries," 121.

6. Kaplan, *Questions of Travel*, 117.

7. T. Mitchell, Introduction to *Questions of Modernity*, xiii.

8. Prakash, *Another Reason*, 234.

9. Gilroy, *The Black Atlantic*, 17.

10. T. Mitchell, Introduction to *Questions of Modernity*, xiii.

11. Gaonkar, "On Alternative Modernities," 17.

12. Cooper, *Colonialism in Question*, 131.

13. Ibid., 147.

14. Gupta, *Postcolonial Developments*, 36.

15. T. Mitchell, Introduction to *Questions of Modernity*, xii, xi.

16. Ibid., xvi.

17. Gupta, *Postcolonial Developments*, 36.

18. Bear, "Traveling Modernity," 1.

19. Simpson, *Trafficking Subjects*, xxii.

20. Thorner, *Investment in Empire*, viii.

21. Thorner, "The Pattern of Railway Development in India," 85.

22. Ibid., 94.

23. Ibid., 83.

24. Ibid., 93.

25. Ahuja, "'The Bridge-Builders,'" 95.

26. Thorner, "The Pattern of Railway Development in India," 91.

27. Kerr, *Building the Railways of the Raj*, 4–5.

28. Railway Report, 1862–63, 27; quoted in Kerr, *Building the Railways of the Raj*, 4.

29. Danvers, *Indian Railways*, 27.

30. Kerr, Introduction to *Railways in Modern India*, 10.

31. Dalhousie, "Minute by Lord Dalhousie to the Court of Directors," II-25.

32. Ibid., II-25.

33. Arnold, *Science, Technology, and Medicine in Colonial India*, 121–22.

34. Vicajee, *Political and Social Effects of Railways in India*, 19.

35. Ibid., 21.

36. Anderson, *Imagined Communities: Reflections on the Origin and Spread of Nationalism*, 37.

37. Mitchell, *The Wheels of Ind*, 34.

38. Ibid., 34.

39. Ibid., 34.

40. Gardiner, "Indian Railways," 23.

41. Jagga, "Colonial Railwaymen and British Rule," 104.

42. Clifford, *Routes*, 2.

43. Freeman, *Railways and the Victorian Imagination*, 19.

44. Robbins, *The Railway Age*, 50.

45. Schivelbusch, *The Railway Journey*, 73.

46. Smith, *The Works of the Rev. Sydney Smith*, 670.

47. Giddens, Foreword to *NowHere: Space, Time, and Modernity*, xi.

48. Metcalf, *Ideologies of the Raj*, x.

49. Arnold, *Science, Technology, and Medicine in Colonial India*, 5.

50. Prakash, *Another Reason*, 174.

51. Dalhousie, *Parliamentary Papers*, 16.

52. De Certeau, *The Practice of Everyday Life*, 110.

53. Prakash, *Another Reason*, 3.

54. Headrick, *The Tools of Empire*, 182.

55. Karl Marx, "The Future Results of the British Rule in India," 33.

56. Ibid., 36.

57. Danvers, *Indian Railways*, 7.

58. W. D. S. [pseud.], "The Night Mail-Train in India," 405.

59. "Modes of Travelling in India," 284.

60. Wheeler, Introduction to *The Travels of a Hindoo to Various Parts of Bengal and Upper India*, xii.

61. Chunder, *The Travels of a Hindoo to Various Parts of Bengal and Upper India*, 141.

62. Ibid., 141.

63. *Railway Times*, January 15, 1853, 59.

64. Marx, "The Future Results of the British Rule in India," 36.

65. S. Bayly, *Caste, Society, and Politics in India from the Eighteenth Century to the Modern Age*, 98.

66. Ibid., 97.

67. Kaye, *A History of the Sepoy War in India 1857–1858*, 190–91.

68. Metcalf, *Ideologies of the Raj*, 36, 135.

69. Wheeler, Introduction to *The Travels of a Hindoo to Various Parts of Bengal and Upper India*, xx.

70. Danvers, *Indian Railways*, 28.

71. Davidson, *The Railways of India*, 3.

72. W. D. S. [pseud.], "The Night Mail-Train in India," 405.

73. Goswami, *Producing India*, 108.

74. Simpson, *Trafficking Subjects*, xxii.

75. Indo-American [pseud.], "Railways in India and America," 120.

76. A. Chatterjee, "Traffic by Railway," 192–93.

77. Freeman, *Railways and the Victorian Imagination*, 109–16.

78. Kerr, "Reworking a Popular Religious Practice," 314, 316.

79. Goswami, *Producing India*, 120.

80. Jenkins, Bengal Proceedings, June 21, 1869.

81. Mookerjee, May 20, 1869, letter to Magistrate and Collector of Burdwan.

82. Bear, *Lines of the Nation*, 52–53.

83. Mookerjee, May 20, 1869, letter to Magistrate and Collector of Burdwan.

84. Bear, *Lines of the Nation*, 135–37.

85. Ibid., 151–53.

86. Ibid., 9.

87. Ibid., 9.

88. Masters, *Bhowani Junction*, 249.

1. The Permanent Way

1. Richards, *Rudyard Kipling: A Bibliography*, 92.

2. "An inside view from one of the earliest first class carriages," 109.

3. Mrs. Shoosmith [M. C. Reid], "A Railway Soliloquy."

4. Ibid.

5. Thomas R. Metcalf, *Ideologies of the Raj*, x.

6. De Certeau, *The Practice of Everyday Life*, 110.

7. Ibid., 110.

8. Mitchell, *The Wheels of Ind*, 21.

9. Mrs. Shoosmith [M. C. Reid], "A Railway Soliloquy."

10. "Honeymooning In India," in *The Ladies' Treasury*, 320.

11. McClintock, *Imperial Leather*, 33.

12. De Certeau, *The Practice of Everyday Life*, 111.

13. Metcalf, *Ideologies of the Raj*, 66.

14. Pratt, *Imperial Eyes*, 4.

15. De Certeau uses the term "slender blade" to refer to the liminal space between the inside and outside of the railway carriage. *The Practice of Everyday Life*, 112.

16. "An Indian railway station (on the Bombay and Tannah railway)," in the *Illustrated London News*, 208.

17. Trevelyan, *The Competition Wallah*, 24.

18. Ibid., 28.

19. Furnell, *From Madras to Delhi and Back via Bombay*, 123.

20. Ibid., 124.

21. Mitchell, *The Wheels of Ind*, 21.

22. Goswami, *Producing India*, 117.

23. Ibid., 119.

24. Trevelyn, *The Competition Wallah*, 5.

25. Furnell, *From Madras to Delhi and Back via Bombay*, 124.

26. Mitchell, *The Wheels of Ind*, 21.

27. Trevelyn, *The Competition Wallah*, 25.

28 Ibid., 27.

29. Ibid., 27.

30. Furnell, *From Madras to Delhi and Back via Bombay*, 124.

31. Forster, *A Passage to India*, 143.

32. Ibid., 141–42.

33. Ibid., 150.

34. Ibid., 150.

35. Ibid., 178.

36. Kerr, "Reworking a Popular Religious Practice," 304–27.

37. "Case 56," in *The Journal of Indian Art*, 23.

38. Wheeler, Introduction to *The Travels of a Hindoo to Various Parts of Bengal and Upper India*, xii.

39. "Modes of Travelling in India," in the *Illustrated London News*, September 19, 1863.

40. Chunder, *The Travels of a Hindoo to Various Parts of Bengal and Upper India*, 139.

41. Ibid., 140.

42. Ibid., 161.

43. Foucault, "Of Other Spaces," 24.

44. Said, *Culture and Imperialism*, 134.

45. Prakash, *Another Reason*, 167.

46. Kipling, "The Bridge-Builders," 206.

47. Ibid., 221.

48. Ibid., 226.

49. Ibid., 227.

50. Sullivan, *Narratives of Empire*, 15.

51. Ibid., 118.

52. Parry, *Delusions and Discoveries*, 228.

53. Ibid., 229.

54. Ibid., 98.

55. Kipling, "The Bridge-Builders," 218.

56. Kipling, *Kim*, 249.

57. Ibid., 74–83; 188–90; 250–251.

58. Ibid., 189–90.

59. Ibid., 249.

60. Ibid., 75.

61. Ibid., 76.

62. Ibid., 74.

63. Ibid., 79.

64. Ibid., 331.

65. Ibid., 331.

66. Ibid., 332.

67. Moore-Gilbert, *Kipling and "Orientalism,"* 123.

68. Steel, "In the Permanent Way," 144.

69. Ibid., 144.

70. Ibid., 157.

71. Ibid., 155.

72. Ibid., 159.

73. Ibid., 142.

2. The Machine of Empire

1. "First Impressions and First Impulses of Railway Traveling," *Bengal Hurkaru and India Gazette*, 183.

2. Stephenson, "Report upon the Practicality and Advantages of the Introduction of Railways into British India," 37.

3. Osborne, "India Under Lord Lytton," 554.

4. Of course, many of the so-called spiritualists were also social critics. The rough term "social critics" is used here to focus on the arena of reform that preoccupied this first group of writers.

5. Goswami, *Producing India*, 128.

6. Roy, *The Economic History of India, 1857–1947*, 13.

7. Dutt, *The Economic History of India in the Victorian Age*, 174–75.

8. Davis, *Late Victorian Holocausts*, 332.

9. Naoroji, "Memorandum on Mr. Danver's Papers of 28 June 1880 and 4th January 1879," 457.

10. Frank, "The Development of Underdevelopment," 159.

11. Joshi, *Writings and Speeches*, 671.

12. The lack of this development, according to some historians, constituted a bias or strategy on the part of the British to keep India an agricultural country dependent on the industrial resources of Britain. See Pacey, *Technology in World Civilization*, 147.

13. Joshi, *Writings and Speeches*, 687–88.

14. Davis, *Late Victorian Holocausts*, 317.

15. Goswami, *Producing India*, 104.

16. Roy, *The Economic History of India*, 13.

17. Ibid., 62.

18. B. Chandra, *The Rise and Growth of Economic Nationalism in India*, 180.

19. G. K. Gokhale, quoted in B. Chandra, *The Rise and Growth of Economic Nationalism in India*, 171.

20. *Dainik-o-Samachar Chandrika*, May 31, 1891; *Indu Prakash*, November 30, 1904. Quoted in B. Chandra, *The Rise and Growth of Economic Nationalism in India*, 181.

21. Tilak, quoted in B. Chandra, *The Rise and Growth of Economic Nationalism in India*, 180. Tilak would otherwise fit among the spiritualists, but his comment is included here as part of this particular discussion on the public sphere.

22. The publishing of Kipling's "The Bridge-Builders" provides a notable exception.

23. Naoroji, "Memorandum on Mr. Danver's Papers of 28 June 1880 and 4th January 1879," 457.

24. Steel, "In the Permanent Way," 144.

25. G. S. Iyer, address to the Madras Provincial Conference at Madura, May 22, 1901. Quoted in B. Chandra, *The Rise and Growth of Economic Nationalism in India*, 182.

26. Gardiner, "Indian Railways," 23–24; Danvers, *Indian Railways*, 6. The British had promoted the railways as protection against famine and as a way to improve the

economic position of the Indian people by increasing domestic and international trade and expanding agricultural and mineral resources.

27. Davis, *Late Victorian Holocausts*, 26.

28. Cotton, *The Madras Famine*, 5.

29. Nightingale, "Letters to the Editor," in *Illustrated London News*, June 29, 1877.

30. "An Indian Stock and Railway Shareholder" in *The Times*, March 25, 1861.

31. Digby, *"Prosperous" British India, a Revelation from Official Records*, 140.

32. Davis, *Late Victorian Holocausts*, 35–36.

33. Nash, *The Great Famine and Its Causes*, 165.

34. Scientific writers argued that embankments stopped the flow of water, causing drought and creating the stagnant water that fostered the conditions for malaria. A 1910 article in the *Modern Review* describes the effect of embankments in creating breeding grounds for mosquitoes as well as the role of the train in the spread of the disease. A Votary of Science [pseud], "Malaria and Its Remedy," 522.

35. Cotton, *Extracts*, 309–27.

36. Indo-American [pseud.], "Railways in India and America," 118.

37. Kelsall and Ghose, 14 September 1844, 37.

38. Danvers, *Indian Railways*, 21.

39. Kerr, *Building the Railways of the Raj: 1850–1900*, 168.

40. Jagga, "Colonial Railwaymen and British Rule, 1919–1922," 107.

41. Kerr, *Building the Railways of the Raj*, 156–58.

42. Ibid., 161–62.

43. Jagga, "Colonial Railwaymen and British Rule," 108.

44. Kerr, *Building the Railways of the Raj*, 166.

45. A. Chatterjee, "Traffic by Railway," 191–92.

46. Ibid., 192–93.

47. Jagga, "Colonial Railwaymen and British Rule," 106.

48. Indo-American [pseud.], *Railways in India and America*, 120.

49. Bear, *Lines of the Nation: Indian Railway Workers, Bureaucracy, and the Intimate Historical Self*, 55.

50. Ibid., 56–57.

51. *Sahachar*, April 30, 1884; cited in B. Chandra, *The Rise and Growth of Economic Nationalism in India*, 181.

52. Indo-American [pseud.], *Railways in India and America*, 118.

53. Jagga, "Colonial Railwaymen and British Rule, 106.

54. Bose, "The Spirit and Form of an Ethical Polity," 131.

55. Nandy, *The Illegitimacy of Nationalism*, 1–2.

56. For another discussion of this aspect of their work, see Adas, "Contested Hegemony: The Great War and the Afro-Asian Assault on the Civilizing Mission Ideology," 31–63.

57. Vivekananda, "Our Present Social Problems," 489–90.

58. Ibid.

59. Dalton, *Indian Ideal of Freedom*, 96.

60. Heehs, "The Centre of the Religious Life of the World," 75.

61. Ghose, *The Life Divine*, 1247.

62. Nandy, *The Intimate Enemy*, 85.

63. Ghose, *War and Self-Determination*, 4.

64. Ibid., 3.

65. Gandhi, "Gandhi's Letter to H. S. L. Polak," *Gandhi*, 130.

66. Gandhi, "The Condition of India (cont.): Railways," in *Gandhi*, 47.

67. Marx, "The Future Results of the British Rule in India," 34.

68. Gandhi, "Machinery," in *Gandhi*, 107

69. Gandhi, "Gandhi's Letter to Lord Ampthill," in *Gandhi*, 135.

70. Gandhi, "The Morals of Machinery," in *Gandhi*, 761.

71. Gandhi, "Supplementary Writings," in *Gandhi*, 167.

72. Ibid., 168.

73. Young, *Postcolonialism*, 320.

74. P. Chatterjee, *Nationalist Thought and the Colonial World*, 93.

75. Ibid., 90.

76. Ibid., 113.

77. Ibid., 96.

78. Boehmer, *Empire, the National, and the Postcolonial*, 51.

79. Michael Adas argues: "Unlike Gandhi, Tagore did not reject the industrial civilization of Europe and North America per se, but concluded that if it was to endure, the West must draw on the learning of the 'east' which had so much to share." "Contested Hegemony," 53.

80. Tagore, "The Call of Truth," 423.

81. Adas, "Contested Hegemony," 53.

82. Tagore, *The Waterfall*, 12.

83. Ibid., 12.

84. Ibid., 7.

85. Ibid., 6.

86. Ibid., 7.

87. Ibid., 28.

88. Tagore, *Red Oleanders.*, 26.

89. Ibid., 242.

90. Ibid., 113.

91. Young, *Postcolonialism*, 317.

92. Arnold, *Gandhi: Profiles in Power*, 66, 54.

93. Ibid., 330. Ironically, Gandhi used the railway extensively in his political campaigns. See Y. P. Anand, *Mahatma Gandhi and the Railways*.

94. Adas, "Contested Hegemony," 52.

95. Adas, *Machines as the Measure of Men*, 395–96.

96. Benjamin, "Theses on the Philosophy of History: IX," 257–58.

97. Goswami, *Producing India*, 128.

98. Tagore, "Railway Station," 114.

99. Ibid., 114.

100. Ibid., 114.

101. Ibid., 114.

102. Radice, "Notes," 168.

103. Tagore, "Railway Station," 115.

104. Ibid., 114.

105. Gandhi, *Gandhi*, 107.

106. Ibid., 47.

107. Goswami, *Producing India*, 128.

3. Partition and the Death Train

1. Manto, "Hospitality Delayed," 97.

2. Butalia, *The Other Side of Silence*; Menon and Bhasin, *Borders and Boundaries*.

3. Daiya, *Violent Belongings*, 6.

4. Talbot, *Freedom's Cry*, 161.

5. Khosla, *History of the Indian Railways*, 193.

6. Report of Chief Commissioner, Indian Railways, November 13, 1947.

7. Khosla, *History of the Indian Railways*, 193.

8. "Indian Railways," *British Railway Gazette*, October 3, 1947, 390.

9. For a collection of these photographs, see those by Margaret Bourke-White in a special edition of the novel. Roli Books, 2006.

10. See, for example, memoirs in Hasan, *India Partitioned*; Urvashi Butalia, *The Other Side of Silence*.

11. Daiya, *Violent Belongings*, 5; Talbot, *Freedom's Cry*, 143.

12. See Chatterjee, *The Nation and Its Fragments*; Sangeeta Ray, *En-Gendering India*.

13. Kaul, "Introduction" to *The Partitions of Memory*, 10.

14. Vanaik, *The Furies of Indian Communalism*, 34.

15. David Ludden, "Introduction. Ayodhya: A Window on the World," 12.

16. Vanaik, *The Furies of Indian Communalism*, 36.

17. Balibar and Wallerstein, *Race, Nation, Class*, 95.

18. See Pandy, *Remembering Partition*.

19. Khwaja Iftikhar, *Jab Amritsar jal rahā thā*; quoted and translated by Talbot, *Freedom's Cry*, 180.

20. Letter by Miss. Mridula Sarabhai to Dr. John Mathai, September 23, 1947.

21. Ibid., 6.

22. Letter by Karnail Singh, railway area officer in Amritsar, letter to Miss. Mridula Sarabhai, October 8, 1947.

23. Butalia, "An Archive with a Difference," 214–15.

24. Shauna Singh Baldwin, *What the Body Remembers*.

25. Daiya, *Violent Belongings*, 14.

26. Parmar, "Trains of Death: Representations of the Railways in Films on the Partition of India."

27. Ibid., 2.

28. Kaul, "Introduction" to *The Partitions of Memory*, 6.

29. Didur, *Unsettling Partition*, 4.

30. Swami, "Evoking Horrors of Partition—and Hopes of a Peaceful Future."

31. Butalia, "Listening for a Change: Narratives of Partition," 133–36.

32. See, for example, respectively, Nahal, *Azadi*; Sharma, *Gadar*; Hosain, *Sunlight on a Broken Column*; Manto, "Toba Tek Singh"; and Sidhwa, *Cracking India (Ice-Candy Man)*.

33. That literature has only recently begun to receive more critical attention, and it has not achieved the iconic status representing Partition that depictions of the Punjab have. See Fraser, Introduction to *Bengal Partition Stories*, for alternate images of Bengal's partition.

34. Kipling, *Kim*, 75.

35. Quoted in Kerr, *Engines of Change*, 144.

36. Giddens, *The Consequences of Modernity*, 17.

37. De Certeau, *The Practice of Everyday Life*, 110.

38. Quoted and translated in Talbot, *Freedom's Cry*, 180.

39. Vatsayan, "Getting Even," 121.

40. Singh, *Train to Pakistan*, 4.

41. Ibid., 5.

42. Schivelbusch, *The Railway Journey*, 44.

43. Singh, *Train to Pakistan*, 77.

44. Ibid., 176.

45. Ibid., 178.

46. Chander, "Peshawar Express," 79–88.

47. Singh, *Train to Pakistan*, 44.

48. Ibid., 180.

49. Ibid., 77.

50. Ibid., 78.

51. Daiya, *Violent Belongings*, 51.

52. Daly, *Literature, Technology, and Modernity, 1860–2000*, 2.

53. Ceserani, "The Impact of the Train on Modern Literary Imagination."

54. See Parmar, "Trains of Death," for another discussion of this music sequence and film in general.

55. De Certeau, *The Practice of Everyday Life*, 111.

56. Ibid., 110.

57. Bhisham Sahni, "We Have Arrived in Amritsar," 119.

58. De Certeau, *The Practice of Everyday Life*, 110.

59. Sahni, "We Have Arrived in Amritsar," 114–115.

60. Ibid., 115.

61. Ibid., 118.

62. Kesavan, *Looking through Glass*, 53.

63. Singh, *Train to Pakistan*, 91.

64. Kesavan, *Looking through Glass*, 91.

65. Ibid., 91.

66. Ibid., 188.

67. Ibid., 188.

4. New Destinations

1. Bhattacharya, "Develop-mentalist Turn," 25.

2. Quoted in Kerr, *Engines of Change*, 144.

3. Nehru, *National Herald*. Lucknow, India, 21 June 1939, quoted in B. Chakrabarty, "Jawaharlal Nehru and Planning, 1938–41: India at the Crossroads," 284.

4. Kerr, *Engines of Change*, 144.

5. Ibid., 162.

6. Goswami, *Producing India*, 131.

7. Kerr, "Reworking a Popular Religious Practice," 325.

8. Freeman, *Railways and the Victorian Imagination*, 121.

9. Williams, *The Country and the City*, 296.

10. Ibid., 264.

11. Ibid.

12. Gupta, *Postcolonial Developments*, 49.

13. Nanda, *Jawaharlal Nehru*, 209.

14. Narayan, *The Guide*, 31.

15. Ibid., 36.

16. The 1965 film version of the novel lessens the defining role of the railway. *The Guide*, directed by Vijay Anand.

17. Narayan, *The Guide*, 19.

18. Ibid., 8.

19. Although Ray introduces the prominent image of the train in his works, his films are based on the book *Pather Panchali* by Bibhutibhushan Banerji.

20. Nyce, *Satyajit Ray*, 3.

21. Ibid., 14.

22. Neepa Majumdar calls the train a "memory-saturated image" for both Apu and for the audience of the three films, a symbol recalling the relationship between the brother and sister as well as the tragic loss of the sister. "*Pather Panchali* (1955) Satyajit Ray," 512.

23. Ganguly, *Satyajit Ray*, 28.

24. Renu, *The Third Vow and Other Stories*, 65.

25. Ibid., 64.

26. Ibid., 65–66.

27. In 1995, Amitav Ghosh revisited "The Fragrance of a Primitive Night" in his science-fiction novel *Calcutta Chromosome*. Ghosh transforms the paradigm of movement into a liberating experience and makes the railway the primary sign of that liberation—reversing Renu's stance on mobility.

28. Tagore, "Railway Station," 25.

29. Rushdie, *Midnight's Children*, 519.

30. V. Chandra, "Shanti," 239.

31. Michel de Certeau calls the liminal space between the inside and the outside of the railway carriage a slender blade: De Certeau, *The Practice of Everyday Life*, 110.

32. Nair, *Ladies Coupé*, 1.

33. Ibid., 2.

34. Ibid., 1.

35. Ibid., 17.

36. Ibid., 42.

37. Ibid., 2.

38. Badami, *Tamarind Mem*, 154.

39. Futehally, *Reaching Bombay Central*, 112.

40. Ibid., 17.

41. Ibid., 17.

42. Ibid., 5.

43. Ibid., 3, 22, 25.

44. Ibid., 119.

45. Theroux, *The Great Railway Bazaar*, 166.

46. Desai, *The Inheritance of Loss*, 42.

47. Ibid., 41.

48. Rushdie, *Imaginary Homelands*, 10.

5. Bollywood on the Train

1. Gopalan, *Cinema of Interruption*, 9; Ganti, *Bollywood*, 33.

2. Gopalan, *Cinema of Interruption*, 66.

3. Kern, *The Culture of Time and Space*, 124.

4. Gopalan, *Cinema of Interruption*, 9.

5. By the end of the film, Desai tempers this stronger message with a romance that conquers even the train—the hero and heroine use a cardboard train to perform a song-and-dance number comparing love to a train; they then continue their song in a train. The train here becomes part of the fantasy aspect of the romance genre.

6. In India, the relation between the train and the character of "Fearless Nadia" in the silent films of the Wadia brothers offers an interesting exception. Nadia scales the train and otherwise takes control of it. See the 1936 film *Miss Frontier Mail*, directed by Homi Wadia. For a discussion of this film, see Thomas, *"Miss Frontier Mail."*

7. Ibid., 86.

8. Laura Bear, *Lines of the Nation*, 49.

9. Wheeler, Introduction to *The Travels of a Hindoo to Various Parts of Bengal and Upper India*, xii.

10. Chunder, *The Travels of a Hindoo to Various Parts of Bengal and Upper India*, 130.

11. Brown, "The Seen, the Unseen, and the Imagined: Private and Public Lives," 503.

12. See Bear, *Lines of the Nation*, 50–53 for extended discussion of this debate.

13. Ibid., 53–54.

14. Ibid., 53–54.

15. Ibid., 52.

16. The widow and child that Madhu joins shortly afterward are not depicted as subject to the same harassment. They appear inside a private (or at least a deserted) waiting room, and the child provides a kind of security in the visible legitimacy it imparts.

17. Kerr, "Reworking a Popular Religious Practice," 312.

18. Gabriel, "Designing Desire," 49.

19. Reading on the train presents another kind of veil often used to display a woman's modesty, a technique used by Vandana in *Aradhana* and Simran in *Dilwale Dulhania Le Jayege*.

20. Gabriel, "Designing Desire," 56.

21. Ganti, *Bollywood*, 33.

22. Gabriel, "Designing Desire," 54–55.

23. Ibid., 51–52.

24. Sumita S. Chakravarty traces the evolution of courtesan films. *National Identity in Indian Popular Cinema*, 269–305.

25. Jenny Sharpe, "Gender, Nation, and Globalization in *Monsoon Wedding* and *Dilwale Dulhania Le Jayege*," 66.

26. Ganti, *Bollywood*, 40.

27. Sharpe, "Gender, Nation, and Globalization," 60–61.

28. Daly, *Literature, Technology, and Modernity*, 10–33.

29. Schivelbusch, *The Railway Journey*, 131–145; Ian Carter, *Railways and Culture in Britain*, 167–201.

30. Amar's later radio broadcast, which relates the encounter as a melodramatic story, gives the scene a self-reflexivity. The over-the-top quality of Amar's version suggests that the train story is by now a cliche in Indian cinema.

31. The song-and-dance sequence is reproduced at the beginning of the musical production *Bombay Dreams;* both feature the choreography of Farah Khan.

32. Virdi, *The Cinematic ImagiNation*, 189.

Conclusion

1. *The Great Indian Railway,* directed by William Livingston.

2. McEwan, *Saturday*, 15.

3. Zulaika and Douglass, *Terror and Taboo*, 10.

4. Rao, "How to Read a Bomb: Scenes from Bombay's Black Friday," 576.

5. Barthes, "Rhetoric of the Image," 45.

6. Ibid., 39.

7. Davis, *Buda's Wagon*, 4–12.

8. Boehmer, "Postcolonial Writing and Terror," 5.

9. Zulaika and Douglass, *Terror and Taboo*, 22.

10. Schivelbusch, *The Railway Journey*, 84–88.

11. "The Globe" (1863) epigraph. Quoted in Smullen, *Taken for a Ride*, 131.

12. Daly, *Literature, Technology, and Modernity*, 25.

13. Ibid., 2.

14. Mistry, *A Fine Balance*, 601.

15. V. Chandra, "Shanti," 234.

16. Daly, *Literature, Technology, and Modernity, 1860–2000*, 2.

17. Ibid., 2.

18. V. Chandra, "Shanti," 235.

19. Lahiri, *The Namesake*, 17.

20. Ibid., 17.

21. Ibid., 17.

22. Schivelbush, *The Railway Journey*, 66.

23. Lahiri, *The Namesake*, 14.

24. Ernst Bloch, *Spuren;* quoted and translated in Schivelbusch, *The Railway Journey*, 132.

25. Schivelbusch, *The Railway Journey*, 132.

26. Kirby, *Parallel Tracks*, 3.

27. Schivelbusch, *The Railway Journey*, 133.

28. Felix Tourneux, *Encyclopédia des chemines de fer et des machines à vapeur;* quoted and translated in Schivelbusch, *The Railway Journey*, 134.

29. Banerjee, "Childhood Voices from the Machine Age," 4.

30. Schivelbusch, *The Railway Journey*, 131.

31. Mrs. Shoosmith [M.C. Reid], *Bengal Nagpur Railway Magazine*.

32. Daly, *Literature, Technology, and Modernity*, 10–33.

33. Ibid., 2.

34. Lahiri, *The Namesake*, 19.

35. Kirby, *Parallel Tracks*, 61.

36. Davis, *Buda's Wagon*, 9.

37. Harpham, "Symbolic Terror," 573.

38. Zulaika and Douglass, *Terror and Taboo*, 25.

39. Heehs, *Nationalism, Terrorism, Communalism*, 10–11.

40. Baudrillard, "The Spirit of Terrorism," 13.

41. D. Chakrabarty, "Early Railwaymen in India," 540.

42. Kerr, *Building the Railways of the Raj*, 161–62.

43. Arnold, "Industrial Violence in Colonial India," 240.

44. Goswami, *Producing India*, 119.

45. Jagga, "Colonial Railwaymen and British Rule," 106.

46. Heehs, *Nationalism, Terrorism, and Communalism*, 15.

47. M. Chatterjee, *Do and Die*, 219–24.

48. Presner, *Mobile Modernity*, 3.

49. Harpham, "Symbolic Terror," 573.

50. Presner, *Mobile Modernity*, 10.

51. Remo Ceserani, "The Impact of the Train on Modern Literary Imagination."

52. Carter, *Railways and Culture in Britain*, 208.

53. An inquiry led by Supreme Court Judge Umesh Chandra Banerjee in January 2005 ruled the fire an accident. BBC News, "India Train Fire 'Not Mob Attack.'"

54. Swami, "Evoking Horrors of Partition—and Hopes of a Peaceful Future."

55. Davis, *Buda's Wagon*, 9.

56. Reuters, "India Militants Threaten More 'Gruesome Acts.' Claim Responsibility for Train Bomb Attack That Killed Dozens."

57. Press Trust of India News Agency, "UK's Indian Muslims Welcome Indian Top Court Ruling on Riots."

58. Associated Press, "Death Toll from Mumbai Blast Hits 200."

59. Saunders, "Deliverance in Mumbai."

60. Ibid.

61. Press Trust of India News Agency, "India: Charges Framed Against 13 People in Multiple Train Blasts Case."

62. Mehta, "Indian Bomb Attacks: Analysis."

63. Saunders, "Deliverance in Mumbai."

64. Ibid.

65. Baudrillard, "The Spirit of Terrorism," 13.

66. Reuters, "Police Kill Mumbai Bombing Suspect," *National Post.*

67. Rushdie, *Imaginary Homelands*, 10.

68. Daly, *Literature, Technology, and Modernity*, 23.

69. Rao, "How to Read a Bomb: Scenes from Bombay's Black Friday," 569.

70. De Certeau, *The Practice of Everyday Life*, 111.

71. Schivelbusch, *The Railway Journey*, 164.

72. Wax, "India Debates Siege Suspect's Legal Rights."

73. Harvey, "The Political Economy of Public Space," 19.

74. Swami, "Evoking Horrors of Partition—and Hopes of a Peaceful Future."

75. Houen, *Terrorism and Modern Literature, from Joseph Conrad to Ciaran Carson*, 10.

76. Harpham, "Symbolic Terror," 573.

77. Rushdie, *Imaginary Homelands*, 72.

78. Goswami, *Producing India*, 118

79. Justin Huggler, "At least 66 burned alive after bomb attacks on Friendship Express."

80. *BBC Worldwide Monitoring*, "India bans non-passengers from train station platforms."

81. De Certeau, *The Practice of Everyday Life*, 110.

82. Saunders, "Deliverance in Mumbai."

83. The Global Fund for Children Worldwide, "Who We Are."

84. Schivelbusch, *The Railway Journey*, 164.

85. Nair, *Ladies Coupé*, 176.

86. Rushdie, *Midnight's Children*, 71.

87. *Slumdog Millionaire*, directed by Danny Boyle.

89. De Certeau, *The Practice of Everyday Life*, 110.

89. Adas, *Machines as the Measure of Men*, 134.

90. Trevelyan, *The Competition Wallah*, 27.

91. De Certeau, *The Practice of Everyday Life*, 110.

92. Goswami, *Producing India*, 128.

93. Schivelbusch, *The Railway Journey*, 19.

Bibliography

Adas, Michael. *Machines as the Measure of Men: Science, Technology, and Ideologies of Western Dominance*. Ithaca: Cornell University Press, 1989.

———. "Contested Hegemony: The Great War and the Afro-Asian Assault on the Civilizing Mission Ideology." *Journal of World History* 15, no. 1 (2004): 31–63.

Ahuja, Ravi. "'The Bridge-Builders': Some Notes on Railways, Pilgrimage, and the British 'Civilizing Mission' in Colonial India." In *Colonialism as Civilizing Mission: Cultural Ideology in British India*, edited by Harald Fischer-Tiné and Michael Mann, 95–116. London: Anthem Press, 2004.

Anand, Y. P. *Mahatma Gandhi and The Railways*. Ahmedabad: Navajivan Publishing House, 2002.

Anderson, Benedict. *Imagined Communities: Reflections on the Origin and Spread of Nationalism*. London: Verso, 1983.

Arnold, David. "Industrial Violence in Colonial India." *Comparative Studies in Society and History* 22 (April 1980): 234–55.

———. *Science, Technology, and Medicine in Colonial India*. The New Cambridge History of India, III, 5. Cambridge, UK: Cambridge University Press, 2000.

———. *Gandhi: Profiles in Power*. London: Longman, 2001.

Associated Press. "Death Toll from Mumbai Blast Hits 200," MSNBC, July 12, 2006, http://www.msnbc.msn.com/id/10958641/ (accessed May 20, 2008).

Aurobindo, Ghose. *War and Self-Determination*. Pondicherry, India: Aurobindo Sri Ashram, 1957.

———. *The Life Divine*. Pondicherry, India: Sri Aurobindo Ashram, 1960.

Badami, Anita Rau. *Tamarind Mem*. London: Viking, 1996.

Baldwin, Shauna Singh. *What the Body Remembers*. New York: N. A. Talese, 1999.

Balibar, Etienne, and Immanuel Wallerstein. *Race, Nation, Class: Ambiguous Identities*. Translated by Chris Turner. London: Routledge, Chapman, and Hall, 1991.

Banerjee, Sumantra. "Childhood Voices from the Machine Age: Popular Culture on the Arrival of Technology in Colonial Bengal." *Indian Horizons* 48, no. 1 (2001): 1–10.

Banerji, Bibhutibhushan. *Pather Panchali: Song of the Road*. Translated by T. W. Clark and Tarapada Mukherji. New Delhi: HarperCollins Publishers, 1999.

Barthes, Roland. "Rhetoric of the Image." In *Image Music Text*, translated by Stephen Heath, 32–51. New York: Hill and Wang, 1977.

Baudrillard, Jean. "The Spirit of Terrorism." In *The Spirit of Terrorism and Other Essays*, translated by Chris Turner, 1–34. London: Verso, 2003.

Bayly, C. A. *Empire and Information: Intelligence Gathering and Social Communication in India, 1780–1870*. Cambridge, UK: University of Cambridge Press, 1996.

Bayly, Susan. *Caste, Society, and Politics in India from the Eighteenth Century to the Modern Age*. The New Cambridge History of India, 4, 3. Cambridge, UK: Cambridge University Press, 1999.

Bear, Laura. "Traveling Modernity: Capitalism, Community, and Nation in the Colonial Governance of the Indian Railways." Ph.D diss., University of Michigan, 1998.

———. *Lines of the Nation: Indian Railway Workers, Bureaucracy, and the Intimate Historical Self*. New York: Columbia University Press, 2007.

Behdad, Ali. *Belated Travelers: Orientalism in the Age of Colonial Dissolution*. Durham, N.C.: Duke University Press, 1994.

Bengal Hurkaru and India Gazette. "First Impressions and First Impulses of Railway Travelling." August 23, 1854, 183.

Benjamin, Walter. "Theses on the Philosophy of History: IX." In *Illuminations: Essays and Reflections*, edited by Hannah Arendt; translated by Harry Zohn, 253–59. New York: Schocken Books, 1968.

Bhattacharya, Sourin. "Develop-mentalist Turn: Recovering Ray's *Panchali*." In *Apu and After: Re-visiting Ray's Cinema*, edited by Mainaka Bisvasa, 19–36. London: Seagull Books, 2006.

Boehmer, Elleke. *Empire, the National, and the Postcolonial, 1890-1920: Resistance in Interaction*. Oxford, UK: Oxford University Press, 2002.

———. "Postcolonial Writing and Terror." *Wasafiri* 51, no. 22:2 (Summer 2007): 4–7.

Bond, Ruskin, ed. *The Penguin Book of Indian Railway Stories*. New Delhi: Penguin Books India, 1994.

Bose, Sugata. "The Spirit and Form of an Ethical Polity: A Meditation on Aurobindo's Thought." *Modern Intellectual History* 4, no. 1 (2007): 129–44.

Bourke-White, Margaret. Illustrations in Khushwant Singh, *Train to Pakistan*. Delhi: Roli Books, 2006.

British Railway Gazette. "Indian Railways." October 3, 1947, 390.

Brown, Sarah Graham. "The Seen, the Unseen, and the Imagined: Private and Public Lives." In *Feminist and Postcolonial Theory: A Reader*, edited by Reina Lewis and Sara Mills, 502–29. New York: Routledge, 2003.

Bury, Harriet. "Novel Spaces, Transitional Moments: Negotiating Text and Territory in Nineteenth-Century Hindi Travel Accounts." In *27 Down: New*

Departures in Indian Railway Studies, edited by Ian J. Kerr, 1–38 New Delhi: Orient Longman, 2007.

Butalia, Urvashi. *The Other Side of Silence: Voices from the Partition of India.* Durham, N.C.: Duke University Press, 2000.

_____. "An Archive with a Difference: Partition Letters." In *The Partitions of Memory: The Afterlife of the Division of India,* edited by Suvir Kaul, 208–41. Bloomington: Indiana University Press, 2002.

_____. "Listening for a Change: Narratives of Partition." In *Pangs of Partition: The Human Dimension (Vol. II),* edited by S. Settar and Indira Baptista Gupta, 133–36. New Delhi: Manohar, 2002.

Carter, Ian. *Railways and Culture in Britain: The Epitome of Modernity.* Manchester, UK: Manchester University Press, 2001.

"Case 56." *The Journal of Indian Art.* London, W. Griggs & Sons (January 1913), 23.

Ceserani, Remo. "The Impact of the Train on Modern Literary Imagination." *Stanford Humanities Review* 7, no. 1 (1999). Accessed August 4, 2009. http://bibpurl.oclc.org/web/7266.

Chakrabarty, Bidyut. "Jawaharlal Nehru and Planning, 1938–41: Indian at the Crossroads." *Modern Asian Studies* 26, no. 2 (May 1992): 275–87.

Chakrabarty, Dipesh. "Early Railwaymen in India: 'Dacoity' and 'Train-Wrecking.'" In *Essays in Honour of Prof. S.C. Sarkar,* edited by Diptendra Banerjee, Boudhayan Chattopadhyay, Binoy Chaudhuri, Barun De, Aniruddha Ray, Asok Sen, Mohit Sen, and Pradip Sinha, 523–50. New Delhi: People's Publishing House, 1976.

Chakravarty, Sumita S. *National Identity in Indian Popular Cinema: 1947–1987.* Austin: University of Texas Press, 1993.

Chander, Krishan. "Peshawar Express." In *Orphans of the Storm: Stories on the Partition of India,* edited by Saros Cowasjee and K. S. Duggal. New Delhi: UBS Publishers, 1995.

Chandra, Bipan. *The Rise and Growth of Economic Nationalism in India.* New Delhi: People's Publishing House, 1966.

Chandra, Vikram. "Shanti." In *Love and Longing in Bombay,* 229–68. Boston: Back Bay Books, 1998.

Chatterjee, Abinash Chandra. "Traffic by Railway." *Modern Review* 7, no. 2 (February 1910): 192–93.

Chatterjee, Manini. *Do and Die: The Chittagong Uprising: 1930–34.* New Delhi: Penguin Books, 1999.

Chatterjee, Partha. *Nationalist Thought and the Colonial World: A Derivative Discourse.* Minneapolis: University of Minnesota Press, 1986.

_____. *The Nation and Its Fragments: Colonial and Postcolonial Histories.* Princeton, N.J.: Princeton University Press, 1993.

Christie, Agatha. *Murder on the Orient Express.* New York: Bantam Books, 1983.

Chunder, Bholanatha. *The Travels of a Hindoo to Various Parts of Bengal and Upper India*. London: N. Trübner, 1869.

Clifford, James. *Routes: Travel and Translation in the Late Twentieth Century*. Cambridge, Mass.: Harvard University Press, 1997.

Cooper, Frederick. *Colonialism in Question: Theory, Knowledge, History*. Berkeley: University of California Press, 2005.

Cotton, Sir Arthur. "Extracts from the Memorandum by Sir Arthur Cotton on the Report of the Select Committee of the House of Commons on Public Works in India, 1899." In *General Sir Arthur Cotton, R.E. K.C.S.I.: His Life and Work*. Edited by Elizabeth Reid Hope. Appendix, 309-27. London: Hodder and Stoughton, 1900.

_____. *The Madras Famine*. London: Simpkin, Marshall, & Co., 1877.

Daiya, Kavita. *Violent Belongings: Partition, Gender, and National Culture in Postcolonial India*. Philadelphia, Penn.: Temple University Press, 2008.

Dalhousie, Lord [James Andrew Broun Ramsay], "Minute by Lord Dalhousie to the Court of Directors." April 20, 1853. In *Railway Construction in India: Select Documents*. General editor S. Settar; editor, Bhubanes Misra, II-23-II-57. New Delhi: Indian Council of Historical Research, Northern Book Centre, 1999.

_____. *Parliamentary Papers* (House of Commons), vol. 45, col. 256 (1856), 16.

Dalton, Dennis Gilmore. *Indian Idea of Freedom: Political Thought of Swami Vivekanda, Aurobindo Ghose, Mahatma Gandhi, and Rabindranath Tagore*. Haryana, India: The Academic Press, 1982.

Daly, Nicholas. *Literature, Technology, and Modernity, 1860–2000*. Cambridge, UK: Cambridge University Press, 2004.

Danvers, Sir Juland. *Indian Railways: Their Past History, Present Condition, and Future Prospects*. London: Effingham Wilson, Royal Exchange, 1877.

Davidson, Captain Edward. *The Railways of India: With an Account of Their Rise, Progress, and Construction*. London: E. & F. N. Spon, 1878.

Davis, Clarence B., Kenneth E. Wilburn, Jr., and Ronald E. Robinson. *Railway Imperialism*. New York: Greenwood Press, 1991.

Davis, Mike. *Late Victorian Holocausts: El Niño Famines and the Making of the Third World*. London: Verso, 2001.

_____. *Buda's Wagon: A Brief History of the Car Bomb*. New York: Verso, 2007.

de Certeau, Michel. *The Practice of Everyday Life*. Translated by Steven F. Rendall. Berkeley: University of California Press, 1984.

Deloche, Jean. *Transport and Communications in India Prior to Steam Locomotion*. Translated by James Walker. Delhi: Oxford University Press India, 1994.

Desai, Kiran. *The Inheritance of Loss*. New York: Atlantic Monthly Press, 2006.

Didur, Jill. *Unsettling Partition: Literature, Gender, Memory*. Toronto: University of Toronto Press, 2006.

Digby, Sir William. *"Prosperous" British India, a Revelation from Official Records*. New Delhi: Sagar Publications, 1969.

D'Souza, Sebastian. "A gunman walks through the Chatrapathi Sivaji [sic] Terminal railway station in Mumbai, India, Wednesday, November 26, 2008." (AP Photo/Mumbai Mirror, Sebastian D'Souza) #5. "Mumbai Under Attack," The Big Picture, Boston.com, http://www.boston.com/bigpicture/2008/11/mumbai_under_attack.html (accessed May 20, 2009).

Dutt, Romesh. *The Economic History of India in the Victorian Age*. 1902. Reprint, London: Routledge & Kegan Paul, 1956.

Ellis, C. Hamilton. *Railway Art*. Boston: New York Graphic Society, 1977.

Forster, E. M. *A Passage to India*. New York: Harcourt Inc., 1984.

Foucault, Michel. "What Is Enlightenment?" Translated by Catherine Porter. In *The Foucault Reader*, edited by Paul Rabinow, 32–50. New York: Pantheon Books, 1984.

———. "Of Other Spaces." *Diacritics* 16, no. 1 (1986): 22–27.

Frank, Andre Gunder. "The Development of Underdevelopment." In *From Modernization to Globalization: Perspectives on Development and Social Change*, edited by J. Timmons Roberts and Amy Hite, 159–66. Malden, Mass.: Blackwell, 2000.

Fraser, Bashabi. Introduction to *Bengal Partition Stories: An Unclosed Chapter*, 1–58. London: Anthem Press, 2006.

Freeman, Michael. *Railways and the Victorian Imagination*. New Haven, Conn.: Yale University Press, 1999.

Furnell, Michael Cudmore. *From Madras to Delhi and Back via Bombay*. Madras: C. Foster and Co., 1874.

Futehally, Shama. *Reaching Bombay Central*. New Delhi: Viking, 2002.

Gabriel, Karen. "Designing Desire: Gender in Mainstream Bombay Cinema." In *Translating Desire: The Politics of Gender and Culture in India*, edited by Brinda Bose, 48–80. New Delhi: Katha, 2002.

Gandhi, M. K. "The Morals of Machinery," April 15, 1926. In *Young India 1924–1926*, edited by Mohandas Gandhi, 760–62. New York: The Viking Press, 1927.

———. *Gandhi: "Hind Swaraj" and Other Writings*, edited by Anthony Parel. Cambridge, UK: Cambridge University Press, 2003.

Ganti, Tajaswini. *Bollywood: A Guidebook to Popular Hindi Cinema*. New York: Routledge, 2004.

Gaonkar, Dilip Parameshwar. "On Alternative Modernities." *Public Culture* 11, no. 1 (1999): 1–18.

Gardiner, Lieut.-Colonel R. E. "Indian Railways." In *The Journal of Indian Art*. London: W. Griggs and Sons, January 1913, 23–24.

Ganguly, Surajan. *Satyajit Ray: In Search of the Modern*. Lanham, Md.: Scarecrow Press, 2000.

Ghosh, Amitav. *Calcutta Chromosome: A Novel of Fevers, Delirium, and Discovery*. New York: Avon Books, 1995.

Giddens, Anthony. *The Consequences of Modernity*. Stanford, Calif.: Stanford University Press, 1990.

_____. Foreword to *NowHere: Space, Time and Modernity*, edited by Roger Friedland and Deirdre Boden, xi–xiii. Berkeley: University of California Press, 1994.

Gilroy, Paul. *The Black Atlantic: Modernity and Double Consciousness*. Cambridge, Mass.: Harvard University Press, 1993.

The Global Fund for Children Worldwide. "Who We Are." http://www.globalfundforchildren.org/ourwork/ (accessed May 20, 2008).

Gopalan, Lalitha. *Cinema of Interruption: Action Genres in Contemporary Indian Cinema*. London: British Film Institute Publishing, 2002.

Goswami, Manu. *Producing India: From Colonial Economy to National Space*. Chicago: University of Chicago Press, 2004.

Grewal, Inderpal. *Home and Harem: Nation, Gender, Empire, and the Culture of Travel*. Durham, N.C.: Duke University Press, 1997.

Gupta, Akhil. *Postcolonial Developments: Agriculture in the Making of Modern India*. Durham, N.C.: Duke University Press, 1998.

Habermas, Jürgen. *The Philosophical Discourse of Modernity: Twelve Lectures*, trans. Frederick G. Lawrence. Cambridge, Mass.: MIT Press, 1992.

Harpham, Geoffrey Galt. "Symbolic Terror." *Critical Inquiry* 28, no. 2 (Winter 2002): 573–79.

Harvey, David. "The Political Economy of Public Space." In *The Politics of Public Space*, edited by Setha Low and Neil Smith, 17–34. New York: Routledge, 2005.

Hasan, Mushirul, ed. *India Partitioned: The Other Face of Freedom*. New Delhi: Lotus Collection, 1995.

Headrick, Daniel. *The Tools of Empire: Technology and European Imperialism in the Nineteenth Century*. New York: Oxford University Press, 1981.

Heehs, Peter. *Nationalism, Terrorism, Communalism: Essays in Modern Indian History*. New York: Oxford University Press, 1998.

_____. "'The Centre of the Religious Life of the World': Spiritual Universalism and Cultural Nationalism in the Work of Sri Aurobindo." *Hinduism in Public and Private: Reform, Hindutva, Gender, and Sampraday*, edited by Antony Copley, 66–83. New Delhi: Oxford University Press India, 2003.

Hobsbawm, Eric. *Industry and Empire: An Economic History of Britain Since 1750*. London: Weidenfeld & Nicolson, 1968.

"Honeymooning in India." *The Ladies' Treasury* (London, England). May 1, 1895, 320.

Hosain, Attia. *Sunlight on a Broken Column*. 1961. Reprint, New Delhi: Penguin, 1988.

Houen, Alex. *Terrorism and Modern Literature, from Joseph Conrad to Ciaran Carson*. Oxford, UK: Oxford University Press, 2002.

Huggler, Justin. "At Least 66 Burned Alive after Bomb Attacks on Friendship Express." *Independent* (London). February 20, 2007, http://www.lexis-nexis. com/ (accessed May 20, 2008).

"India Bans Non-passengers from Train Station Platforms." *BBC Worldwide Monitoring.* July 29, 2006, http://www.lexis-nexis.com/ (accessed May 20, 2008).

Illustrated London News. "An Indian railway station (on the Bombay and Tannah Railway)." Illustration. September 9, 1854, 208.

Illustrated London News. "Modes of Travelling in India_____Tramps_____Hindoo Pilgrim_____Palky Dawk_____Travelling Beggar_____Camel Caravan_____ Charry Dawk_____A Bhylie_____Riding Elephant_____Am Ekha_____The East Indian Railway," Illustration. September 19, 1863, 284.

Indian Train Fire "Not Mob Attack," BBC News, Monday, January 17, 2005, http:// news.bbc.co.uk/2/hi/south_asia/4180885.stm/ (accessed May 20, 2008).

Indo-American [pseud.], "Railways in India and America," Illustration. *Modern Review* 7, no. 2 (February 1910): 118–23.

"An Inside View from One of the Earliest First-class Carriages," Illustration. *Central Railway Centenary: Central Railway Magazine* (April 1953): 109.

Jagga, Lajpat. "Colonial Railwaymen and British Rule: A Probe into Railway Labour and Agitation in India, 1919–1922." *Studies in History* 11, no. 1–2 (1981): 103–45.

Jenkins, R. P., Commisioner of Patna, June 21, 1869. Bengal Proceedings. Public Works Department: Railway Branch, September 1869, no. 99 (no. 205).

Joshi, Rao Bahadur G. V. *Writings and Speeches.* Poona: Arya Bhushan Press, 1912.

Kaplan, Caren. *Questions of Travel: Postmodern Discourses of Displacement.* Durham, N.C.: Duke University Press, 2005.

Kaye, Sir John. *A History of the Sepoy War in India.* London: W. H. Allen and Co., 1864.

Kelsall, Mssr. and Ghose, Messr. [Baboo Ram Ghopaul Ghose]. Mssrs. Kelsall and Ghose to R. MacDonald Stephenson, September 14, 1844. In "Report upon the Practicality and Advantages of the Introduction of Railways into British India," by R. Macdonald Stephenson, 35–37. London: Kelly & Co, 1845.

Kern, Stephen. *The Culture of Time and Space 1880–1918.* Cambridge, Mass.: Harvard University Press, 1983.

Kerr, Ian J. *Building the Railways of the Raj: 1850–1900.* Delhi: Oxford University Press, 1995.

_____. Introduction to *Railways in Modern India*, edited by Ian J. Kerr, 1-61. New Delhi: Oxford University Press India, 2001.

_____. "Reworking a Popular Religious Practice: The Effects of Railways on Pilgrimage in 19th- and 20th-Century South Asia." In *Railways in Modern India*, edited by Ian Kerr, 304–27. New Delhi: Oxford University Press India, 2001.

_____. "On the Move: Circulating Labor in Pre-Colonial, Colonial, and Post-Colonial India." *IRSH* 51 (2006): S85–S109.

_____. *Engines of Change: The Railroads That Made India*. Westport, Conn.: Praeger, 2007.

Kesavan, Mukul. *Looking through Glass*. Delhi: Ravi Dayal Publisher, 1995.

Khosla, G. S. *History of the Indian Railways*. New Delhi: Ministry of Railways (Railway Board) and A. H. Co., 1988.

Kipling, Rudyard. "The Bridge-Builders." In *Tales of East and West*. 1893. Reprint, selected by Bernard Bergonzi and illustrated by Charles Raymond, 203–30. Avon, Conn.: The Heritage Press, 1973.

_____. *Kim*. 1901. Reprint, edited by Edward Said. New York: Penguin Group, 1987.

Kirby, Lynne. *Parallel Tracks: The Railroad and Silent Cinema*. Durham, NC: Duke University Press, 1997.

Kolatkar, Arun. *Jejuri*. 1974; New York: New York Review of Books, 2005.

Lahiri, Jhumpa. *The Namesake*. Boston: Houghton Mifflin Co., 2003.

Lazarus, Neil. *Nationalism and Cultural Practice in the Postcolonial World*. Cambridge, UK: Cambridge University Press, 1999.

Ludden, David. "Introduction. Ayodhya: A Window on the World." In *Contesting the Nation: Religion, Community, and the Politics of Democracy in India*, edited by David Ludden, 1–26. Philadelphia: University of Pennsylvania Press, 1996.

Majumdar, Neepa. "*Pather Panchali* (1955) Satyajit Ray." In *Film Analysis: A Norton Reader*, edited by Jeffrey Geiger and R. L. Rutsky, 510–27. New York: W. W. Norton, 2005.

Manto, Saadat Hasan. "Hospitality Delayed" ("Kasre-Nafsi"). In *India Partitioned: The Other Face of Freedom, Vol. 1*, edited by Mushirul Hasan, translated by Mushirul Hasan, 97. New Delhi: Roli Books, 1995.

_____. "The Return." In *Kingdom's End and Other Stories*, translated by Khalid Hasan, 35–38. London: Verso, 1987.

_____. "Toba Tek Singh." In *Kingdom's End and Other Stories*, translated by Khalid Hasan, 11–18. London: Verso, 1987.

Markovits, Claude, Jacques Pouchepadass, and Sanjay Subrahmanyam. Introduction to *Society and Circulation: Mobile People and Itinerant Cultures in South Asia, 1750–1950*, edited by Claude Markovits, Jacques Pouchepadass, and Sanjay Subrahamanyam, 1-22. Delhi: Permanent Black, 2003.

Marx, Karl. "The Future Results of the British Rule in India." In *The First Indian War of Independence: 1857–1859*. 1853. Reprint, 28–32, Moscow: Foreign Languages Publishing House, 1959.

Marx, Leo. *The Machine in the Garden: Technology and the Pastoral Ideal in America*. 1964. Reprint, Oxford, UK: Oxford University Press, 2000.

Masters, John. *Bhowani Junction*. New York: The Viking Press, 1954.

McEwan, Ian. *Saturday*. New York: Anchor Books, 2005.

McClintock, Anne. *Imperial Leather: Race, Gender, and Sexuality in the Colonial Contest*. New York: Routledge, 1995.

Mehta, Suketu. "Indian Bomb Attacks: Analysis." *Washington Post*, July 11, 2009, www.washingtonpost.com (accessed May 20, 2009).

Menon, Ritu, and Kamela Bhasin. *Borders and Boundaries: Women in India's Partition*. New Brunswick, N.J.: Rutgers University Press, 1998.

Metcalf, Thomas R. *Ideologies of the Raj*. The New Cambridge History of India, 3, 4, Cambridge, UK: Cambridge University Press, 1995.

Meyer, Eric. "Labour Circulation Between Sri Lanka and South India in Historical Perspective." In *Society and Circulation: Mobile People and Itinerant Cultures in South Asia, 1750–1950*, edited by Claude Markovits, Jacques Pouchepadass, and Sanjay Subrahmanyam, 55–88. Delhi: Permanent Black, 2003.

Mistry, Rohinton. *A Fine Balance*. New York: Vintage International, 1997.

Mitchell, John William. *The Wheels of Ind*. London: Thornton Butterworth, 1934.

Mitchell, Timothy. Introduction to *Questions of Modernity*, edited by Timothy Mitchell, xi–xxvii. Contradictions of Modernity, Vol. 11. Minneapolis: University of Minnesota Press, 2000.

Mookerjee, Baboo Joykishen. May 20, 1869, letter to Magistrate and Collector of Burdwan, Bengal Proceedings. Public Works Department: Railway Branch, no. 202, June 4, 1869.

Moore-Gilbert, B. J. *Kipling and "Orientalism."* London: Croom Helm, 1986.

Nahal, Chaman. *Azadi*. New Delhi: India Paperbacks, 1975.

Nair, Anita. *Ladies Coupé*. New York: St. Martin's Griffin, 2004.

Nandy, Ashis. *The Intimate Enemy: Loss and Recovery of Self under Colonialism*. Delhi: Oxford University Press, 1983.

_____. *The Illegitimacy of Nationalism: Rabindranath Tagore and the Politics of Self*. Delhi: Oxford University Press, 1994.

Nanda, B. R. *Jawaharlal Nehru: Rebel and Statesman*. Delhi: Oxford University Press, 1995.

Naoroji, Dadabhai. "Memorandum on Mr. Danver's Papers of 28 June 1880 and 4th January 1879." In *Essays, Speeches, Addresses, and Writings (on Indian Politics)*, edited by Chunilal Lallubhai Parekh, 441–64. Bombay: Caxton Printing Works, 1887.

Narayan, R. K. *The Guide*. 1958. Reprint, New York: Penguin Books, 2006.

_____. *Swami and Friends*. East Lansing: Michigan State College Press, 1954.

Nash, Vaughan. *The Great Famine and Its Causes*. London: Longmans, Green, and Co., 1900.

Nehru, Jawaharlal. *The Discovery of India*. New York: The John Day Co., 1946.

_____. *Toward Freedom: The Autobiography of Jawaharlal Nehru*. Boston: Beacon Press, 1967.

Nightingale, Florence. "Letters to the editor." *Illustrated London News,* June 29, 1877.

Nyce, Ben. *Satyajit Ray: A Study of His Films.* New York: Praeger, 1988.

Osborne, Lt.-Col. Robert D. "India Under Lord Lytton." *Contemporary Review* 36 (September–December 1879) London: Strahan and Co. Ltd, 553–73.

Pacey, Arnold. *Technology in World Civilization: A Thousand-Year History.* Cambridge, Mass.: MIT Press, 1992.

Pandey, Gyanendra. *Remembering Partition: Violence, Nationalism, and History in India.* Cambridge, UK: Cambridge University Press, 2001.

Parmar, Prabhjot. "Trains of Death: Representations of the Railways in Films on the Partition of India." In *27 Down: New Departures in Indian Railway Studies,* edited by Ian J. Kerr, 68–100. Hyderabad: Orient Longman, 2007.

Parry, Benita. *Delusions and Discoveries: Studies on India in the British Imagination 1880–1930.* London: Allen Lane the Penguin Press, 1972.

Paterson, George. "The Paterson Diaries." November 23, 1770, British Library, Oriental and India Office Collections, MS Eur.E379/2.

Prakash, Gyan. *Another Reason: Science and the Imagination of Modern India.* Princeton, N.J.: Princeton University Press, 1999.

Pratt, Mary Louise. *Imperial Eyes: Travel Writing and Transculturation.* New York: Routledge, 1992.

Presner, Todd Samuel. *Mobile Modernity: Germans, Jews, Trains.* New York: Columbia University Press, 2007.

Press Trust of India News Agency. "India: Charges Framed Against 13 People in Multiple Train Blasts Case," *BBC Worldwide Monitoring,* August 8, 2007, http://www.lexis-nexis.com/ (accessed May 20, 2008).

———. "UK's Indian Muslims welcome Indian top court ruling on riots," *BBC Worldwide Monitoring,* March 27, 2008, http://www.lexis-nexis.com/ (accessed May 20, 2008).

Radice, William. "Notes." In *Selected Poems* by Rabindranath Tagore, edited and translated by William Radice, 167–68. Harmondsworth, UK: Penguin Books, 1994.

Railway Times, January 15, 1853, London, vol. 16.

Rao, Vyjayanthi. "How to Read a Bomb: Scenes from Bombay's Black Friday." *Public Culture* 19, no. 3 (Fall 2007): 567–92.

Ray, Sangeeta. *En-Gendering India: Woman and Nation in Colonial and Postcolonial Narratives.* Durham, N.C.: Duke University Press, 2000.

Renu, Phanishwar Nath. *The Third Vow and Other Stories.* Translated by Kathryn G. Hansen. Delhi: Chanakya, 1986.

Report of Chief Commissioner, Indian Railways, November 13, 1947, Mountbatten Papers, University of Southampton, MB1/D276.

Reuters. "India Militants Threaten More 'Gruesome Acts.' Claim Responsibility for Train Bomb Attack that Killed Dozens," *Toronto Star* (Canada), January 4, 1997, http://www.lexis-nexis.com/ (accessed May 20, 2009).

_____. "Police Kill Mumbai Bombing Suspect," *National Post* (Canada), August 22, 2006, http://www.lexis-nexis.com/ (accessed May 20, 2008).

Richards, David Alan. *Rudyard Kipling: A Bibliography*. New Castle, Del.: Oak Knoll Press, 2009.

Robbins, Michael. *The Railway Age*. London: Routledge, Kegan, and Paul, 1962.

Roy, Thirthankar. *The Economic History of India, 1857–1947*. New Delhi: Oxford University Press, 2000.

Rushdie, Salman. *Midnight's Children*. New York: Penguin Books, 1980.

_____. *Imaginary Homelands: Essays and Criticism: 1981–1991*. London: Penguin Press, 1991.

Sahni, Bhisham. *Tamas*. Translated by Bhisham Sahni. New Delhi: Penguin Books, 2001.

_____. "We Have Arrived in Amritsar" ("Amritsar Aa Gaya Hai"). In *India Partitioned: The Other Face of Freedom*, edited by Mushirul Hasan, 113–24. New Delhi: Lotus Collection, 1995.

Said, Edward. *Culture and Imperialism*. New York: Alfred A. Knopf, 1993.

Sarabhai, Mridula. Letter to Dr. John Mathai, November 1948, "Pani Wala Ko Kaho Kih Pani Chhor De," Relief Work Done for a Muslim Refugee Train Derailed at Amritsar on 23-9-47. National Archive, New Delhi, India, RT Nov. 48, 3–4

Satow, Michael, and Ray Desmond. *Railways of the Raj*. New York: New York University Press, 1980.

Saunders, Doug. "Deliverance in Mumbai," *Globe and Mail* (Canada), July. 15, 2006, http://www.lexis-nexis.com/ (accessed May 20, 2008).

Schivelbusch, Wolfgang. *The Railway Journey: Trains and Travel in the 19th Century*. Translated by Ansel Hollo. New York: Urizen Books, 1977.

Sharpe, Jenny. "Gender, Nation, and Globalization in *Monsoon Wedding* and *Dilwale Dulhani Le Javenge*." *Meridians: Feminism, Race, Transnationalism*. 6, no. 1 (2005): 58–81.

Shoosmith, Mrs. (M. C. Reid). *Bengal Nagpur Railway Magazine*, University of Cambridge, Cambridge South Asian Archive, n.d. Box 2.

Sidhwa, Bapsi. *Cracking India (Ice Candy Man)*. Minneapolis, Minn.: Milkweed Editions, 1991.

Simpson, Mark. *Trafficking Subjects: The Politics of Mobility in Nineteenth-Century America*. Minneapolis: University of Minnesota Press, 2005.

Singh, Karnail. Railway Area Officer in Amritsar, letter to Miss Mridula Sarabhai, 8/10/47. Relief Work Done for a Muslim Refugee Train Derailed at Amritsar on 23-9-47. RT Nov. 48 (11).

Singh, Khushwant. *Train to Pakistan*. 1956. Reprint, New York: Grove Weidenfeld, 1990.

Smith, Sydney. *The Works of the Rev. Sydney Smith*. London: Longman, Brown, Green, and Longmans, 1850.

Smullen, Ivor. *Taken for a Ride: A Distressing Account of the Misfortunes and Misbehaviour of the Early British Railway Traveller*. London: Jenkins, 1968.

Steel, Flora Annie. "In the Permanent Way." In *Indian Scene: Collected Short Stories of Flora Annie Steel*, 142–59. London: Edward Arnold & Co., 1933.

Stephenson, Macdonald R. "Report upon the Practicality and Advantages of the Introduction of Railways into British India." London: Kelly & Co, 1845.

Sullivan, Zohreh T. *Narratives of Empire: The Fiction of Rudyard Kipling*. Cambridge, UK: Cambridge University Press, 1993.

Swami, Praveen. "Evoking horrors of Partition—and hopes of a peaceful future." *Hindu* (India) February 20, 2007, http://www.hindu.com/ (accessed August 5, 2009).

Syal, Meera, and Thomas Meehan. *Bombay Dreams*. A play directed by Steven Pimlott. Apollo Victoria Theatre, London, June 19, 2002.

Tagore, Rabindranath. *Red Oleanders: A Drama in One Act [Raktakarabi]*. Calcutta: Macmillan and Co., 1925.

_____. "Railway Station." In *Selected Poems*. Edited and translated by William Radice. Harmondsworth, UK: Penguin Books, 1994.

_____. *The Waterfall [Muktadharaa]*. Kolkata: Rupa Books, 2002.

Talbot, Ian. *Freedom's Cry: The Popular Dimension in the Pakistan Movement and Partition Experience in North-West India*. Karachi: Oxford University Press, 1996.

Taylor, Charles. "Modern Social Imaginaries." *Public Culture* 14.1 (2002): 121.

Theroux, Paul. *The Great Railway Bazaar: By Train Through Asia*. New York: Penguin Books, 1995.

_____. *Ghost Train to the Eastern Star: On the Tracks of the Great Railway Bazaar*. Boston: Houghton Mifflin, 2008.

Theroux, Paul, and Steve McCurry. *The Imperial Way*. Boston: Houghton Mifflin, 1985.

Thomas, Rosie. "Miss Frontier Mail: The Film That Mistook Its Star for a Train." In *Sarai Reader 07: Frontiers*, edited by Monica Narula, Shuddhabrata Sengupta, Jeebesh Bagchi, and Ravi Sundaram, 294–309. Delhi: Centre for the Study of Developing Societies, 2007.

Thorner, Daniel. *Investment in Empire: British Railway and Steam Shipping Enterprise in India, 1825–1849*. Philadelphia: University of Pennsylvania Press, 1950.

_____. "The Pattern of Railway Development in India." In *Railways in Modern India*, edited by Ian J. Kerr, 80–96. Oxford, UK: Oxford University Press, 2001.

Times (London). "An Indian Stock and Railway Shareholder." March 25, 1861, 6.

Tomlinson, John. *Globalization and Culture.* Chicago: University of Chicago Press, 1999.

Trevelyan, George Otto. *The Competition Wallah.* London: Macmillan and Co., 1866.

Vanaik, Achin. *The Furies of Indian Communalism: Religion, Modernity, and Secularization.* London: Verso, 1997.

Vatsayan, S. H. (Ajneya). "Getting Even," translated by Alok Raj. In *Stories About the Partition of India, Vol. I,* edited by Alok Bhalla, 119–25. New Delhi: Indus, 1994.

Vicajee, Framjee R. *Political and Social Effects of Railways in India.* London: R. Clay, Sons, and Taylor, 1875.

Virdi, Jyotika. *The Cinematic ImagiNation: Indian Popular Films as Social History.* New Brunswick, N.J.: Rutgers University Press, 2003.

Visram, Rozina. *Asians in Britain: 400 Years of History.* London: Pluto Press, 2002.

Vivekananda, Swami (Narendranath Datta). "Our Present Social Problems." In *The Complete Works of Swami Vivekananda, Volume IV,* 488–92. Calcutta: Advaita Ashrama, 1972.

A Votary of Science [pseud.]. "Malaria and its Remedy." *Modern Review* 8, no. 5 (1910): 518–22.

Wax, Emily. "India Debates Siege Suspect's Legal Rights; Some Lawyers Refuse to Accept Case of Only Surviving Gunman," *Washington Post,* December 21, 2008, http://www.lexis-nexis.com/ (accessed May 20, 2008).

W. D. S. [pseud.] "The Night Mail-Train in India." *Fraser's Magazine* 52, no. 664 (1857): 404–8.

Wheeler, J. Talboys. Introduction to *The Travels of a Hindoo to Various Parts of Bengal and Upper India,* by Bholanatha Chunder, xi–xxv. London: N. Trübner, 1869.

Williams, Raymond. *The Country and the City.* New York: Oxford University Press, 1973.

Young, Robert J. C. *Postcolonialism: An Historical Introduction.* Oxford, UK: Blackwell Publishers, 2001.

Zulaika, Joseba, and William A. Douglass. *Terror and Taboo: The Follies, Fables, and Faces of Terrorism.* New York: Routledge, 1996.

Filmography

27 Down Bombay–Varanasi Express. Filmstrip. Directed by Avtar Krishna Kaul. Bombay: National Film Development Co., 1973.

Aparajito. DVD. Directed by Satyajit Ray. 1956; Culver City, Calif.: Sony Picture Classics, 2003.

Apur Sansar. DVD. Directed by Satyajit Ray. 1959; Culver City, Calif.: Sony Picture Classics, 2003.

Aradhana. DVD. Directed by Shakti Samanta. 1969; Burke, Va.: Baba Digital Media, 2000.

Before Sunrise. DVD. Directed by Richard Linklater. 1995; Burbank, Calif.: Warner Home Video, 1999.

Bhowani Junction. Directed by George Dewey Cukor. 1956; Los Angeles, Calif.: MGM/UA Home Video, 1991.

The Burning Train. DVD. Directed by Ravi Chopra. 1980; Mumbai: Shemaroo Video, 2003.

Chhalia. DVD. Directed by Manmohan Desai. 1960; Springfield, Va.: Baba Digital Media, 2000.

Coolie. DVD. Directed by Manmohan Desai. 1983; New Delhi: Time-n-Tune, 2005.

Darjeeling Limited. Directed by Wes Anderson. DVD. 2007; Beverly Hills, Calif.: 20th Century Fox Home Entertainment, 2008.

Derailed. DVD. Directed by Mikael Hafstrom. 2005. Solana Beach, CA: Genius Products, 2006.

Devdas. DVD. Directed by Bimal Roy. 1955; New York: Yash Raj Films, 2000.

Dil Se. DVD. Directed by Mani Ratnam. 1998; London: Eros International, 2003.

Dilwale Dulhania Le Jayenge. DVD. Directed by Aditya Chopra. 1995; Mumbai: Yash Raj Films Home Entertainment, 2007.

Earth. DVD. Directed by Deepa Mehta. New York: New Yorker Video, 1999.

Gadar: Ek Prem Katha. Directed by Anil Sharma. Edison, N.J. : Video Sound, 2001.

The Great Indian Railway. DVD. Directed by William Livingston. Washington, D.C.: National Geographic Society, 1995.

The Guide. DVD. Directed by Vijay Anand. 1965; Secaucus, N.J.: Eros International, 2002.

Guru. DVD. Directed by Mani Ratnam. New Delhi: Kaleidoscope Entertainment Pvt. Ltd, 2007.

Jab We Met. DVD. Directed by Imtiaz Ali. Fort Lee, N.J.: Studio 18, 2007.

Kati Patang. DVD. Directed by Shakti Samanta. 1970; Jackson Heights, N.Y.: Sky Entertainment, 2003.

Lady Vanishes, The. DVD. Directed by Alfred Hitchcock. 1938; New York: The Criterion Collection, 2007.

Mere Huzoor. DVD. Directed by Vinood Kumar. 1968; Sacramento, Calif: Bollywood Entertainment, 2008.

Miss Frontier Mail. Directed by Homi Wadia. Bombay: Wadia Movietone, 1936.

Mumbai Meri Jaan. DVD. Directed by Nishikant Kamat. Mumbai: UTV Motion Pictures, 2008.

Nayak. DVD. Directed by Satyajit Ray. 1966; New York: New York Film Annex, 2006.

North by Northwest. Directed by Alfred Hitchcock. 1959; Burbank, Calif: Warner Home Video, 2004.

Pakeezah. DVD. Directed by Kamal Amrohi. 1971; London: Gurpreet Video International, 2000.

Pather Panchali. DVD. Directed by Satyajit Ray. 1955; Culver City, Calif: Sony Picture Classics, 2003.

Sholay. DVD. Directed by Romesh Sippy. 1975; London: Eros International, 1998.

Slumdog Millionaire. DVD. Directed by Danny Boyle; co-director (India) Loveleen Tanden. Los Angeles, Calif.: Fox Searchlight, 2008.

Strangers on a Train. DVD. Directed by Alfred Hitchcock. 1951; Burbank: Warner Home Video, 2004.

Tamas. VHS. Directed by Govind Nihalani. Bombay: Blaze Entertainment, 1987.

The Train. Filmstrip. Directed by Hasnain Hyderabadwala and Raksha Mistry. Mumbai: Diddhi Vinayak Creations, 2007.

Train to Pakistan. DVD. Directed by Pamela Rooks. 1997; New Delhi: Eagle Home Entertainment, 2004.

Zamaane Ko Dikhana Hai. DVD. Directed by Nasir Hussain. Secaucus, N.J.: Eros Entertainment, 2000.

Index

Waddedar, Pritilata, 162, 167
Westerns, U.S. film genre of, 131–32
Wheeler, J. Talboys, 15, 16, 35, 134
Williams, Raymond, 105–6
women, 19–21, 59, 76; and mobility,
    121–26; and railway travel, 134–38,
    181. *See also* gender
wonder, discourse of, 34–37

World War I, 63, 69, 163
World War II, 163. *See also* Nazism

Young, Robert, 65, 69

Zamaane Ko Dikhana Hai (film), 144, 176
zenana, 20, 134–36, 139
Zulaika, J., 161

MARIAN AGUIAR is associate professor of English in the Literary and Cultural Studies Program at Carnegie Mellon University.